Studies in Renaissance Literature

Volume 1

THE THEOLOGY OF JOHN DONNE

John Donne has rarely been treated seriously as an original religious thinker; his prose and poetry have been discussed in theological contexts for the purposes of highlighting their devotional nature and of seeking to identify Donne's sectarian allegiance, but critics have largely neglected Donne as a theologian in his own right, and his response to the religious controversies of his day. This new study describes the distinguishing features of Donne's theology, as revealed primarily in his extant sermons, and also reads a variety of his individual sermons in context as applications of his own theological vision. Topics addressed are: the doctrine of the Trinity; common prayer; sight and spectacle; the doctrine of repentance; the doctrine of grace.

JEFFREY JOHNSON is Associate Professor of English at College Misericordia in Dallas, Pennsylvania.

T0326792

Studies in Renaissance Literature

ISSN 1465–6310

General editor: John T. Shawcross

Editorial board
John T. Shawcross
Helen E. Wilcox
John N. King
Graham Parry

Studies in Renaissance Literature offers investigations of topics both spanning the sixteenth and seventeenth centuries and growing out of medieval concerns, up to the Restoration period. Particularly encouraged are new examinations of the interplay between the literature of the English Renaissance and its cultural history.

Proposals or queries may be sent directly to the editors at the addresses given below; all submissions will receive prompt and informed consideration.

Professor John T. Shawcross, Department of English, University of Kentucky, Lexington, Kentucky 40506, USA

Professor Helen E. Wilcox, Rijksuniversiteit Groningen, Broerstraat 5, POB 72,9700 AB, Groningen, The Netherlands

Dr John N. King, Department of English, the Ohio State University, Columbus, Ohio 43210, USA

Professor Graham Parry, Department of English, University of York, Heslington, York YO1 5DD, UK

THE THEOLOGY OF
JOHN DONNE

Jeffrey Johnson

D. S. BREWER

© Jeffrey Johnson 1999

All Rights Reserved. Except as permitted under current legislation
no part of this work may be photocopied, stored in a retrieval
system, published, performed in public, adapted, broadcast,
transmitted, recorded or reproduced in any form or by any means,
without the prior permission of the copyright owner

The right of Jeffrey Johnson to be identified as
the author of this work has been asserted in accordance with
sections 77 and 78 of the Copyright, Designs and Patents Act 1988

First published 1999
D. S. Brewer, Cambridge

Transferred to digital printing

ISBN 978-0-85991-620-2

D. S. Brewer is an imprint of Boydell & Brewer Ltd
PO Box 9, Woodbridge, Suffolk IP12 3DF, UK
and of Boydell & Brewer Inc.
668 Mt Hope Avenue, Rochester, NY 14620, USA
website: www.boydellandbrewer.com

A CiP catalogue record for this book is available
from the British Library

This publication is printed on acid-free paper

CONTENTS

Contents

for Lee

PREFACE

With surprisingly few exceptions, John Donne has not been treated seriously as a religious thinker. His prose and poetry have been discussed in theological contexts for the purpose of highlighting their devotional nature, but in doing so critics have neglected Donne as a theologian in his own right who is worthy of study in the development of seventeenth-century theology and in the history of the Church of England. There is little doubt that modern assessments have been unduly influenced by T. S. Eliot who, in his essay on Lancelot Andrewes, laments that Donne belonged to the category of such persons "who seek refuge in religion from the tumults of a strong emotional temperament which can find no complete satisfaction elsewhere" and about whom, therefore, "there hangs the shadow of the impure motive."[1] Evelyn Simpson also undervalues Donne as a religious thinker, contending that the *Sermons* reveal the mind, not of a theologian, but of a "poet who grasps certain ideas by intuition, not by logical reasoning."[2] Further, she concludes that simply because he did not produce in the *Sermons*, or anywhere else for that matter, a fully articulated polemic system of theology, "Donne was not a great speculative or constructive theologian."[3] In addition, David Nicholls also contends that Donne has been largely ignored as a theologian not only because the tenor of his thought is "a far cry from that optimistic 'incarnationalism' which frequently passes for Anglicanism," but also because Donne himself "has generally been consigned to the field of 'Eng. Lit.'"[4]

More recent studies of Donne's *Sermons* have, on the one hand, neglected their theological significance by affording a disproportionate attention to their political dimensions, often following the lead of John Carey and Debora Shuger in appropriating bits and pieces from the *Sermons* in order to confirm "the impure motive" of Donne's ambition and absolutism. However, Gale Carrithers and James Hardy are exactly right in their contention that while "John Donne was *ipso facto* a political figure in his preaching, no matter what he said," his politics, nevertheless, "may best be construed largely, in terms of his theology and the Prayer Book liturgy, the tropes of religious life, and the

---

[1] Eliot, *Selected Essays*, pp. 352, 345.
[2] Simpson, *A Study of the Prose Works of John Donne*, p. 76.
[3] Ibid., p. 111.
[4] Nicholls, "The Political Theology of John Donne," pp. 47–48.

fact of dialogue."[5] The *Sermons* have, on the other hand, also been tapped in selective ways in order to reach a rather limiting, and often oversimplified, determination of Donne's sectarian allegiance, and the critical impulse to do so by and large ignores Donne's own desire to rise above the divisive wrangling that characterized the Church in his day.[6] Every such uncontextualized reading of Donne's *Sermons* suffers the risk of theological misinterpretation that can, as Jeanne Shami writes, "produce Donne the Puritan and Donne the Arminian without assessing how and why the sermons allow for such extremes."[7]

The purpose of this study is to describe the distinguishing features of Donne's theology, as revealed in the most extensive record of his mature thought, the *Sermons*,[8] and to read the historical/political circumstances in which he preached in relation to these theological foundations. The *Sermons*, of course, do not provide anything like a systematic theology, yet they do present a clear theological vision (Donne's own eclectic *via media* as it were) by which to navigate the religious controversies of the period. The initial chapter, "So Steepy a Place," examines the doctrine of the Trinity, which Donne espouses as the fundamental and distinguishing belief for regulating Christian faith and practice. Grounding his discussions of the Trinity within the framework of creation, and specifically Genesis 1:1, 26, Donne conceives of the essential nature of the godhead as a divine community that through mutual consultation enlarged itself to create and then embrace humankind. This image of dialogic unity serves for Donne as the model for individuals to conform themselves to the triune God specifically through a liturgical participation in the Church. The chapter includes a reading of Donne's two-part sermon on Genesis 1:26 (April 1629), which not only provides the most extensive explanation of his views on this doctrine, but which also applies his theology to the immediate context of Charles I's dissolution of Parliament (March 1629) in order to influence his King to maintain political unity through a dialogic process. As his theological first principle, the doctrine of the Trinity informs every aspect of Donne's religious thought and lays the foundation for the subsequent chapters of this study.

The second chapter, "To Batter Heaven," explores both the liturgical practice of common prayer Donne articulates in the *Sermons* and the private prayers that he made publicly available in his *Devotions upon Emergent Occasions*. In many ways, the crucial religious struggle for Donne concerns

[5] Carrithers and Hardy, "Love, Power, Dust Royall, Gavelkinde: Donne's Politics," p. 39.

[6] On this last point, see, for example, "The Preface" to *Pseudo-Martyr*, pp. 13–14; the *Essays in Divinity*, pp. 50–52; and Donne's 9 April 1612 letter to Henry Goodyer (*Letters to Severall Persons of Honour, 1651*), p. 132.

[7] Shami, "Donne's Sermons and the Absolutist Politics of Quotation," p. 392.

[8] I concur with Paul Stanwood ("Donne's Earliest Sermons and the Penitential Tradition") who asserts that "Donne's ideas were well formulated by 1615" and that his style "did not markedly change or 'develop' over the period of his ordained ministry" (pp. 372, 366).

his understanding of the Church and the theological necessity he himself feels for being identified within the common body of Christ. The benefit of prayer, then, is for those who complete the double motion of the relationship between the divine and human by exercising what Donne refers to as "religious impudency," and the purpose of common prayer is to remember, and thereby affirm, the promise of God's grace. The chapter includes a reading of the sermon Donne preached at Whitehall on 5 April 1628 before Charles I. Rather than a homily on the fast the King had ordered because of repeated military disasters in seeking to liberate the Protestants at Île de Rhé, Donne offers his royal auditor instead a theologically nuanced explanation that prayer should precede and inform acts of penitence such as fasting. By offering this orthodox corrective to Charles, Donne illustrates in this sermon the manner in which common prayer properly defines the communion of saints.

Donne's response to the iconoclastic controversy of his day is detailed in the third chapter, "Through His Own Red Glasse," which analyzes Donne's iteration throughout the *Sermons* that sight is preeminent among the human senses. His persistent plea for a use of pictures and images, both those tangible representations created by human hands and those painted in the mind by the spoken and written word, informs his understanding of the sacrament of baptism, including the signing of the cross. In addition, his views on sight and spectacle speak to one's responsibility for religious self-fashioning, especially for those in authority such as ministers and nobles, by perceiving and reflecting images worthy of imitation. This last idea is dramatically illustrated in the sermon Donne preached at Hanworth on 25 August 1622, where he was invited by James Hay to participate in the celebration for the release of Hay's father-in-law, Henry Percy, from the Tower. In this sermon, Donne seeks to adjust the spiritual vision of both patrons, specifically Hay's penchant for lavish outward display and Percy's inclination toward Stoic resignation, by directing their sight to the spectacle of Christ crucified. As Donne learned from Augustine, and as he exemplifies in the Hanworth sermon, seeing leads to knowing, and to loving union with, God.

Chapter four, "Voice of the Turtle," addresses the theological imperative Donne places on the doctrine of repentance. To the extent that he perceives the central gospel message as one of repentance, Donne relates his own sense of calling to his responsibility to preach this doctrine faithfully, as illustrated in the readings this chapter provides of his two extant churching sermons and of his Valediction sermon. The former sermons, the one for the Countess of Bridgewater and the other for Lady Doncaster, are both extended homilies on this doctrine and reveal Donne's desire to move his auditors beyond a strictly liturgical or a culturally delimiting understanding of the churching service even as he fulfills his vocational duty to lead them to humble confession. The latter explicates the sermon Donne preached at Lincoln's Inn prior to serving as chaplain for the embassy led by James Hay to mediate between Catholics and Protestants in Bohemia, and is read in conjunction with the poem he composed for this same occasion, "A Hymne to Christ, at the Authors last going into Germany." These texts complement Donne's concern expressed throughout the *Sermons* that proper repentance is accompanied by purifying tears of contrition, as a type of baptism, and is best accomplished in the communal contexts of prayer, preaching, and the Sacraments.

The final chapter, "O Taste and See," locates Donne's views on the topic that incited so much debate and division during this period, the doctrine of grace. Throughout his homiletic discussions of this doctrine, Donne reiterates his desire for unity in the Church, including Puritans and Roman Catholics, yet he clarifies in the *Sermons* that while God's prevenient grace precedes all, those in the Church must actively pursue subsequent grace to complete the salvific process; that justification, as a consequence, comes through both faith and works; and that the Word and Sacraments are together the effectual means of grace. The chapter culminates with an overview of Donne's response to the theological point of contention regarding Christ's presence in the Lord's Supper. Eschewing both the transubstantiation of the Roman Catholics and the memorialism of the low-church Protestants, Donne espouses that the real presence of Christ is manifested in worthy communicants as they eat the bread and drink the wine. As such, the Lord's Supper involves the Church in a liturgically-sanctioned act of assimilation; the tasting/seeing that provides a saving knowledge of God is for Donne the antitype for the eating of the forbidden fruit and the knowing of good and evil that separates individuals from God and from one another. Therefore, the assimilation of oneself to God in the Church is for Donne the only theologically informed response to the Trinity's dilating its own community to enfold humankind.

ACKNOWLEDGMENTS

In completing this study, I owe a debt of thanks to a great many people over a long period of time, beginning with my parents who have always provided me with opportunity and encouragement throughout my education and scholarly career. The person who introduced me to the study of Donne is my mentor and friend John R. Roberts, who is always in my prayers. Further, I benefited greatly from the Summer Research Grants and the sabbatical leave awarded to me by College Misericordia, and I wish to acknowledge the support I received from Sr. Mary Glennon, Vice President of the College and Dean of Academic Affairs; from Richard Lynch, English Department Chair; and from the staff of the College library. I am also grateful for the assistance I received in the various libraries of the University of Toronto, where I conducted the majority of my research, namely at Robarts; at Trinity College; at the Centre for Renaissance and Reformation Studies, Victoria College; and at Knox College (especially the assistance afforded by Stephen Farris and Kathleen Gibson). In addition, I am indebted to my colleague Scott Blanchard and to my fellow Donne scholar Frances Malpezzi, both of whom read portions of the manuscript and offered valuable criticism. My last and greatest debt of thanks goes to my wife Lee, without whose love, wit and insight this study, and my life, would be incomplete.

Chapter One

SO STEEPY A PLACE

ST. DUNSTAN-IN-THE-WEST

THE passing of Dr. Thomas Whyte on 1 March 1624 left a vacancy at the vicarage of St. Dunstan-in-the-West that would not remain open long. Having been promised the position by the Earl of Dorset sometime before it fell vacant,[1] Donne was formally appointed on March 18 and thereby added to his responsibilities at St. Paul's and its attendant prebend, and at the rectories of Sevenoaks and of Blunham. Whyte's death, however, left another type of vacancy. The strained relationships Whyte had prior to his death with both the Earl of Dorset, with whom he was engaged in a lawsuit, and the parishioners of St. Dunstan's, who through Whyte's lack of attention had acquired a certain discontent, undoubtedly shaped the meeting between Donne and the churchwardens three days after the death of Whyte. Within these troubled circumstances, Bald wonders "whether there had not been some feeling in the parish against Donne and a reluctance to accept him."[2]

Located within Temple Bar, St. Dunstan's, nevertheless, attracted the kinds of city intellectuals with whom Donne must surely have felt comfortable, namely, members of the legal profession, and printers and stationers. While there is some evidence that "Donne had in fact become involved in the affairs of St. Dunstan's even before he succeeded to the vicarage,"[3] Donne's first sermons for this congregation leave little doubt that "the attention that Donne gave to the parish from the outset was so much more than Whyte had given it, for many years at least, that, if there was any initial dissatisfaction, he soon allayed it."[4]

---

[1] R. C. Bald (*John Donne: A Life*) notes that ten days after Donne's appointment the Earl died "and was succeeded in the title and the estates by his brother Sir Edward Sackville, with whom Donne had long been well acquainted" (p. 455).

[2] Ibid., p. 460.

[3] Ibid., p. 457. In particular, Bald cites the vestry minutes for 31 July 1623, which "record that the churchwardens were 'desired to attende the Deane of Paules and the Lo: Keeper to sue out a ne exeat regnum against Captaine Harvye for the more security of recouery of the twoo hundred poundes given by Mr Hares will to the vse of the poore of this parish'" (p. 457).

[4] Ibid., p. 461.

Donne's initial sermon as Vicar of St. Dunstan's, preached on 11 April 1624 and described by Simpson and Potter as "a kind of manifesto setting forth the preacher's view of the reciprocal duties of the pastor and his flock, . . . [and] expressed in language almost homely in its simplicity" (6:9), opens with a familiar idea found throughout his sermons that "From the beginning God intimated a detestation, a dislike of *singularity*" (6:81).[5] Donne immediately situates this idea within the context of Genesis 1:1, noting that God (in the word "Elohim") "is named *Plurally, Creavit Dii, Gods*, Gods in the plurall, Created Heaven and Earth," and further that "As the *Creator* was not *Singular*, so neither were the *creatures*" (6:81). Still within the introductory paragraph, Donne then articulates the controlling metaphor for this sermon, the spiritual marriage "not onely betweene Christ and the whole Church, . . . but in the union between Christs *particular Ministers*, and *particular Churches*" (6:82). The sermon concludes by defining the reciprocal relationship of pastor and congregation:

> If the Pastor *love*, there will bee a *double labour*; if the People *love*, there will bee double respect. . . . For where the Congregation loves the Pastor, hee will forbeare bitter reproofes, and wounding increpations, and where the Pastor loves his Congregation, his *Rebukes*, because they proceed out of *love*, will bee acceptable, and well interpreted by them. . . . [For] *love* being the *root* of all, the *fruit* of all may be peace, *love* being the *soul* of all, the *body* of all may be unity; which the Lord of unity, and concord, grant to us all, for his Sonne Christ Jesus sake, Amen. (6:94)

The second of the St. Dunstan's sermons, preached just two weeks later on April 25, takes as its scripture text Psalm 34:11 ("Come ye children, hearken unto me, I will teach you the fear of the Lord"), on which Donne comments in the *divisio*: "To every Minister and Dispenser of the word of God, and to every Congregation belong these words; . . . There is the *Meum & Tuum*, your part, and our part" (6:95). Continuing his pastoral attentiveness, Donne expands on his metaphor of familial relationships by instructing "his children" that "This then is the operation of the feare of the Lord, this is his working; [there] remaines onely to consider what this feare of the Lord is: And, beloved in him, be not afraid of it; for, this *fear* of God, is the *love* of God" (6:111).

Framed as they are within the context of the plurality of God discovered in Genesis 1:1, 26, the themes of love and unity informing these first sermons at St. Dunstan's illustrate Terry Sherwood's insight that "Creation is the basic [sic] for [Donne's] theology of participation that hinges on the likenesses established between the Creator and his creatures."[6] To be precise, within the framework of creation, Donne persistently articulates the image of the

---

[5] See later in this chapter the section "Unity v. Singularity."
[6] Sherwood, *Fulfilling the Circle*, p. 5.

godhead in terms of a divine community that, through consultation, manifests the relationship between Creator and creatures within the Church, as it liturgically reinscribes the eternal unity of Father, Son, and Holy Spirit. The historical situation surrounding Donne's initial two sermons at St. Dunstan's provides only one application of his understanding of the doctrine of the Trinity, the articulation of which pervades the *Sermons* and serves as the first principle for his theology.

FACIAMUS HOMINEM

The singular critical voice to acknowledge Donne's fundamentally Trinitarian theology is that of David Nicholls, who asserts that "the Trinity is, for Donne, the hub from which radiate the beliefs of the Church, finding in it their unity and coherence" and that "the doctrines of creation, sin, incarnation, atonement, ecclesiology, as well as the sacramental and devotional life of the Church, are held together by a conception of God as plurality in unity."[7] The doctrine of the Trinity defines the Church and shapes its beliefs precisely because for Donne the doctrine establishes the essential community of the godhead, which itself sought to enlarge its own community through the creation of humankind.

In an early sermon preached at Whitehall on 19 April 1618, Donne delineates the communal action of the Trinity in its creative purposes, distinguishing the making of humankind from the rest of creation:

> But when God came to the best of his creatures, to Man, Man was not only made *in verbo*, as the rest were, by speaking a word, but by a Consultation, by a Conference, by a Counsell, *faciamus hominem, let us make Man*; there is a more expresse manifestation of divers persons speaking together, of a concurrence of the Trinity; and not of a saying only, but a mutuall saying; not of a Proposition only, but of a Dialogue in the making of Man: The making of matter alone was *sine verbo*, without any word at all; the making of lesser creatures was *in verbo*, by saying, by speaking; the making of Man was *in sermone*, in a consultation. (1:289)

The opening chapter of Genesis reveals for Donne, first and foremost, that the essential nature of God is communal. Furthermore, the Trinity defines its community through dialogue, through consultation. As a result, because humankind was created "*in sermone*," Donne seems to imply then that the interplay of preacher and congregation ideally imitates the creative council of the Trinity.[8]

This social interplay is illustrated on 26 April 1625 when Donne preached

---

[7] Nicholls, "The Political Theology of John Donne," p. 50.

[8] For an overview of Donne's use of *sermo*, see John Shawcross, "The Concept of *Sermo* in Donne and Herbert."

at Denmark House where the body of King James lay in state, and he opens the sermon by referring directly to Genesis 1:26:[9]

> In the Creation of man, in that one word, *Faciamus, let Vs make man,* God gave such an intimation of the *Trinity,* as that we may well enlarge, and spread, and paraphrase that one word, so farre, as to heare therein, a councell of all the *three Persons,* agreeing in this gracious designe upon Man, *faciamus,* let us make him; *make* him, and *mend* him, and make him *sure:* I, the Father, will make him by my power; if he should fall, Thou the Sonne shalt repayr him, re-edify him, *redeem* him; if he should distrust, that this Redemption belonged not to him, Thou, the *Holy Ghost,* shalt apply to his particular soule, and conscience, this *mercy* of mine, and this *merit* of the Sonnes; and so let *us make him.* (6:280)

The consolation Donne discovers here is the communal action of the Trinity, not only in its initial creative act, but also in its providential work throughout history. Then, in order to enlarge this thought expressed in the opening paragraph, Donne organizes the remainder of the sermon according to the three "persons" implied in his scripture text (Canticles 3:11), "The *Church,* that calls, The *children* that hearken, and *Christ in his Humiliation*" (6:281). As a result, Donne comforts his grieving auditory in the preaching of this sermon by recreating in time and space the divine counsel of creation.

In addition to God's provisions for the tribulations of the world, Donne also perceives God's creative action in the Trinity as applicable for informing the joys of this life. In his St. Paul's sermon on Psalm 90:14, Donne insists, first, that "Charity begins in our selves, but it does not end there, but dilates it selfe to others," and he then explains that "True love and charity is to doe the most that we can, all that we can for the good of others" (5:278). Within this context of explaining how love should dilate from one's self to others, Donne again cites Genesis 1:26:

> When God bestowed upon man, his first and greatest benefit, his making, it is expressed so, *Faciamus hominem, Let us,* All us, *make man;* God seems to summon himselfe, to assemble himselfe, to muster himself, all himselfe, all the persons of the Trinity, to doe what he could in the favour of man. (5:278–79)

Donne concludes this section of the sermon by urging his parishioners, "let us goe Gods way, all the way" (5:279), by reflecting the love of God for humanity in the creation to one another:

> First, *Faciamus hominem ad imaginem nostram,* Let us make that Man according unto our image, let us consider our selves in him, and make our

---

[9] See Nicholls ("The Political Theology of John Donne"), who asserts that "the closely connected but distinct social image of God the Holy Trinity as a model for the life of the nation, play[s] a central and unifying role in the theology of Donne, giving it more coherence than is generally perceived" (pp. 45–46).

case his, and remember how lately he was as well as we, and how soone we may be as ill as he, and then *Descendamus & confundamus*, Let us, us, with all the power we have, remove or slaken those calamities that lie upon them.

(5:279)

Certainly Donne is not unusual in reading Genesis 1:1, 26 in order to inform his understanding of the Trinity.[10] Nevertheless, in so far as they serve to determine the communal nature of the Trinity as a theological first principle, these verses distinguish Donne as a theologian, for this understanding of the doctrine of the Trinity illuminates every corner of his religious imagination. The divine concurrence in creating humanity establishes for Donne the foundation for the divine/human relationship and, as a result, determines every aspect of Christian faith and practice.

REGULA FIDEI

A thorough reading of the *Sermons* leaves little doubt of the significance of the Trinity in Donne's preaching. The seven Trinity Sunday sermons, which form a series comparable to those for Easter and Christmas, and the dozen or so additional sermons that provide substantive discussions of the Trinity are difficult to ignore. Beyond this merely quantitative summation, however, Donne persistently articulates the preeminence of the doctrine of the Trinity in his thought, employing a spectrum of historical occasions, biblical contexts, and illustrative metaphors. Donne asserts, for example, that "the name of God to a Christian, [is] the Trinity" (8:145); that "As there is but one Godhead, so there is no sin against God (and all sin is so) but it is against the whole Trinity" (5:87); and that "perfect blessednesse consists in this, the true knowledge and worship of the Trinity" (3:89). Further, Donne identifies the Trinity as:

> the first letter in his Alphabet, that ever thinks to read his name in the book of life; The first note in his Gammut, that ever thinks to sing his part, in the Quire of the Triumphant Church . . . he hath not learnt to spel, that hath not learnt the Trinity; not learnt to pronounce the first word, that cannot bring three Persons into one God. (9:51)

Two additional passages express the unequivocal necessity of knowing and believing in the Trinity for salvation. In the first, from his St. Paul's sermon on Psalm 90:14, Donne compares catechistical instruction to the manna the Israelites received from God during their forty years in the Wilderness and writes, "Every man is bound to take in his Gomer [of manna], his explicite knowledge of Articles absolutely necessary to salvation; The simplest man, as

---

[10] For an overview of this use of these verses in Donne's time, see Arnold Williams, *The Common Expositor*, pp. 243–45.

well as the greatest Doctor, is bound to know, that there is one God in three persons" (5:276); and in the second, preached at St. Paul's on Christmas day 1621 (John 1:8), he states:

> He that should come to a *Heathen man*, a meere naturall man, uncatechized, uninstructed in the rudiments of the Christian Religion, and should at first, without any preparation, present him first with this necessitie; Thou shalt burn in fire and brimstone eternally, except thou believe *a Trinitie of Persons, in an unitie of one God.* (3:357)

The import of the two selections above is exemplified in one of Donne's personal reminicences. In his first published sermon, that on James' *Directions for Preachers*, Donne tells of "An Artificer of this Citie" who brought his young daughter, "not above nine yeares of age," before Donne in order to demonstrate her ability to recite scripture. Donne recounts, "wee could scarse propose any Verse of any Booke, or Chapter of the *Bible*, but that that childe would goe forward without Booke" (4:203), and then comments that when he undertook "to Catechise this childe," he was amazed that "truly, shee understood nothing of the *Trinitie*, nothing of any of those fundamentall poynts which must save us: and the wonder was doubled, how she knew so much, how so little" (4:203–04).

One of the most telling passages, one that reflects the dimensions of Donne's thought on this subject, appears in the Trinity Sunday sermon Donne preached at St. Dunstan's the year he was appointed Vicar:

> And this mystery of the Trinity, is *Regula fidei*, sayes S. *Hierom*, It is the rule of our faith, this onely regulates our faith, That we beleeve aright of the Trinity; It is *Dogma nostræ Religionis*, sayes S. *Basil*, As though there were but this one Article; It is, sayes he, the foundation, the summe, it is all the Christian Religion, to beleeve aright of the Trinity. By this wee are distinguished from the Jews, who accept no plurality of Persons; And by this we are distinguished from the Gentiles, who make as many severall persons, as there are severall powers, and attributes belonging to God. Our Religion, our holy Philosophy, our learning, as it is rooted in Christ, so it is not limited, not determined in Christ alone; wee are not baptized in his name alone, but our study must be the whole Trinity; for, he that beleeves not in the Holy Ghost, as well as in Christ, is no Christian: And, as that is true which S. *Augustine* sayes, *Nec laboriosius aliquid quæritur, nec periculosius alicubi erratur*, As there is not so steepy a place to clamber up, nor so slippery a place to fall upon, as the doctrine of the Trinity; so is that also true which he addes, *Nec fructuosius invenitur*. There is not so fulfilling, so accomplishing, so abundant an Article as that of the Trinity, for it is all Christianity. And therefore let us keepe our selves to that way, of the manifestation of the Trinity. (6:138–39)

In this passage Donne unequivocally expresses that Christian faith is distinguished through a proper belief in the Trinity, and, more importantly, he celebrates how a vital and active expression of the doctrine both challenges and shapes the Christian life.

REASON AND THE TRINITY

The extended passage above is significant not only because it reiterates, by citing and adopting the Church Fathers, the essential foundation of a proper belief in the Trinity, but also because it acknowledges, through the words of Augustine, the arduousness of such an undertaking, as well as the full potential of its promise. Both as "so steepy a place to clamber up" and as "so fulfilling, so accomplishing, so abundant an Article," the doctrine of the Trinity can only be properly understood in Donne's religious imagination by examining it in relation to reason.

To begin with, Donne clarifies in the *Sermons* that the mystery of the Trinity is unquestionably "above Man, and the extent of his Reason" (3:136); that "God, in the Trinity, is open to no other light, then the light of faith" (8:54); and, finally, that "If we think to see this mystery of the Trinity, by the light of reason, *Dimittemus*, we shall lose that hold which we had before, our naturall faculties, our reason will be perplext, and infeebled, and our super-naturall, our faith not strengthened that way" (8:54–55). Donne, however, is no enemy to reason. On the contrary, as Sherwood has so ably demonstrated, "Donne's conviction of reason's dominant powers lies at the heart of his thought,"[11] and further that the central role of reason in Donne's theology, "as the tripartite soul's primary faculty," is in fact "consistent with its centrality in the life of faith."[12]

In a St. Paul's Cross sermon dated 22 November 1629, Donne addresses the dichotomous tension between reason and faith, stating of the Trinity that

> though we cannot so immediately prove that by *Reason*, nor so intirely, altogether, yet, by these steppes we can; first, that there is nothing in the doctrine of the Trinity *against Reason*; the doctrine of the Trinity implies no *contradiction*; It may be so; and then, that it is so, if we have the word of God, for it, Reason it selfe will conclude, that we have Reason on our side; And that we have the word of God for it, we proceed thus, that for this Book, which we call *the Bible*, which book delivers us the Doctrine of the Trinity, we have far better reasons, and stronger arguments to satisfie any naturall man. (9:114–15)

Knowledge of the Trinity, as Donne often clarifies, is only available by means of revelation. As if to manifest the way in which reason can be appeased in the doctrine of the Trinity, especially as shaped by the scriptures, Donne provides, in his 1620 Lenten sermon before King James at Whitehall, a syllogistic explanation of the Apostles' Creed:

[11] Sherwood, *Fulfilling the Circle*, p. 15.
[12] Ibid., p. 22.

> if I must get Heaven by a Syllogism, my *Major* is *Credo in Deum Patrem, I believe in God the Father,* for, *Pater major,* the Father is greater then all: And my *Minor* shall be, *Credo in Deum Filium, I believe in God the Son, Qui exivit de patre,* he came from God; And my Conclusion, which must proceed from my *Major & Minor,* shall be *Credo in Spiritum Sanctum, I believe in the Holy Ghost,* who proceeds from Father and Son: And this Syllogisme brought me into the Militant Church in my Baptisme, and this will carry me into the Triumphant, in my Transmigration; for, doctrine of Salvation is matter without controversie.
>
> (3:209–10)

In stating that "*if* I must get Heaven by a Syllogism," Donne recognizes that the tensions of reason and faith cannot be resolved logically. He recognizes that "saving 'knowledge,'" a knowledge accounting for the full implications of the Trinity, "can only outdistance reason by using it."[13] The key role in this movement beyond reason is for Donne performed by the Holy Spirit. In his 1630 Whitsunday sermon, Donne asserts that for the certainty of understanding the creation of the world and the unity of the godhead, "I need not Scriptures," and then states:

> but to know this distinction of Persons, That the Son is in the Father, I need the Scriptures, and I need more then the Scriptures, I need this Pentecost, this comming, this illustration of the holy Ghost, to inspire a right understanding of these Scriptures into me. For, if this knowledge might be had without Scriptures, why should not the heathen beleeve the Trinity, as well as I, since they lack no naturall faculties which Christians have? (9:245)

For Donne, the Holy Spirit complements, assists, and satisfies reason; the indwelling work of the Spirit confirms for Donne one's place within the Church.

The passage above from the 1630 Whitsunday sermon becomes all the more poignant when read in its larger context. The scripture text for the sermon is John 14:20, "At that day shall ye know, that I am in my father, and you in me, and I in you," which Donne reads as a prophetic allusion to Pentecost. These words occur in a portion of the gospel in which Christ is attempting, in general, to warn the disciples of his coming death and, in particular, to speak to Philip's request, "Lord, shew us the Father, and it sufficeth us" (14:8). In responding, Christ reveals the Trinity, stating that he and the father are one and that the father will send a helper, "the Spirit of truth" (14:17), and then insists, "I will not leave you as orphans; I will come to you" (14:18). However, as Donne clarifies throughout this sermon, it is not sufficient to know only the father. The mystery of the Trinity comforts Donne in the knowledge that the community of the godhead seeks to enfold humanity in its own community through the indwelling Holy Spirit. As

---

[13] Sherwood, *Fulfilling the Circle,* p. 57.

Sherwood explains, "the full Trinity participates in the human soul through the Spirit's motions," and "the Spirit's recreative motions, divine repair against sin's erosion, reingraves the likeness between the tripartite soul and tripartite God."[14]

As a fundamental belief which, as Donne often reminds his auditors, "distinguishes us from Jews, and Turks, and al other professions" (8:145), the doctrine of the Trinity describes the essential nature of God and, thereby, the created purpose of the individual. On the one hand, reason alone will only frustrate the individual in this pursuit, for "He that seeks proofe for every mystery of Religion, shall meet with much darknesse; but he that beleeves first, shall finde every thing to illustrate his faith." On the other hand, "that man that believes the Trinity, can scarce turne upon any thing, but it assists, and advances, and illustrates that beliefe" (8:40). As a result, the responsibility Donne communicates to his parishioners is to celebrate the mystery of the Trinity in the created world.

VESTIGIA TRINITATIS

What Donne emphasizes throughout the *Sermons* is an Augustinian understanding of the Trinity that reveals and informs the divine/human relationship, which is precisely what he means to communicate when he writes of prayer, preaching, and the sacrament that "this is thy trinity upon earth, that must bring thee to the Trinity in heaven" (9:315). A brief passage from Donne's sermon at Lincoln's Inn, as that congregation prepared to build a new chapel, nicely illustrates this conception of community. The sermon text consists of two verses from the Genesis 28 narration of Jacob's ladder, the details of which Donne interprets as a revelation of the Trinity to the Church:

> Now this ladder is for the most part, understood to be *Christ* himself; whose foot, that touched the earth, is his *humanity*, and his top that reached to heaven, his *Divinity*; The ladder is Christ, and upon him the Angels, (his Ministers) labour for the edifying of the Church; And in this labour, upon this ladder, God stands above it, governing, and ordering all things, according to his providence in his Church. . . . [And] God the father stands upon this ladder, as the *Originall* hath it, *Nitzab*, that he leanes upon this ladder, as the *vulgar* hath it, *Innixus scalæ*, that he rests upon it, as the holy Ghost did, upon the same ladder, that is, upon Christ, in his baptisme. (2:225–26)

In response to this manifestation of the salvific extensions of the Trinity, Donne states that "now it becomes every Christian, to doe something for the advancing of the outward glory, and worship of God in his Church" (2:226).

---

[14] Ibid., p. 57.

Donne's metaphoric expression for this imperative is that the divine descent must be met with a human ascent.[15]

It is in this larger context of defining the divine/human relationship that he writes in his 1620 Trinity Sunday sermon, "And therefore it is a lovely and a religious thing, to finde out *Vestigia Trinitatis*, Impressions of the Trinity, in as many things as we can" (3:144).[16] Yet, by way of caution and as a necessary point of distinction, discovering the Trinity in the creation does not, for Donne, mean seeking out triples in nature in a manner comparable to Sir Thomas Browne's pursuit of the quincunx. It is, instead, just this simple, numerical impulse that Donne speaks against in the fourth stanza of "A Litanie," in which, addressing the Trinity directly, he writes:

> As you distinguish'd undistinct
> By power, love, knowledge bee,
> Give mee a such selfe different instinct,
> Of these let all mee elemented bee,
> Of power, to love, to know, you'unnumbred three. (ll. 32–36)[17]

As Donne clarifies, a pursuit of the Trinity is always a means for better understanding God's incarnational presence: "Let us therefore, with *S. Bernard*, consider *Trinitatem Creatricem*, and *Trinitatem Creatam*, A Creating, and a Created Trinity; A Trinity, which the Trinity in Heaven, Father, Son, and Holy Ghost, hath created in our soules, Reason, Memory, and Will" (3:144–45). The implication here is that the community of the individual soul is a reflection of the divine community and a conduit for the commerce between Creator and creatures.

As is to be expected, Donne delineates the individual roles of St. Bernard's "creating Trinity" in his own idiosyncratic, though consistently orthodox, manner, and this aspect of Donne's thought is described with precision in an extended passage from the concluding paragraph of his 1627 Trinity Sunday sermon at St. Dunstan's:

[15] Donne appropriates his expression of the human ascent as a pattern for humility from Augustine and Bernard of Clairvaux. In his *Homilies of the Psalms*, especially those identified as "Songs of Steps" (120, 121, and 122), Augustine describes this pattern of humility as an ascent of the heart, which in a Platonic manner carries the believer from ignorance and darkness to wisdom and light. Similarly, Bernard's treatise *On the Steps of Humility*, the first of his published works, defines humility as "the fruit of the knowledge of truth," which is born "from this first union of the Word and reason" (*Selected Works*, pp. 103, 117).

[16] See Dennis Klinck, "John Donne's 'knottie Trinitie,'" who briefly discusses Donne and the notion of *Vestigia Trinitatis* in the larger context of the English Renaissance to illustrate what he sees as "a double emphasis in the preoccupation with 'similitudes' of the Trinity: they were not only to be discovered in God's creation but also to be reproduced in the creations of men" (p. 13).

[17] *The Complete Poetry of John Donne*, ed. John T. Shawcross (Garden City, NY: Anchor, 1967), p. 357. All references to Donne's poetry are from this edition, unless otherwise noted, and are cited in this study by line numbers.

But that which distinguishes man from man, that which onely makes his Immortality a blessing, (for, even Immortality is part of their damnation that are damned, because it were an ease, it were a kind of pardon to them to be mortall, to be capable of death, though after millions of generations) is, to conceive aright of the Power of the Father, of the Wisdome of the Son, of the Goodnesse of the Holy Ghost; Of the Mercie of the Father, of the Merits of the Son, of the Applications of the Holy Ghost; Of the Creation of the Father, of the Redemption of the Son, of the Sanctification of the Holy Ghost. Without this, all notions of God are but confused, all worship of God is but Idolatry, all confession of God is but Atheisme; For so the Apostle argues, *When you were without Christ, you were without God.* Without this, all morall vertues are but diseases; Liberality is but a popular baite, and not a benefit, not an almes; Chastity is but a castration, and an impotency, not a temperance, not mortification; Active valour is but a fury, whatsoever we do, and passive valour is but a stupidity, whatsoever we suffer. Naturall apprehensions of God, though those naturall apprehensions may have much subtilty, Voluntary elections of a Religion, though those voluntary elections may have much singularity, Morall directions for life, though those morall directions may have much severity, are all frivolous and lost, if all determine not in Christianity, in the Notion of God, so as God hath manifested and conveyed himself to us; in God the Father, God the son, and God the Holy Ghost, whom this day we celebrate, in the Ingenuity, and in the Assiduity, and in the Totality, recommended in this text, and in this acclamation of the text, *Holy, Holy, Holy, Lord God Almighty, which was, and is, and is to come.* (8:59–60)

Here in this passage, and especially in that magnificent concluding sentence, Donne again articulates his insistence on a proper understanding of the Trinity as the seminal Christian belief; it alone determines all other theological considerations. It is a proper understanding of these individual roles of Father, Son, and Holy Ghost, distinct in their applications yet complementary in their purposes, that inform the tripartite soul and that preserve moral virtues.

In the opening paragraph of his Lincoln's Inn sermon on Psalms 38:2, which he notes is described in the title of the Psalm as "a Psalm of Remembrance," Donne places a description of the tripartite soul directly in the context of Genesis 1:26, stating that the phrase "*faciamus hominem*"

intimates a plurality, a concurrence of all the Trinity in our making, so doth it also a *plurality in that image of God*, which was then imprinted in us; As God, one *God* created us, so wee have a soul, *one soul*, that represents, and is some image of that one God; As the three Persons of the *Trinity* created us, so we have, in our one soul, a *threefold impression* of that image, and, as Saint *Bernard* calls it, *A trinity from the Trinity*, in those *three faculties* of the soul, the *Vnderstanding*, the *Will*, and the *Memory*. (2:72–73)

Immediately following this passage, Donne discounts the effectiveness of the understanding and will for the purpose of leading one to salvation, explaining first that the judgments and intentions of God are beyond human understanding, and then that the children of God are a rebellious lot who habitually exhibit a "stiffe perversenesse" of will. Donne then insists, in that often quoted passage, "But the *memory* is so familiar, and so present, and so ready a faculty, as will always answer, if we will but speak to it, and ask it, *what God hath done for us, or for others.* The art of *salvation*, is but the art of *memory*" (2:73).

Achsah Guibbory observes that while by Donne's time "this Augustinian conception of man's triune soul had become a theological commonplace,"[18] she properly highlights and contextualizes, specifically in terms of Augustine's *De Trinitate* and Book X of his *Confessions*, Donne's idiosyncratic expression of giving "an unusual weight to memory," which Donne finds "most reliable for leading man to God."[19] Later in the article, she states, "memory's supreme value lies in its ability to reestablish the link between man and God,"[20] which is the very idea with which Donne himself concludes. Directly on the heels of his pronouncment that "The art of *salvation*, is but the art of *memory*," Donne provides his justification for this assertion:

> When god gave his people the *Law*, he proposes nothing to them, but by that way, to their memory; *I am the Lord your God, which brought you out of the land of Egypt*; Remember but that. And when we expresse Gods mercy to us, we attribute but that faculty to God, that he *remembers* us. (2:73)

It is in the memory that for Donne the divine/human relationship is established; here is the faculty where Creator and creature find one another.

DONNE AND CALVIN

While Donne's understanding of the tripartite soul (especially in the context of the affinities Louis Martz perceives between Donne's religious verse and Ignatian meditation),[21] and his emphasis on memory have certainly been discussed at some length, the implications of these ideas have not been explored fully for defining the theological framework of Donne's thought.

---

[18] Guibbory, "John Donne and Memory as 'the Art of *Salvation*,'" p. 261.

[19] Ibid., p. 261. Also, Joan Webber (*Contrary Music*) argues that Donne's purpose in the sermons is "to get at the memory, not at the intellect, to remind rather than to teach," and as a result, "he shapes his prose in such a way as to appeal directly to the memory, by use of the long loose 'Senecan' sentence . . . that seems to advance with the progress of thought and emotion, a sentence shaped for exploration and recollection of known truths, rather than for exposition and persuasion" (p. 22).

[20] Guibbory, "John Donne and Memory as 'the Art of *Salvation*,'" p. 269. For additional discussions of this passage, and its larger implications in Donne's thought, see A. M. Guite, "The Art of Memory and the Art of Salvation"; and Elizabeth Tebeaux, "Memory, Reason, and the Quest for Certainty in the *Sermons* of John Donne."

[21] See Martz's *The Poetry of Meditation*, especially pp. 25–56.

Such an exploration reveals the veracity of Sherwood's contention that "Donne's differences from Calvin, whose influence pervaded English Protestantism, have not been defined clearly enough,"[22] especially the theological distinctions. In the midst of the religious/political wranglings of his time (and that occupy so many recent critical attempts to identify Donne's sectarian allegiance),[23] Donne centers his comments throughout the *Sermons* on theological essentials rather than on anthropological points of contention. In other words, Donne is less concerned with the issues of sin and atonement that characterize sectarian points of dispute than he is with defining the communal nature of God and only then establishing the parameters for Christian faith and practice from that theological basis.

To begin with, Donne's expression of the Augustinian tripartite soul marks a telling theological distinction between Donne and Calvin. In writing of the nature of the human soul, Calvin first asserts, "the human soul consists of two faculties, understanding and will" noting that the office of the former is "to distinguish between objects, as each seems worthy of approval or disapproval" while that of the latter is "to choose and follow what the understanding pronounces good, but to reject and flee what it disapproves" (I.xv.7).[24] Calvin then adds, by way of explanation, "let it be enough for us that the understanding is, as it were, the leader and governor of the soul; and that the will is always mindful of the bidding of the understanding, and in its own desires awaits the judgment of the understanding" (I.xv.7).[25] Calvin not only limits the soul to two faculties, and as he concludes, "no power can be found in the soul that does not duly have reference to one or the other of these members" (I.xv.7),[26] but he also excludes the very faculty that for Donne is most essential in the process of salvation.

This discussion of the nature of the soul reveals, further, the primary theological distinction between Donne and Calvin, as intimated specifically in Calvin's hierarchical identification of the understanding as "the guide and governor of the soul." While both Donne and Calvin unquestionably believe in the eternal existence of the Trinity, Calvin, unlike Donne, insists in his discussions of creation on the power and the sovereignty of God as the first principle for determining his tightly woven theological system.[27] As

---

[22] Sherwood, *Fulfilling the Circle*, p. 35.

[23] See, for example, David Chanoff, "Donne's Anglicanism"; E. Randolph Daniel, "Reconciliation, Covenant and Election"; Daniel Doerksen, *Conforming to the Word*; Dennis Flynn, "Donne's Catholicism: I and II"; Paul Sellin, *John Donne and 'Calvinist' Views of Grace*; and Richard Strier, "John Donne Awry and Squint."

[24] Calvin, *Institutes of the Christian Religion*, I:194.

[25] Ibid., I:194.

[26] Ibid., I:195.

[27] Approaching this issue from a perspective complementary to my own, John New (*Anglican and Puritan*) asserts that "only after we stop explaining Puritan behavior in terms of the merely derivative doctrine of predestination, and link it to the central premises, can we remedy some of the injustices of the accepted interpretation" of Puritan belief and practice

a result, Calvin hedges in the *Institutes* on the equality of the persons of the Trinity:

> Indeed, although the eternity of the Father is also the eternity of the Son and the Spirit, since God could never exist apart from his wisdom and power, and we must not seek in eternity a *before* or an *after*, nevertheless the observance of an order is not meaningless or superfluous, when the Father is thought of as first, then from him the Son, and finally from both the Spirit. (I.xiii.18)[28]

Further, in his discussion in the *Institutes* Calvin states, "For power and might are contained under the title *Elohim*" (I.x.2),[29] and his comments on the creation (I.xiv.20–22) emphasize God's "power in sustaining so great a mass, in governing the swiftly revolving heavenly system, and the like" (I.xiv.21) and "his power and grace in ourselves and in the great benefits which he has conferred upon us" (I.xiv.22).[30]

In her discussion of Donne's *Sermons*, Debora Shuger confirms that "Calvin's emphasis on the sovereignty of the divine will pervades English Protestantism" and that the *Institutes*, "with their insistent stress on the 'majesty of God' that 'compel[s] us to obey,'" are characterized by a theology "based on reciprocally implied principles of power and submission, domination and obedience."[31] It is from this foundation that she argues for what she calls Donne's "absolutist theology" or his "theology of power." Shuger then uses Donne's own statements acknowledging God's sovereignty to link him with "Calvin and almost all Reformed theologians"[32] and thereby concludes that such "power dynamics" not only "constitute the totality of Donne's theology," but finally "they are at the center of his conception of God."[33] Arguing that Donne believes in divine sovereignty, which he does, does not, however, allow one to assume that he subscribes to this doctrine as theologically foundational in the same way that Calvin does. As this chapter seeks to demonstrate, if we take Donne at his word, a belief in the communal nature of God in the Trinity is the center of his conception of God.[34]

In contrast to Calvin's insistence on sovereignty as his theological first

---

(p. 19). Identifying the central Calvinist premise as "a belief in man's total depravity [that] heightened the awful sovereignty of God," he adds that "the sharp antimony between man's abject predicament and God's immeasurable power gave Puritanism its distinctive character, and lay at the center of Puritan motivation" (p. 19).

[28] Calvin, *Institutes of the Christian Religion*, I:143.

[29] Ibid., I:98.

[30] Ibid., I:181.

[31] Shuger, *Habits of Thought in the English Renaissance*, p. 160.

[32] Ibid., p. 175.

[33] Ibid., p. 176.

[34] For an informed counterpoint to Shuger's views of Donne's absolutism, see two articles by Jeanne Shami: "Donne's *Sermons* and the Absolutist Politics of Quotation," and "'The Stars in their Order Fought against Sisera': John Donne and the Pulpit Crisis of 1622." See also David Nicholls, "Divine Analogy: The Theological Politics of John Donne."

principle, even to the point of ordering the persons of the godhead, Donne seems intent on avoiding such hierarchical distinctions. Instead, Donne insists on emphasizing, as his own theological first principle, the communal unity of the godhead when he writes that "that *name*, by which God notifies himself to the world, in the very beginning of *Genesis*, which is *Elohim*, as it is a *plural word* there, so it hath no *singular*: they say we cannot name God, but *plurally*" (6:152), and further that in the work of salvation "Christ were not sole, and alone, (for that mercy in the Decree was the joynt-act of the whole Trinity) yet even in that, Christ was equall to the Father, and the Holy Ghost" (5:379).[35] Even when Donne identifies the separate roles of the godhead, as he does in his Trinity Sunday sermon on Psalm 2:12, he emphasizes that the traditionally distinguishing features of Father, Son, and Holy Ghost overlap. Couched in the context of David's sin committed against Uriah and his having "transgressed against all the three Persons, in all their Attributes" (3:328), Donne explains that "those three Attributes of God, Power, and Wisedome, and Goodnesse, be all three in all the three Persons of the Trinity, (for they are all (as we say in the Schoole) *Co-omnipotentes*, they have all a joynt-Almightinesse, a joynt-Wisdome, and a joynt-Goodnesse)" (3:327). In addition, Donne's 1625 Easter sermon articulates an overlapping of their roles in human history:

> We use to ascribe the Creation to the Father, but the Father created by the Word, and his Word, is his Son, Christ; *When he prepared the Heavens, I was there*, (saies Christ, of himselfe in the person of Wisdome) *and when he appointed the foundations of the earth, then was I by him, as one brought up with him*; It is not, as one brought in to him, or brought in by him, but with him; one as old, that is, as eternall, as much God as he. We use to ascribe Sanctification to the Holy Ghost; But the Holy Ghost sanctifies in the Church, And the Church was purchased by the blood of Christ, and Christ remaines Head of the Church, *usque in consummationem*, till the end of the world.
>
> (6:275–76)

Finally, in a sermon preached to the Earl of Exeter in the summer of 1624, Donne writes of "the *sociablenesse*, the *communicablenesse* of God," who prior to the creation was never alone for there was always a Father, Son, and Holy Ghost, and yet, Donne states, "We see [God] proceeded further; he came to a *Creation*" (6:154). The creation of humankind, in particular, is itself a reflection for Donne, not primarily of God's sovereignty, but principally of the divine community:

> [God] enlarged his love, in making *man*, . . . God would not be without man, nor he would not come single, not alone to the making of man; but it is *Faciamus hominem, Let us, us, make man*; God, in his whole counsail, in his

---

[35] Along similar lines, Donne states in another of his sermons that "The hypostaticall union of God and man in the person of Christ, was a work of the whole Trinity" (2:321).

whole Colledge, in his whole society, in the whole Trinity, makes man, in whom the whole nature of all the world should meet. (6:154)

These differences between Donne and Calvin are, Sherwood contends, "by and large determined by Donne's much greater respect for human powers," to the extent that "the Spirit finds much more powerful human efforts in Donne than Calvin."[36] Obviously, Sherwood's comments are made in a chapter in which he is seeking to present the Augustinian foundation for and the Reform influence on Donne's views on reason. Nevertheless, Sherwood is exactly right in calling attention to the need for more clearly defined differences between Donne and Calvin, which, when viewed in terms of their beliefs concerning God's nature in the Trinity and in relation to their perceptions of the human soul, are profound.

APRIL 1629

Throughout the *Sermons*, Donne chooses to make his arguments from a theological, rather than anthropological, perspective in order to move the Church from divisive quarreling and towards a unifying dialogue that reflects the creative action of the Trinity. The sermon he preached before Charles I at court in the spring of 1629 provides an excellent example of Donne applying this Trinitarian theology within a particular historical/political situation. The sermon in question is actually two sermons preached on a single text, Genesis 1:26 ("And God said, let us make man, in our image, after our likeness"), that form a complementary whole. The first is dated April 1629, with no day of the month indicated, while no date of any sort is provided for the second, although Simpson and Potter conjecture that "it probably followed the first at no great interval" (9:1). It is difficult not to read and analyze these companion sermons outside the context of the parliamentary discussions, and the adversarial conditions that existed between certain members of Parliament and Charles I, from 1628 through early March 1629.

During the later half of the 1620s, there was an increasing concern among certain Protestant MPs as English military forces returned home in defeat at the hands of French and Spanish Catholic armies and, correspondingly, as they witnessed the growing power of Charles in matters of both church and state. As a result, it was during the sessions in 1628–29 that, in the words of historian Christopher Thompson, "the House lost its sense of judgement and its members rushed incontinently from one uncompleted subject to the next."[37] In addition, the relationship between Charles and the Duke of Buckingham, who during 1628 was blamed by Parliament as a significant source of England's ills, created further political tension that Charles felt in an

---

[36] Sherwood, *Fulfilling the Circle*, p. 46.
[37] Thompson, "The Divided Leadership of the House of Commons in 1629," p. 245.

especially personal way when Buckingham was murdered in August of that year.[38] All of this frustration and distrust between Parliament and Charles came to a point of crisis early in 1629 and resulted in Charles' dissolution of Parliament on March 10 of that year, after which he began his era of personal rule.

The two issues that dominated the sessions from June 1628 to the dissolution of Parliament, and that became intertwined in the political power struggles, were tonnage and poundage, and religion. Concerning the former, Kevin Sharpe states, "Charles was anxious to have tonnage and poundage which he had collected without statutory authority since 1625 granted for life, as was customary, by parliament."[39] The bill for this had been read in the Commons in April of 1628, and throughout the latter half of that year Charles pushed for it to become law. Concerning the latter, Thompson describes what many in Parliament saw as "the infectious increase in Arminianism,"[40] which, such members as Francis Rous believed, "could undermine true religion and introduce their own erroneous opinions" specifically "by separating the prince from his people or by discovering other, non-parliamentary, sources of income."[41]

Throughout the final year that Parliament sat during Charles I's reign, the King seemed primarily concerned with the issue of tonnage and poundage, expressing his desire to support the English armies. In one speech during this time, he addressed both Houses and, in the words of Thompson, "made it plain that his purpose was conciliatory, explaining that his speech at the end of the previous session had been intended to show the necessity, not the right, by which he took Tonnage and Poundage."[42] Nevertheless, certain MPs (namely, Pym, Rich, Sherland, Harley, and Mildmay) continued to press the issue of Arminianism, and as Conrad Russell observes, "Such an atmosphere of concentration on religion had not been known in any previous Parliament of the decade."[43] Charles responded to these religious concerns, L. J. Reeve contends, "by holding out the prospect of religious reform."[44] In particular, he reinstated the recusancy laws in the summer of 1628, and at that time he "declared to Council that he intended to put all non-conformist Catholics out of office and commission."[45] Furthermore, at the end of November he not only ordered the bishops and judges to execute the

---

[38] For more complete discussions of the significance of Buckingham in this context, see Christopher Thompson, "The Divided Leadership of the House of Commons in 1629," pp. 246–48; and Kevin Sharpe, *The Personal Rule of Charles I*, pp. 46–52.

[39] Sharpe, *The Personal Rule of Charles I*, p. 51.

[40] Thompson, "The Divided Leadership of the House of Commons in 1629," p. 253.

[41] Ibid., p. 253.

[42] Ibid., pp. 251–52.

[43] Russell, *Parliaments and English Politics, 1621–1629*, p. 406.

[44] Reeve, *Charles I and the Road to Personal Rule*, p. 61.

[45] Ibid., p. 60.

recusancy laws, but he also charged the bishops "to maintain true religion, as laid down in the Prayer Book and Thirty-Nine Articles, without innovation."[46]

It was, however, the interpretation of the Thirty-Nine Articles that was at the heart of the religious debate, and what was dangerous about the Arminians, for many MPs, "was that they did claim, to the bewilderment of many members, that theirs was the doctrine of the Church of England."[47] In fact, Digges reminded the Commons at this time, "It seems the Arminians do all agree on the articles, but the difference is on the sense of it."[48] The debate in the Commons foundered precisely because, in its arguments against Arminian teachings on grace, the Calvinists relied on a mixture of statutory and non-statutory authorities that could not effectively exclude the Arminians from "true religion." In its own claim to be the true doctrine of the English Church, Arminianism was, in the words of Francis Rous, "'this Trojan horse,' sent to infiltrate the citadel of English religion: 'For an Arminian is the spawn of a papist.'"[49] As a result, Conrad Russell concludes, "Just as the 1628 House had been driven towards giving legal force to Parliamentary interpretation of the law, the 1629 House was driven towards wishing to give legal authority to Parliamentary interpretation of religion."[50]

When Sir John Eliot submitted his resolution, "which declared favourers of Arminianism, and collectors *or payers* of Tonnage and Poundage to be capital enemies of King and kingdom,"[51] it was obvious that Charles and Parliament had reached a political impasse. The vehemence with which certain MPs condemned innovations in religion and the collection and payment of tonnage and poundage resulted in Charles's dissolving Parliament on 10 March 1629. However, in his declaration to dissolve the assembly, Charles made it clear that "it was the seditious activity of the few in the lower house which had led to the failure of the session,"[52] noting that in the House as a whole "there were amongst them many religious, grave and well-minded men."[53]

Roughly one month after the culmination of these momentous events,

---

[46] Reeve, *Charles I and the Road to Personal Rule*, pp. 61–62. Further in his discussion, Reeve notes both that "in November, Charles also issued a declaration on religion, prefixed to a new edition of the Thirty-Nine Articles," and that "the declaration stated that the Articles were to be read literally and it forbade theological disputation of their meaning" (p. 63). In addition, a slightly expanded summary of these events appears in Peter White, *Predestination, Policy and Polemic*, pp. 250–53.

[47] Russell, *Parliaments and English Politics, 1621–1629*, p. 410.

[48] Ibid., p. 410. See also, Dewey Wallace, *Puritans and Predestination*, pp. 88–90.

[49] Reeve, *Charles I and the Road to Personal Rule*, p. 74.

[50] Russell, *Parliaments and English Politics, 1621–1629*, p. 409.

[51] Ibid., p. 416.

[52] Reeve, *Charles I and the Road to Personal Rule*, p. 88.

[53] Sharpe, *The Personal Rule of Charles I*, p. 57.

Donne preached at Court before Charles. In the wake of these religious/ political wranglings, Donne moves the discussion from sectarian interpretations of the Thirty-Nine Articles, with respect to grace, to the nature of God in the creation and, in doing so, presents a clear and detailed articulation of his theological vision. Donne's choice of text, Genesis 1:26, reveals his intention to center these two sermons on what is for him the theological foundation on the godhead's communal creation of humankind through deliberation and consultation.[54]

The lengthy opening paragraph of the first of these two sermons establishes the creative work of God as theological matter of the first order when Donne writes of the opening chapter of Genesis, "For, for the thing it selfe, there is no other thing to compare it with. For it is All, it is the whole world" (9:47). As a result, Donne divides his examination of the scripture text into the four compass points defining the earth, for as Donne writes, "And since we have the whole world in contemplation, consider in these words, the foure quarters of the world, by application, by fair, and just accommodation of the words" (9:49). These two companion sermons then comprise Donne's homily on the godhead's manifestation of itself to humankind. As Donne, in this opening paragraph, introduces the "frame" of his scripture text and his sermon, he seems to be speaking to the historical situation as well when he states, "Onely, beloved, remember, that a frame may be thrown down in much lesse time, then it was set up" (9:48). Here the Dean of St. Paul's is making a call for theological essentials and the orderly manner in which they must be approached.

In the *divisio*, Donne then describes the scope of the four compass points he uses to analyze his scripture text, east and west for the first sermon, and north and south for the second. The expansion of the text, he explains in the *divisio*, begins in the east, for "in the first word, that God speaks here, *Faciamus*, Let us, us in the plurall, (a denotation of divers Persons in one Godhead) we consider our East where we must beginne, at the knowledge and confession of the Trinity" (9:49). Donne then explains that what he calls the next word, *Faciamus Hominem*, is the west, the mortality of humankind: "Though we be thus made, made by the counsell, made by the concurrence, made by the hand of the whole Trinity; yet we are made but men. . . but earth, but red earth, earth dyed red in bloud, in Soul-bloud, the bloud of our own soules" (9:49).[55]

---

[54] In his "Donne's Political Intervention in the Parliament of 1629," Paul Harland examines Donne's sermon preached at Whitehall on 20 February 1629, in which he explains that Donne warns both Charles I and Parliament "that not to make use of the divine gift of discourse is to sink to a bestial level" (p. 29). Harland then quotes Donne, who writes, "speech is the Glue, the Cyment, the soul of Conversation, and of Religion too" (8:338), a statement that speaks directly to Donne's Trinitarian theology and the divine action of consultation.

[55] In this passage, Donne is alluding to Adam, as revealed in another sermon in which he specifies that the name "Adam" "signifies nothing but *red earth*; Let it be earth red with blood, let it be earth red with blushing" (2:200).

However, Donne consoles his listeners, stating that the next words "designe a North, a strong, and powerfull North, to scatter, and disipate these clouds" of decay and death and reveal that "we are made according to a pattern, to an image, to a likenesse, which God proposed to himselfe for the making of man" (9:49). Finally, Donne expresses that being created not just to any pattern, but specifically in the image of God "is our Meridionall height, our noon, our south point, our highest elevation" (9:50).

The expansion of the text in part one originates with the light of the east, "the manifestation of the Trinity" (9:51), and as he states later in this section, "We exercise not faith, (and *without faith it is impossible to please God*) till we come to that, which is above nature, till we apprehend a Trinity," for "We know God, we beleeve in the Trinity" (9:52). Following his distinction between natural philosophy, "the foure elements, which God made" (9:51), and supernatural philosophy, "the three elements, which God is" and which "notifie God to us, Father, Sonne, and holy Ghost" (9:51), Donne then raises the question that drives this first part of the sermon: "But though in our *Doctrine* we keep up the Trinity aright; yet, God knowes, in our *Practice* we doe not. I hope it cannot be said of any of us, that he beleeves not the Trinity, but who amongst us thinkes of the Trinity, considers the Trinity?" (9:53). This question articulates Donne's persistent concern for the practical application of the doctrine. In fact, Donne prefaces this practical concern with his own comment on the recent historical debates and actions:

> Truly it is a sad Contemplation, to see Christians scratch and wound and teare one another, with the ignominious invectives, and uncharitable names of Heretique, and Schismatique, about Ceremoniall, and Problematicall, and indeed but Criticall verbal controversies: and in the meane time, the foundation of all, the Trinity, undermined by those numerous, those multitudinous Anthills of *Socians*, that overflow some parts of the Christian world, and multiply every where. (9:52–53)

Here Donne seeks to remind his auditors that the fundamental unifying belief for all Christians, including, it would seem, both Calvinists and Arminians, is a proper belief in the Trinity. To emphasize his point concerning the doctrine that he believes should unify the English Church, Donne identifies what he sees as a truly serious threat to doctrinal essentials, the Socians, who denied the divinity of Christ. Yet, even here, Donne is less concerned with enumerating who does and who does not belong among the "true religious" than he is with establishing theological foundations.

Donne proceeds by exploring four areas of practical application that discover "*Vestigia Trinitatis*" in the Church universal. He first reminds his audience that being baptized in the name of the Father, Son, and Holy Ghost is a seal that reimprints the Trinity on the soul "in our second Creation, our

Regeneration, in Baptisme."[56] Next, he questions why Christians are not instead called Trinitarians, and then responds, "the professing of the name of Christ, [is] the professing of the whole Trinity," for "as Christ is the manifestation of the Father, so the holy Ghost is the application of the Sonne," and similarly, "because, as the Father sent him [Christ], so he sent the holy Ghost" (9:56). Third, Donne explains that ministers are invited to participate in the divine imperative of this scripture text:

> *Faciamus,* Let us, us both together, you and we, make a man; join mine Ordinance (your preaching) with my Spirit, (says God to us) and so make man. Preach the oppressor, and preach the wanton, and preach the calumniator into another nature. Make that ravening Wolfe a Man, that licentious Goate a man, that insinuating Serpent a man, by thy preaching. (9:58)

Finally, Donne addresses Charles I directly, in the context of discussing the opening word of Genesis 1:26 as a royal plural. Although he begins by emphasizing the reverence due the King by his subjects, Donne moves on to remind Charles that "this rule goes thorough all nations, that in that disposition, and posture, and action of the body which in that place is esteemed most humble, and reverend, God is to be worshipped" (9:59). As a result, Donne then declares that in prayer "there is no difference, one humiliation is required of all" (9:60) and thereby uses a Trinitarian application of the act of prayer to define for the King his royal limitations.[57] The section devoted to the east concludes with a meditation on the comfort afforded by the Trinity in daily life:

> But I coine my gold into currant money, when I apprehend God, in the severall notions of the Trinity. That if I have been a prodigall Sonne, I have a father in heaven, . . . That if I be a decayed Father, and need the sustenation of mine own children, I have a Sonne in heaven, . . . If I be dejected in spirit, there is a holy Spirit in heaven, which shall beare witnesse to my spirit, that I am the child of God. (9:61)

These are the theological essentials to which Donne would move the King and members of court beyond the delimiting sectarian battles that persisted during this time.

The tone Donne seeks to establish in the second part, the west, is one of humility, yet in reminding his auditory of the truth of human mutability, he

---

[56] See the section in chapter 3 entitled "God's Wardrobe" for a discussion of Donne's views on baptism.

[57] On the limits of absolutism, see Nicholls, "Divine Analogy," in which he argues convincingly, "Donne insisted again and again that the analogy between divine and civil structures of authority does not imply a univocal similarity between God and the king" (p. 575) and that it would "be a mistake to suggest that Donne's conception of God was merely an ideological tool for justifying by analogy the kind of polity of which he approved," for "his trinitarianism is too closely bound up with other aspects of his religion for this to be credible" (p. 580).

does so in terms of the assurance and comfort found in the divine community. After briefly reviewing the four Hebrew names for man and their respective meanings (Ish, Enosh, Gheber and Adam), Donne notes that the scripture text uses the last of these, indicating that "Man is but an earthern vessel" (9:62). He then elaborates this metaphor, noting that so long as God is the potter Donne is content to be the vessel, in order to establish the point of "let me be any thing, so that that I am be from my God" (9:62). To emphasize this point further, he modifies and extends the metaphor, explaining his contentment to be a sheep if God will be his shepherd, to be a cottage if God his builder, to be rye or wheat if God his husbandman, and to be either leather or silk if God his merchant.

Only after securing the assurance of his desire to belong to God does Donne move on to enumerate the humbling and leveling truth that in the grave "all dusts are equall" (9:63). Yet, Donne goes further by placing this idea poignantly in its historical immediacy:

> No limbeque, no weights can tell you, This is dust Royall, this Plebeian dust: no Commission, no Inquisition can say, This is Catholique, this is Hereticall dust. All lie alike; and all shall rise alike: alike, that is, at once, and upon one Command. The Saint cannot accelerate; The Reprobate cannot retard the Resurrection. (9:64)

In its context, this brief passage offers an interesting example of Donne's inclusive understanding of the Christian community. On the one hand, he names Catholics as distinct from heretics, and on the other hand, he uses the decidedly Calvinist word "reprobate."[58] Again, this time through a reminder of the humbling effects of death, Donne shows his concern for the unity of the Church universal that reflects the divine community.

Donne concludes his section on the west, as well as the first of the two sermons, with a warning that although "White is the colour of dilatation; [for] goodnesse onely enlarges the Throne" (9:66), yet whiteness can also indicate leprosy:

> It is *Whole-pelagianisme*, to thinke nature alone sufficient; *Halfe-pelagianisme*, to thinke grace once received to be sufficient; *Super-pelagianisme*, to thinke our actions can bring God in debt to us, by merit, and supererogation, and *Catharisme*, imaginary purity, in canonizing our selves, as present Saints, and condemning all, that differ from us, as reprobates. All these are white spots, and have the colour of goodnesse; but are indications of leprosie. (9:67)

[58] In his attempt to describe Donne's Anglicanism, Nicholls ("The Political Theology") notes: To regard Donne as belonging to some kind of Arminian party would be to misconceive the situation. At the time of the Synod of Dort (1618–19), Donne clearly supported a moderate Calvinism, firmly rejecting the Arminianism of the Remonstrants on the one hand and the ultra-Calvinism of the "supralapsarians," like Gomarus, on the other. (p. 49)

Although this passage offers important and useful distinctions concerning Donne's views on grace and free will, it would be a mistake to use this passage only to attempt to identify Donne's sectarian allegiance.[59] The conclusion of this first sermon is a definition not of "true religion," but of goodness, as discerned by the ways in which people treat one another. Therefore, Donne explains that to pretend to do good and not mean it, or to do good but not for good ends both have the color of goodness, but are in fact "mischievous leprosie" (9:67), for "There is no good whiteness, but a reflection from Christ Jesus, in an humble acknowledgement that wee have none of our own, and in a confident assurance, that in our worst estate we may be made partakers of his" (9:67). In the light of the divine community that is the Trinity, the fact of our mortality, Donne believes, provides the humility necessary for the Church to find its own unity in that of the godhead.

The second of the two sermons Donne preached on Genesis 1:26 offers at the start a rather extensive summary of the first, reiterating, with respect to the east, "the fundamentall knowledge of the Trinity" (9:68), and, with respect to the west, "the over-valuation of our own purity, and the uncharitable condemnation of all that differ from us" (9:69–70). The connection Donne perceives, as he sails from one quarter of his text to the next, is that humankind's "Eastern dignity," being created as the work of the whole Trinity, "falls under a Westerne cloud," that the Trinity "made us but earth," and yet, Donne continues, "then blowes our North, and scatters this cloud; that this earth hath a nobler forme, then any other part or limbe of the world," namely, that "we are made by a fairer pattern, by a nobler Image, by a higher likenesse" (9:70). This is the "fair weather" Donne describes coming from the North and that he introduces in the context of Canticles 4:16: "Awake, O north wind; and come, thou south; blow upon my garden, that the spices thereof may flow out. Let my beloved come into his garden, and eat his pleasant fruits." By alluding directly to this passage from Canticles, which Donne understood typologically as an epithalamium celebrating the love of Christ for his Church, he once again emphasizes that the assurance and comfort we receive from this north wind is that of being in loving communion with God.

From here, however, this first part of the second sermon takes a curious turn. Donne notes that theologians have offered a variety of observations concerning the distinctions between the words from the scripture text translated as "image" and "likeness," and then he launches into a lengthy section based on the contention, "I know it is a good rule, that *Damascen* gives, *Parva, parva non sunt, ex quibus magna proveniunt:* Nothing is to be neglected as little, from which great things may arise" (9:70–71). After presenting an array of examples (from the Council of Ephesus to the Council of Chalcedon to the Council of Nicæa) related to changes in words, syllables

---

[59] Donne's views on grace are examined in chapter 5.

and letters, as well as examples representing changes in syntax and changes from declaratives to interrogatives, that have had significant interpretive effects, Donne repeats, "Sounds, voices, words must not be neglected," for "Great inconveniences grew upon small tolerations" (9:72). What is puzzling here is that following nearly three pages of reasons seemingly in favor of why it is necessary to distinguish between the words "image" and "likeness," Donne promptly dismisses the need for doing so. "This might be done," he writes, and then immediately explains:

> but that that must be done, will possesse all our time; that is, to declare, (taking the two words for this time to be but a farther illustration of one another, *Image*, and *likenesse*, to our present purpose, to be all one) what this *Image*, and this *likenesse* imports; and how this North scatters our former cloud; what our advantage is, that we are made to an Image, to a pattern; and our obligation to set a pattern before us, in all our actions. (9:73)

As a result, Donne seems to dismiss this extended digression as a squabble over "things indifferent" (or *adiaphora*) and, as such, generates a pattern for resolving such contentions by shifting the focus away from linguistic dissections resulting in charges of heresy and sectarian splinterings of the Church.[60]

Yet, Donne complicates the issue even further. At the end of the paragraph following the digression, he directly comments on grace and free will, which were, of course, the points of religious controversy during the parliamentary debates that occurred just prior to the sermon:

> In man his [God's] administration is this, that he hath imprinted in him a faculty of will, and election; and so hath something to reward in him. . . . But the free will of man God visits, and assists with his grace to doe supernaturall things. . . . When man does any thing conducing to supernaturall ends, though the worke be Gods, the will of man is not merely passive. The will of man is but Gods agent; . . . For, the will considered, as a will, (and grace never destroyes nature, nor, though it make a dead will a live will, or an ill will a good will, doth it make the will, no will) might refuse or omit that that it does. (9:75)

---

[60] For an examination of the ubiquitousness of this concept throughout the English Reformation, see Bernard Verkamp, *The Indifferent Mean*, in which he explains that for the English reformers:

> the very definition of adiaphora along theological lines as those things which had been "neither commanded, nor forbidden" by Scripture, implied that so far at least as the immediate will of God was concerned such matters were lacking in any necessity of means or precept, and to that extent could not, in themselves and apart from any legislation in their regard by church or civil officials, be considered necessary to salvation. But, of course, the heart of the matter lay elsewhere. The more critical question was whether things which by theological definition were adiaphora and "not necessary to salvation" might upon legislation by church or civil officials lose their adiaphoristic character and become necessary to salvation by at least a necessity of precept. (pp. 40–41)

This view of the human will as the agent of God is the pattern, Donne asserts, that the Church should follow. What Donne has written here concerning the need of human efforts in the work of grace would undoubtedly have pleased Charles and the Arminians, yet Donne's purpose here is not primarily to choose sides in this sectarian battle. On the contrary, he clarifies that even though this is the pattern he prefers for the Church, yet he warns (himself as well as his auditory):

> Never say, There is no Church without error: therefore I will be bound by none; but frame a Church of mine owne, or be a Church to my selfe. What greater injustice, then to propose no Image, no pattern to thy selfe to imitate; and yet propose thy selfe for a pattern, for an Image to be adored? Thou wilt have singular opinions, and singular ways differing from all other men; and yet all that are not of thy opinion must be heretiques; and all reprobates, that goe not thy wayes. (9:75)

The fundamental pattern from which Donne has argued throughout these companion sermons is the communal unity of the Trinity, but here Donne acknowledges that, existing as it does under the mark of original sin, the visible Church is imperfect.[61] Thus, even though Donne argues against strict Calvinism and for a necessary exercise of free will, it is theologically significant that with respect to the issue of grace he does not exclude the Calvinists as heretics, as they themselves (in the House of Commons) sought to do with the Arminians. Because of his understanding of the doctrine of the Trinity, Donne's theological impulse always moves towards inclusion rather than exclusion, which is what he develops further in the fourth, and final, compass direction.

Donne initiates the section designated the south by noting, "when we seek the Image of God in man, we beginne with a negative; This Image is not in his body" (9:76), but instead, he explains, in the soul. The location of the image of God serves as the basis for Donne's word of caution in calling anyone a heretic, specifying, "for I dare call an opinion heresie for the matter, a great while before I dare call the man that holds it an *heretick*" (9:77). The outward actions are more easily discerned and judged than are the inward essence, for as Donne elaborates, "It must be matter of faith, before the matter be heresie," and "there must be pertinacy after convenient instruction, before that man be an heretique" (9:77). Donne then extends his warning to an

---

[61] See Nicholls, "The Political Theology," who explains, "Donne did not adopt in consequence the Lutheran concept of an invisible church but, following Hooker, saw the institutional churches as concrete and necessary, though always imperfect, embodiments of Christ's one, holy, Catholic, and apostolic Church" (p. 63). See also, Dominic Baker-Smith, "John Donne's *Critique of True Religion*," in which, in the context of his discussion of "Satyre III," he asserts that Donne's view of the Church "is directly indebted to the concept of the *via media* outlined by such Henrician apologicists as Thomas Starkey and John Bekinshaw and massively fulfilled in Hooker" (p. 418).

occasion for instruction by asserting that wit and learning are better applied in proving the Incarnation and Judgment of Christ to the nations, as well as one's own conscience, "then to have filled the world, and torne the Church, with frivolous disputations," and then admonishes, "Wo unto fomentors of frivolous disputations" (9:79). Donne calls such activity "frivolous" precisely because it gives inordinate weight and attention to surfaces and appearances. While Donne knows that the body matters, he also knows that the body does not bear the divine image and, therefore, is not the exclusive, or even primary, focus of divine attention: "God lookes not for the gilding, or enamelling, or painting of that: but requires the labour, and cost therein to be bestowed upon the table it selfe, in which this Image is immediately, that is the soule. And that's truly the *Vbi*, the place where this Image is" (9:79).

The soul, consisting of the memory, understanding and will, is the wax, Donne explains, that receives the seal of the Trinity (9:80). By means of the word "seal" Donne introduces a metaphor that he pursues to remind the politically powerful of their limitations. "No Image," he writes, "but the Image of God can fit our soule" (9:80), and based on this principle of what is fitting and proper, Donne insists that civil officials and rulers should conform to this pattern, only exercising the authority their particular seals allow:

> The magistrate is sealed with the Lion; The woolfe will not fit that seale: the Magistrate hath a power in his hands, but not oppression. Princes are sealed with the Crown; The Miter will not fit that seale. Powerfully, and gratiously they protect the Church, and are supreme heads of the Church; But they minister not the Sacraments of the Church. (9:80)

Read in relation to the parliamentary issues of tonnage and poundage and the threat of Arminianism, this passage seems to be a statement about not using political power to punish innocents under the guise of religion. It may refer to Charles' rather recent reinstatement and execution of the recusancy laws, or to the resolution sent forward by Sir John Eliot to punish any who paid or received monies for tonnage and poundage, or both of these together. Whatever the specific application, Donne remains firm in his purpose to pursue matters of religious controversy from the foundation of a clear Trinitarian theology. The remainder of this fourth part consists of a detailed and rather lengthy account of the relation between the tripartite soul and the persons of the Trinity, an account which corresponds to the ideas found earlier in this chapter. The sermon as a whole then concludes, in its final sentence, with an injunction for the audience to attend to the words of the sermon and for Charles himself to be a pattern for his subjects: "For that's the heighth of Gods malediction upon a Nation, when the assiduity of preaching, and the example of a Religious Prince, does them no good, but aggravates their fault" (9:91).

There is no evidence indicating how this sermon was received by Charles or by the members of court in attendance, either the Calvinist or the Arminian sympathizers. Clearly throughout this double text Donne supports Charles, but he does so from a decidedly theological, and not a merely political, basis. In spite of the passages affirming human efforts in the work of grace that are sprinkled throughout these two sermons, which the King and the Arminians would have favored, Donne's theological vision suggests that he would not have been pleased with the dissolution of Parliament, fundamentally since such action stands in the face of his Trinitarian model of consultation and deliberation.[62]

In addition to the national implications of this sermon on Genesis 1:26, it also had personal implications for Donne a short while later. A little more than a year after preaching this sermon before the King at court, Donne posed in a winding sheet, according to Izaak Walton, for the portrait that Donne kept by his bedside until his death and that Nicolas Stone afterwards used for the marble sculpture that stands in St. Paul's. The statue faced east in the old cathedral,[63] and the epitaph above the statue that Donne composed for himself reaffirms in its closing sentence the theological significance of that compass direction: "*HIC LICET IN OCCIDVO CINERE/ ASPICIT EVM CVIVS NOMEN/ EST ORIENS*"[64] ("Here, though in western dust, he looks towards Him whose name is the East").[65] In the *divisio* of his April 1629 sermon on Genesis 1:26, Donne explains that "Christs name is *Oriens*, the *East*," and then adds, "if we will be named by him, (called Christians) we must look to this East, the confession of the Trinity" (9:49). Read in the context of his clerical career and writings, this statue and its accompanying epitaph provide, within the edifice of the Church, testimony of Donne's desire for the individual members of the Church universal to find their life and unity in the Trinity.

---

[62] See Harland ("Donne's Political Intervention in the Parliament of 1629") who, in the context of challenging critics charging Donne with "sycophantic behavior towards the king" (p. 30), describes Donne's implied message throughout the 20 February 1629 sermon at Whitehall:

> if the king can expect to be honoured with thanksgiving and submission in the admission of error, he must also be willing to hear the needs of his people, such as those continually presented in Parliament. On the other hand, those charged with advising the king have a duty to speak to him without flattery, even when it is difficult. (p. 26)

[63] See Izaak Walton, *The Lives of John Donne, Sir Henry Wotton, Richard Hooker, George Herbert, and Robert Sanderson*, who describes Donne standing on a wooden urn "with his eyes shut, and with so much of the sheet turned aside as might shew his lean, pale, and death-like face, which was purposely turned toward the East, from whence he expected the second coming of his and our Saviour Jesus" (p. 78).

[64] *The Variorum Edition of the Poetry of John Donne*, gen. ed. Gary Stringer, vol. 8, p. 193.

[65] Nigel Foxell, *A Sermon in Stone*, p. 6.

WHITSUNTIDE

At several prominent moments in the April 1629 sermon to Charles I, Donne writes of the person of the Holy Spirit, urging his auditors to reflect seriously on the all too often neglected workings of the Spirit:

> But for the holy Ghost, who feels him, when he feels him? Who takes knowledge of his working, when he works? Indeed our Fathers provided not well enough for the worship of the whole Trinity, nor of the holy Ghost in particular, in the endowments of the Church, and Consecrations of Churches, and possessions in their names. (9:53)

Sounding a more personal note, Donne asks, "Shall I ever forget who gave me my comfort in sicknesse? Who gave me my comfort, in the troubles, and perplexities, and diffidencies of my conscience?" and then responds, "The holy Ghost brought you hither [and] the holy Ghost opens your eares, and your hearts here" (9:54). As an extension of the Spirit's comfort, Donne even imagines it in terms of the final judgment, stating, "Till in all your distresses, you can say, *Veni Creator Spiritus*, come holy Ghost, and that you feel a comfort in his comming: you can never say *Veni Domine Jesu*, come Lord Jesus, come to Judgement," for as Donne reasons, it is a fearful thing not to consider the day of judgment, "But," he adds, "to consider the day of Judgement, without the comfort of the holy Ghost, is a thousand times more fearfull" (9:54).

One of the most distinctive features of Donne's Trinitarian theology is his emphasis on the Holy Spirit and the Spirit's role concerning human efforts, both to the individual and in the Church. It is the Holy Spirit who, as Donne states in this same sermon on Genesis 1:26, "applies the mercies of the Father, and the merits of the Sonne to my soule" (9:56). Further, Donne specifically links the workings of the Spirit to the memory and the Spirit's distinguishing characteristics of goodness and love (9:84),[66] such as when he explains that in the memory a person "may reade many a history of Gods goodnesse to him" so that "truly the Memory is oftner the Holy Ghosts Pulpit that he preaches in, then the Understanding" (8:261–62). As a result, if "the art of *salvation*, is but the art of *memory*" (2:73), then it is crucial to know how Donne conceives of the workings of the Holy Spirit.

In the earliest of his Whitsunday sermons, Donne writes, "And as the Trinity is the most mysterious piece of our Religion, and hardest to be comprehended, So in the Trinity, the Holy Ghost is the most mysterious person, and hardest to be expressed" (5:46). Of the sermons Donne prepared

---

[66] Donne's aligning of the Holy Spirit with the faculty of memory is a departure from Augustine who in *De Trinitate* seems to align the Holy Spirit with the will (XV.xxi), although Donne concurs with Augustine that the person of the Spirit is characterized by love (XV.xvii).

for publication, no less than ten are Whitsunday sermons, a fact that accentuates the prominence of the Holy Spirit in Donne's religious imagination. Addressing the parishioners of St. Dunstan's on Trinity Sunday 1624, Donne seeks to rectify the problem that "neither doe we bend our thoughts upon the consideration of the Holy Ghost, so much as we ought to doe" by explaining that "there are two processions of the holy Ghost, *Æterna*, and *Temporaria*, his proceeding from the Father, and the Son, and his proceeding into us" (6:127).[67] Of the first, Donne asserts, "we shall never understand, if we reade all the books of the world," and of the second, "we shall not choose but understand, if we study our own consciences" (6:127–28). Although he avoids discussing the former here in this sermon, Donne offers an evocative metaphoric description of the Spirit's procession from the Father and Son in his 1630 Whitsunday sermon. Insisting on the equality of the persons of the Trinity, Donne notes, referring to the Spirit, "But the Father sent him, and the Son sent him, as a tree sends forth blossomes, and as those blossomes send forth a sweet smell, and as the Sun sends forth beames, by an emanation from it selfe" (9:240). Because Donne can hardly mention the Spirit without shifting to the latter procession (as these agricultural and celestial metaphors suggest by emphasizing their reception through the senses), Donne concludes his aside in this sermon, stating, "Though nothing be more mysterious then the knowledge of God in the Trinity, yet nothing is more manifest unto us, then, by the light of this person, the Holy Ghost, so much of both the other Persons, as is necessary for our Salvation" (9:241).

To return then to the 1624 St. Dunstan's sermon, Donne enlarges his discussion of the Spirit proceeding into us by launching into a detailed explanation of the relationship between "our Creation, which is commonly attributed to the Father," "our Redemption, which belongs to the Son," and the work of sanctification performed by the Spirit:

> this Spirit disposes, and dispenses, distributes, and disperses, and orders all the power of the Father, and all the wisdome of the Son, and all the graces of God. It is a Center to all. . . . That office which the soule performes to our body, the holy Ghost performes in the body of Christ, which is the Church. (6:128–29)

Donne situates this reference to the soul and the mediating office of the Holy Ghost immediately in terms of the triune counsel of creation and concludes, "let us be sure to hold this that is nearest us, to keep a neare, a familiar, and daily acquaintance, and conversation with the holy Ghost, and to be watchfull to cherish his light, and working in us" (129).

As these passages suggest, as well as the earlier discussion in the section on "Reason and the Trinity," the Holy Spirit performs the key role of manifesting the other two persons of the Trinity to the individual members

---

[67] Donne's views on the *filioque* controversy that divided the Eastern and Western Churches are, not surprisingly, derived primarily from Augustine's *De Trinitate*, Books IV, IX, and XV.

of the Church. Preached 16 June 1619 to the Prince and Princess Palatine, Donne's Heidelberg sermon identifies the coming of Christ "to our heart, in the working of his grace" as "the internal operation of the holy Ghost, in infusing grace" (2:260, 261). It is the Holy Spirit, as Donne explains to his royal auditors, that "tels thy soul that all this that the Father had promised, and the Son had performed, was intended by them, and by the working of their spirit, is now appropriated to thy particular soul" (2:261).

Overall in his *Sermons*, Donne is much less interested in analyzing the theological nuances of the Holy Spirit's relation to the rest of the godhead than he is with clarifying the ways in which the Spirit enfolds the Church in the divine community. David Nicholls highlights this very point when he notes that Donne "does not speak of the Church as an extension of the Incarnation, as many Anglicans have done, but as a creation of the Holy Spirit in the context of the saving work of Christ," and, as a result, "ecclesiology is, for him, more closely related to soteriology than to Christology."[68] Two Whitsunday sermons, one that falls next to last in the chronology and another that appears as first in the series, reveal Donne's mature thought on the role of the Spirit.

Donne begins his 1629 Whitsunday sermon, the text for which is Genesis 1:2 ("And the Spirit of God moved upon the face of the waters"), by emphasizing that "The Holy Ghost is the God, the Spirit of Comfort" (9:92). He later summarizes this opening paragraph by explaining how the Spirit manifests its comfort to us:

> So that, as the Holy Ghost is the Comforter, so is this Comfort exhibited by him to us, and exercised by him upon us, in this especially, that he hath gathered us, established us, illumined us, and does governe us, as members of that body, of which Christ Jesus is the Head; that he hath brought us, and bred us, and fed us with the meanes of salvation, in his application of the merits of Christ to our soules, in the Ordinances of the Church. (9:92)

In order to illustrate the workings of the Spirit's comfort more fully, Donne discusses later in the sermon the word in the text that is translated as "moved." Specifically, Donne articulates the paradoxical double meaning of the word itself: "it signifies *motion*, and it signifies *rest*" (9:98). Yet, the double possibility of meaning has for Donne a single context, namely the Spirit's work in nurturing humanity: "This word, we translate, *As the Eagle fluttereth over her young ones*, so it is a word of Motion; And S. *Hierom* upon our Text expresses it by *Incubabat, to sit upon her young ones, to hatch them, or to preserve them*, so it is a word of rest" (9:98). The whole point of this etymological discussion is to articulate the way in which the Spirit reveals the Creator to humankind, for, as Donne explains, "this is the office of the holy Ghost, to manifest and apply God to us" (9:99), or again as he states later,

[68] Nicholls, "The Political Theology," p. 60.

"This is the person, without whom there is no Father, no Son of God to me, the holy Ghost" (9:101).

One final metaphor of the Spirit's workings is worthy of note in this sermon, and it too enlarges the image of God by complementing God's role as creator:

> The moving of the holy Ghost upon me, is, as the moving of the mind of an Artificer, upon that piece of work that is then under his hand. A Jeweller, if he would make a jewell to answer the form of any flower, or any other figure, his minde goes along with his hand, nay prevents his hand, and he thinks in himselfe, a Ruby will conduce best to the expressing of this, and an Emeraud of this. The holy Ghost undertakes every man amongst us, and would make every man fit for Gods service, in some way, in some profession; and the holy Ghost sees, that one man profits most by one way, another by another, and moves their zeal to pursue those wayes, and those meanes, by which, in a rectified conscience, they finde most profit. And except a man have this sense, what doth him most good, and a desire to pursue that, the holy Ghost doth not move, nor stir up a zeale in him. (9:101–2)

This passage is intriguing for a whole variety of reasons; however, for my purposes here, two points are especially illuminating. The first is the emphasis on human efforts and artifice, insisting that it is necessary for individuals to have the self-awareness and the desire in order to enable the Spirit to "stir up a zeale" in them. The second is the point expressed early in the passage that the Spirit makes individuals fit for service, some "by one way" and "another by another," which is an idea that implies an understanding of the Church that is, in its intention, more inclusive than a strict sectarian allegiance.

The earliest of Donne's extant Whitsunday sermons, that preached at Lincoln's Inn on Acts 10:44, further clarifies the way in which the Spirit draws humanity into the divine community and, by extension, into community with one another as the body of Christ. In this sermon Donne speaks of the humility of the Spirit's motions: "In all his workings, the Holy Ghost descends, for there is nothing above him . . . ; so that whatsoever he doth, is a descent, a diminution, a humiliation, and an act of mercy, because it is a Communication of himselfe, to a person inferiour to himselfe" (5:48). Beyond highlighting the virtue of humility, Donne also defines in this passage, yet again, the workings of the Spirit as communicative. A paragraph later, Donne offers reasons for the purpose of the Spirit's descent, which "was not such a particular insinuation of the Holy Ghost, as that he convaied himselfe into those particular men, for their particular good, and salvation, and determined there" (5:49). Instead, Donne interprets his sermon text, which refers to the falling of the Spirit on the day of Pentecost, by stating, "So the Holy Ghost fell upon these men here, for the benefit of others," and further that the falling of the Spirit was "not meerly an infusing of justifying grace, but an infusing of such gifts, as might edifie others" (5:50). The significance of this passage is the way in which it develops Donne's view of the Spirit, and the Spirit's relation to the Trinity, as a theology that defines the Church in ways calling for human efforts responding to the divine initiative mediated by the Spirit and reflecting the divine unity.

UNITY V. SINGULARITY

In language that is virtually identical to that in his first sermon at St. Dunstan's, Donne opens one of his christening sermons by declaring, "Almighty God ever loved *unity*, but he never loved *singularity*; God was always *alone* in heaven, there were no *other Gods* but he; but he was never *singular*, there was never any time, when there were not *three persons* in heaven" (5:113). As if to illustrate the full extent of this concept, Donne applies, in his 1629 Christmas sermon, the plurality of the godhead to the very nature of sublunary existence, noting, "*Chajim*, which is the [Hebrew] word for *life*, hath no singular number" (9:149). As a further extension of his theology of communal participation, Donne offers, in another of his christening sermons, a lengthy discussion of the three witnesses in heaven (Father, Son, and Holy Spirit) and, in the context of Christ's encounter with Nicodemus in John 3, explains:

> Christ could not be *Singular testis*, a single witness; He was always more then one witnesse, because he had alwayes more then *one nature*; God and man; and therefore Christ instructing *Nicodemus*, speakes plurally, *we speake, that we know, we testifie that we have seene*, and you receive not *Testimonium nostrum*, our witnesse; he does not say *my witnesse*, but *ours*, because although a singular, yet he was a plurall person too. (5:141–42)

Not surprisingly, then, this theological insistence on unity over singularity, as well as community versus hierarchy, shapes Donne's interpretation of the scriptures. In his sermon on Matthew 9:13, which was preached at Whitehall on 30 April 1626, Donne explains that the text is neither singular nor universal, for "it is neither in one onely, nor in all the Evangelists" (5:142). Yet, because the text appears in three of the four Gospels, Donne claims that it has "(as they speak in the Law) an interpretative universality, a presumptive universality," and then concludes, "for that which hath a plurality of voices, is said to have all; and this Text hath so" (5:142). By means of his legal analogy, Donne expresses yet again that truth is revealed most clearly in a community of voices. Elsewhere Donne details a similar point when he writes of St. Paul's delight for "that sociable syllable, *Syn, Con, Conregnare*, and *Convificare*, and *Consedere*," and then draws the parallel that "As much also doth God delight in it, from us, when we expresse it in a Conformity, and Compunction, and Compassion, and Condolency" (3:376). In one final example of this sort, Donne opens his sermon on 1 Timothy 1:15 by defining the genre of the New Testament epistle in terms of its communal application: "An Epistle is *collocutio scripta*, saies Saint *Ambrose*, Though it be written far off, and sent, yet it is a Conference, and *seperatos copulat*, sayes hee; by this meanes wee overcome distances, we deceive absences, and wee are together even then when wee are asunder" (1:285).

The community of God is the center from which Donne's theology radiates, and the primary application Donne perceives for this revealed truth is in terms of defining the Church and informing the Christian life. In a Trinity Sunday sermon, Donne acknowledges, on the one hand, the unapproachable mystery of God and, on the other hand, the accessibility afforded through the Trinity:

> And though [God] be in his nature incomprehensible, and inaccessible in his light, yet this is his infinite largenesse, that being thus infinitely One, he hath manifested himselfe to us in three Persons, to be the more easily discerned by us, and the more closely and effectually applied to us. (3:263)

Along similar lines, his 1627 Christmas sermon preached at St. Paul's comments once again that "God loves not singularity" (8:155) and then expands on God's inclusive, communal nature as the pattern for the Church:

> As God loves Sympathy, God loves Symphony; God loves a compassion and fellow-feeling of others miseries, that is Sympathy, and God loves Harmony, and fellow-beleeving of others Doctrines, that is Symphony; No one man alone makes a Church; no one Church alone makes a Catholique Church. (8:155)

Even though Donne obviously attacks the "one man alone" governing the Roman Church, the emphasis here is primarily a dialogic one. In this same passage, Donne explains that the God who dwells in us "will make us Tutelar Angels to one another" and that "in good conversation," we will keep each other "from many sinfull actions, which we would commit if we were alone" (8:155).

The principle that Donne implies in the passage above is one that he articulates directly in his second sermon at St. Dunstan's when he discusses individuals who are "afraid to crosse the vices of the Time, so far, as by being vertuous in their owne particular," and then states that these individuals are afraid their actions "will be called a *singularity*, and a *schismaticall* and *seditious* disposition" (6:107).[69] This connection between singularity and schism is expressed clearly in the sermon Donne preached at The Hague on 19 December 1619 while attached to Viscount Doncaster's mission to

---

[69] For a parallel of this idea in the *Devotions upon Emergent Occasions*, see the end of the seventh expostulation, in which Donne addresses God, stating, "That for thy great *Helpe*, thy *Word*, I may seeke that, not from *corners*, nor *Conventicles*, nor *schismatical singularities*; but from the assotiation, & communion of thy *Catholique Church*, and those persons, whom thou hast alwayes furnished that *Church* withall" (p. 39).

Germany. Specifically, Donne asserts, "Christ loves not singularity; he called not one alone; He loves not schisme neither between them whom he cals" (2:280), which he states in response to defining the name and nature of the Church:

> God loves not singularity; The very name of Church implies company; It is *Concio, Congregatio, Cœtus,* It is a Congregation, a Meeting, an assembly; . . . The Church loves the name of Catholique; and it is a glorious, and an harmonious name; Love thou those things wherein she is Catholique, and wherein she is harmonious, that is, *Quod ubique, quod semper,* Those universall, and fundamentall doctrines, which in all Christian ages, and in all Christian Churches, have beene agreed by all to be necessary to salvation; and then thou art a true Catholique. (2:279, 280)

The message Donne articulates here is not simply, "Take heed of singular, of schismatical opinions" (4:349); it is finally a message that celebrates communal participation:

> The Dove is *animal sociale,* a sociable creature, and not singular; and the Holy Ghost is that; And Christ is a Sheep, *animal gregale,* they flock together: Embrace thou those truths, which the whole flock of Christ Jesus, the whole Christian Church, hath from the beginning acknowledged to be truths, and truths necessary to salvation. (4:349)

Over and over again throughout the *Sermons* it is the community of the body of Christ reflecting the community of the Trinity that pervades and characterizes Donne's theology.[70] "The whole Church of God is one household," Donne contends, "as long as they agree in the unity of that doctrine which the Apostles taught, and adhere to the supreme head of the whole Church, Christ Jesus" (3:138). One final sermon further clarifies the theological implications of Donne's views on Trinitarian unity and the manner in which that model shapes his vision of the Church.

Donne's sermon to the Earl of Exeter, preached at the Earl's chapel at St. John's on 13 June 1624, exposes the parameters of Donne's views on the doctrine of the Trinity. Part one of the sermon examines at length "the *sociablenesse,* the *communicablenesse* of God; He loves holy meetings, he loves the *communion of Saints,* the *household of the faithful*" (6:152).[71] Of this contemplation of the Trinity and the Church, Donne writes, "It is a garden

---

[70] See Nicholls, "The Political Theology," pp. 60–64, who concludes, "Donne saw the Church of England, then, as a national embodiment of the Catholic Church – in alliance with the Protestant churches of the Continent, but at the same time as an integral part of a Christian commonwealth, which took as its model the social life of the Trinity" (p. 64).

[71] For a different application of this idea, see Dennis Klinck, "John Donne's 'knottie Trinitie,'" who argues that for Donne the doctrine of the Trinity is a response to a problem of the Many and the One, and yet in a manner that accords with my point here, he states that "the Trinity, as a principle of *unity,* is a principle of being" (p. 241).

worthy of your walking in" (6:152). A bit further into the argument, Donne then ponders the existence of God prior to the creation and asks, "but yet was God alone, any one minute of al this?", a question which he answers with another, this one rhetorical: "was there not alwais a *Father* and a *Son*, and a *holy Ghost*?" (6:153). With a third question Donne explains the reason for creation in terms of God's need to enlarge the divine community: "Had God company enough of himselfe; was he satisfied in the *three Persons*? We see he proceeded further; he came to a *Creation*" (6:153–54). Nevertheless, Donne argues, in spite of the fullness of creation and God's own pronouncement that it was "very good," God had further need:

> And still our large, and our Communicable God, affected this association so, as that having *three Persons* in himselfe, and having *Creatures* of divers natures, and having collected all natures in *man*, who consisted of a spirituall nature, as well as a bodily, he would have one liker himselfe, than man was; And therefore he made *Christ*, God and Man, in one person, Creature and Creator together.
> (6:154–55)

Yet, even this was not sufficient, for as Donne writes, "Beyond all this, God having thus maried soule and body in one man, and man and God, in one Christ, he maries this Christ to the Church," and yet even to those of the Church, "all met upon *whitsunday*," Donne writes, "the *holy Ghost* came so as that they were enabled, by the *gift of tongues*, to convey, and propagate, and derive God, (as they did) *to every nation under heaven*" (6:155). As a result, Donne asks of the Earl and his guests:

> so much does God delight in man, so much does God desire to unite and associate man unto him; and then, what shall disappoint, or frustrate Gods desires and intentions so farre, as that they should come to him, but singly, *one by one*, whom he *cals*, and *wooes*, and *drawes* by thousands, and by whole Congregations? (6:155)

*

This chapter began by outlining the circumstances surrounding Donne's appointment as Vicar of St. Dunstan-in-the-West. In his initial sermons to that congregation, Donne seeks to woo the parishioners, employing familial metaphors of husbands and wives, and of parents and children. Donne develops these familiar biblical metaphors in the context of creation and the unified plurality of God. Creation itself, which Donne understands as the Trinity's seeking to dilate its own community, is an act of love. As he articulates at the conclusions of the first two St. Dunstan's sermons, it is an act that defines the model for all relationships, including that between a minister and a congregation, for without a proper understanding of the doctrine of the Trinity, the Church, Donne contends, is in danger of losing its identity.

In an analogous manner, Donne's decidedly triune understanding of God inextricably intertwines itself with his understanding of the self. In the introduction to her edition of *Donne's Prebend Sermons*, Janel Mueller notes the continuing influence of Augustine's *De Trinitate* on Donne's preaching and, especially, Augustine's interpretation of Genesis 1:26, explaining that "the workings of the human consciousness reflect the relations of the Persons of the Trinity, and St. Augustine traces the reflections in what he considered to be the two essential activities of the soul – knowing and loving."[72] She comments further that for Augustine "knowledge and love are illustrations of the operative unity of Father, Son, and Holy Ghost," and that because "knowledge of God is the means to love of God," therefore, "creation and redemption constitute a correspondence in process between man and God."[73]

Donne cannot conceive of God outside of community and the creative and redemptive acts of God that enfold humankind within the divine relationship. Biblical history reveals then for Donne God's will for community with and among the creatures, which is itself an expression of the godhead's faithfulness to its own eternal, communal existence. Seen in this light, Donne's expression of the doctrine of the Trinity portrays God as the one who creates not as a demonstration of absolute power, but instead as an expression of the love that both defines God's essence and unites the Trinity itself. Vulnerable, rather than coercive, the triune God Donne portrays in the *Sermons* displays a sacrificial extension of itself that therefore risks the divine self and that then necessarily results in the suffering of God in Christ. It is in response to the Incarnation and Crucifixion that the individual believer, within the Church and through the workings of the Holy Spirit, shares in the sufferings of Christ and, as a result, finds a place in the enlarged community of God, all of which will be explored in the subsequent chapters.

If we take Donne at his word in the *Sermons*, that a right understanding of the doctrine of the Trinity defines Christian belief and regulates Christian faith and practice, then knowing Donne's particular views on this doctrine ought to clarify his theology, which in fact it does. As the subsequent chapters of this study make clear, Donne's understanding of the role of the Church universal and of the individual's responsibilies within the body of Christ are dependent on his view of the triune nature of God. Furthermore, the ideas developed in this chapter provide a theological context for reevaluating not only Donne's clerical career, but also the political contexts that shaped the most extensive record we have of his mature thought, the *Sermons*.

---

[72] Mueller, *Donne's Prebend Sermons*, pp. 30–31. These ideas are most clearly spelled out in *De Trinitate*, Books IX and XV.

[73] Ibid., p. 31.

Chapter Two

TO BATTER HEAVEN[1]

LINCOLN'S INN CHAPEL

O N Ascension Day in 1623, Donne returned to Lincoln's Inn to dedicate the chapel that was under construction while he served there as Reader. The printed edition of the sermon, dedicated "To the Masters of the Bench, and the rest of the Honourable Societie of Lincolnes Inne," is prefaced by a prayer of blessing for the new chapel. Donne asks that the chapel "mayest bee all unto all" – a treasure "to them that love *Profit* and *Gaine*," marrow and fatness "to them that love *Pleasure*," and a kingdom "to them that love *Preferment*" (4:363). It is a prayer of inclusion, a prayer that reflects Donne's wishes not simply for the new chapel, but finally for the Church as a whole to transform sinful pursuits into righteous ones. Brief as it is, this prayer expresses Donne's ideal for the Church to fulfill human desire and aspiration within a truly Catholic community that reflects the Trinity. In fact, the prayer opens by invoking the three persons of the divine community: "O Eternall, and most gracious *God*, Father of our Lord *Iesus Christ*"; followed by the request, "make us so much his [Christ's], as that we may be like him"; and then for the chapel, "Bee this thine *Arke*, and let thy *Dove*, thy blessed *Spirit*, come in and out, at these *Windowes*" (4:363). Donne's prayer for the chapel and his view of the Church universal rely entirely on his understanding of the Trinity, as revealed both in this text and throughout the *Sermons*.

In the sermon preached for this dedicatory occasion, Donne directs the attentions of his former congregation to the function of the new chapel:

> it is a frivolous contention, whether *Churches* be for *preaching*, or for *praying*. But if *Consecration* be a kind of *Christning* of the *Church*, and that at the *Christning* it have a name, wee know what name *God* hath appoynted for his House, *Domus mea, Domus orationis vocabitur. My House shall bee called the House of Prayer.* (4:373)

Donne often quotes in his *Sermons* this passage from Isaiah 56:7 in order, as he does here, to remind his auditors how God himself describes the Church,

---

[1] An abbreviated version of this chapter appeared as my article "Wrestling with God: John Donne at Prayer."

the members of which congregate, as Donne states, for "no other Service, but Common prayer" (4:374). Furthermore, in stating, "it is a frivolous contention, whether *Churches* be for *preaching*, or for *praying*," Donne touches one of the sectarian battlegrounds of the time, of which the decidedly Calvinist congregation at Lincoln's Inn would have been keenly aware.[2] However, Donne is not so much choosing sides here as he is focusing his audience on the theologically essential nature of prayer as it conforms the Church to the dialogic unity of the Trinity.

One of the most significant, and possibly the most visible, of Donne's religious struggles derives from his understanding of the Church. Reacting to the difficulties Donne experienced in his personal life in converting to the Church of England, as well as the inquiries he raises in the poems "Show me deare Christ" and "Satyre III," many critics have analyzed his religious conflicts in ways that tend to isolate and overemphasize the issue of his sectarian allegiance. To cite only a few examples, John Carey reduces the issue by simply labeling Donne an apostate. Interpreting Donne's life and faith exclusively as a betrayal of his Catholic upbringing, Carey states that "though Donne eventually came to accept Anglicanism, he could never believe that he had found in the Church of England the one true church outside which salvation was impossible."[3] Next, in an article that discusses Donne's life at Mitcham from 1607–10, those years which R. C. Bald describes as "the most disturbed and anxious years of Donne's life,"[4] Dennis Flynn argues that although Donne began, during these years, to perceive himself as "an Anglican with reservations," he still "could not fully accept Anglicanism as long as he felt a deep division between his private religious feelings and the institutional religion to which he subscribed."[5] Citing letters that Donne wrote to Goodyer during this period, Flynn insists that Donne's "private habits of prayer continued to reflect his Catholic background" and that throughout this period in his life Donne "emphasizes the value of a private devotion as opposed to the public ritual of his church."[6]

Even those critics who seek to define Donne as a Calvinist reach markedly different conclusions about Donne's Calvinism. Richard Strier, for example,

---

[2] In her "'The Stars in their Order Fought Against Sisera': John Donne and the Pulpit Crisis of 1622," Jeanne Shami contends, "The Puritan leaning of Lincoln's Inn, and the fact that Donne was preceded by Thomas Gataker and succeeded by John Preston in his role as Reader there, has also never been sufficiently emphasized" (p. 7). In the context of the debate over preaching and sacraments, I would argue that Daniel Doerksen (*Conforming to the Word*) is too rigid in his insistence that Donne is a Calvinist conformist because he values preaching (cf. pp. 104–06). While Donne does in fact hold preaching in high regard, his views on preaching must be read in the light of his understanding of the Church and its defining communal act, common prayer.

[3] Carey, *John Donne: Life, Mind and Art*, p. 15.

[4] Bald, p. 235.

[5] Flynn, "Donne's Catholicism: II," pp. 185, 186.

[6] Ibid., pp. 187, 188.

reacting to John Stachniewski's attempt to read the *Divine Poems* as consistently Calvinistic, argues that "the pain and confusion in many of the 'Holy Sonnets' is not that of the convinced Calvinist but rather that of a person who would like to be a convinced Calvinist but who is both unable to be so and unable to admit that he is unable to be so."[7] According to Strier, Donne's theological irresolution concerning the Church and his relation to it surfaces in the *Holy Sonnets* because of his inability to rest in the comfort afforded by the doctrine of predestination. Nevertheless, in his readings of the *Sermons* Daniel Doerksen finds Donne's position in the Church of England to be "in general that of the Calvinist majority leadership, marked by 'fair entreaty, gentle persuasion' rather than a harsh imposition of rules and penalties," and further that Donne is "an active believer in predestination."[8] Finally, Debora Shuger expresses the view that Donne's theology "is characteristic of the 'High Church Calvinism' of men like Downame, Bridges, Carleton, Hall and Montague (James, not Richard)," and she adds that "he is 'soft' on predestination" and that he "clearly opposes supralapsarian Calvinism."[9]

Critical discussions such as these ignore that Donne himself eschews such sectarian labeling because of the divisive wrangling it represents and, more importantly, often overlook the theological emphasis Donne perceives between the Church, as the body of Christ, and its liturgical expression within the world, common prayer. In fact, Donne's extant statements about prayer, especially those found in the *Sermons*, consistently reiterate the efficacy of communal prayer:

> In a Sermon, God speaks to the Congregation, but he answers onely that soule, that hath been with him at Prayers before. A man may pray in the street, in the fields, in a fayre; but it is more acceptable and more effectuall prayer, when we shut our doores, and observe our stationary houres for private prayer in our Chamber; and in our Chamber, when we pray upon our knees, then in our beds. But the greatest power of all, is in the publique prayer of the Congregation. (7:311)

Within this context, in which one's devotional life finds its highest potential within common prayer, Donne identifies what he refers to in several sermons as "St. Augustine's Holy Circle," which is "to pray, that we may heare Sermons profitably, and to heare Sermons that we learn to pray acceptably" (9:194). What one discovers in reading the *Sermons* is that for Donne prayer, and specifically public prayer, is an activity so central to Christianity that for him it transcends sectarian allegiances. As a result, Donne pursued a definitional, rather than dogmatic, understanding of prayer which was

---

[7] Strier, "John Donne Awry and Squint: The 'Holy Sonnets,' 1608–1610," p. 361. Strier is responding to Stachniewski, "John Donne: The Despair of the 'Holy Sonnets.'"

[8] Doerksen, *Conforming to the Word*, pp. 85, 109.

[9] Shuger, *Habits of Thought in the English Renaissance*, pp. 164–65, 177.

idiosyncratic, blending quite orthodox teachings with his own highly stylized devotional practice.

THE CARE AND PIETY OF THE CHURCH

In his Second Prebend sermon, explaining that all that is undertaken wisely and well is accomplished by following a pattern, Donne raises the question with his congregation at St. Paul's, "If [God] aske me an Idea of my prayers, shall I not be able to say, It is that which my particular necessities, that which the forme prescribed by thy Son, that which the care, and piety of the Church, in conceiving fit prayers, hath imprinted in me?" (7:61). It is within this three-part pattern – the teachings of the Church, the model of Christ, and the particular needs of the self – that Donne couches his discussions of prayer.

The teachings of the Christian Church (whether Catholic or Protestant) are in accord with respect to the primary purpose and significance of prayer. In spite of what Peter Kaufman has recently labeled "the prayer wars of the 1590s,"[10] the controversies at this time over the prescribed forms of prayer, namely liturgically scripted versus extemporary expressions,[11] were not viewed by Donne as theologically essential. While he himself clearly favors written forms of prayer, Donne acknowledges, in his sermon on Luke 23:24, the overall lack of controversy surrounding prayer, stating that "Of all the conduits and conveyances of Gods graces to us, none hath been so little subject to cavillations, as this of prayer," and further that "Almost every meanes between God and man, suffers some adulteratings and disguises: But prayer least" (5:232). In spite of some relatively minor areas of disagreement between Catholic and Protestant practices, specifically over praying for the dead and praying to saints,[12] theologians from various camps consistently identify prayer as the chief act of religion and as the highest service to God.

Aquinas, in accordance with earlier Church Fathers, explains in Question 83 of his *Summa Theologiae* (Second Part of the Second Part) that because all things showing honor to God belong to religion, prayer itself is an act of religion since through it believers subject themselves to God by confessing dependence on the Creator (cf. Article 3). This dependence, by which Aquinas asserts that "prayer and desire are synonymous," defines prayer as "an appetitive act," in which "union with God is effected through love."[13] Aquinas further contends that, as an act belonging to the will, prayer is "the most important act of religion, since man's intellect thereby is directed by

---

[10] Kaufman, *Prayer, Despair and Drama*, see especially pp. 26–32.
[11] For a good overview of this debate, see Horton Davies, *Worship and Theology in England*, I:268–73.
[12] For Donne's views against praying for the dead, see sermon number 6 in volume VII of the Simpson and Potter edition, and for an engaging discussion of Donne's ideas concerning praying to saints, see Roman Dubinski's "Donne's 'A Litanie' and the Saints."
[13] Aquinas, *Summa Theologiae*, XXXIX:47 (Article 1).

religion to God."[14] As a result, Aquinas repeatedly defines prayer as "*the lifting up of the mind to God*," as an action in which "*we unveil our mind in his presence*" and, thereby, "*surrender ourselves to God and unite ourselves to Him.*"[15]

Reformed dogma propounds a similar understanding of prayer to that of Roman Catholicism. Calvin, noting that "words fail to explain how necessary prayer is" (III.xx.2), reaffirms prayer as an appetitive act, stating that "in our petitions we ever sense our own insufficiency, and earnestly pondering how we need all that we seek, join with this prayer an earnest – nay, burning – desire to attain it" (III.xx.6).[16] Further, Calvin explains that in prayer believers call on God "to reveal himself as wholly present to us," and, therefore, the benefit of prayer is discovered in that "communion of men with God by which, having entered the heavenly sanctuary, they appeal to him in person concerning his promises in order to experience, where necessity so demands, that what they believed was not vain" (III.xx.2).[17]

In a similar understanding of the purpose and significance of prayer, Hooker first raises the question in his *Ecclesiastical Polity* (V.xxiii–xl), "Is not the name of prayer usuall to signifie even all the service that ever wee doe unto God?", and then continues, "And that for no other cause, as I suppose, but to show that there is in religion no acceptable dutie which devoute invocation of the name of God doth not either presuppose or inferre" (V.xxiii.1).[18] Hooker describes prayer as the act of acknowledging God "our soveraigne good," and as a "concurrence with him in desiringe that wherewith his verie nature doth most delight" (V.xxiii.1).[19] Hooker imagines doctrine and prayer as angels, the former descending to earth and the latter ascending heavenward, and that, as a result, God's "heavenly inspirations and our holie desires are as so many Angels of entercorse and comerce betwene God and us" (V.xxiii.1).[20] Prayer is, according to this Anglican apologist, a "holie and religious dutie of service towardes God" (V.xxiv.1),[21] a duty with respect to the love God has extended

---

[14] Ibid., XXXIX:55 (Article 3).
[15] Ibid., XXXIX:51, 47 (Article 1).
[16] Calvin, *Institutes of the Christian Religion*, II:851 and 856.
[17] Ibid., II:851.
[18] Hooker, *The Folger Library Edition of the Works of Richard Hooker*, II:110.
[19] Ibid., II:110.
[20] Ibid., II:110.
[21] Ibid., II:111. In the section following (V.xxv.4–5) Hooker states unequivocally his views against extemporal prayer:

> if the liturgies of all ancient Churches throughout the world be compared amongst them selves, it may be easilie perceaved they had all one originall mould, and that the publique prayers of the people of God in Churches throughlie setled did never use to be voluntarie dictates proceedinge from any mans extemporall witt. To him which considereth the grievous and scandalous inconveniences whereunto they make them selves dailie subject, with whome anie blinde and secret corner is judged a fit house of common prayer; the manifolde confusions which they fall into where everie mans privat Spirit and guift (as they terme it) is the onlie Bishop that ordeineth him to this

41

to us and a service accounted more worthy when accomplished as a common body.

Donne's sermon on Psalm 32:6 discusses the duty of prayer not only as a public act, but also as a surrendering of the mind, and therefore the will, to God. Donne delineates in his exegesis that prayer is the duty of every godly person who desires to be more godly; that the object of prayer is God alone, for as Donne states, "God alone can heare, and God alone can give"; that the subject of prayer, according to the model provided by David in the Psalms, is the confession of and forgiveness for one's sins, which is better accomplished through the prayers "recommended to us by the Church, then to extemporall prayers of others, or of our owne effusion"; and, finally, that the time for prayer is now and always, whether in time of calamity or of prosperity, for any time one may "seeke him with a whole heart, seeke him as a Principall" (9:328). Yet in urging his auditors to this central duty, Donne never forgets that charity is the wellspring of prayer since devout petitions motivated by charity bring people into community with one another.

It is just this communal emphasis that Donne pursues when he recounts in a Lincoln's Inn sermon an extended stay "lying at *Aix*, at *Aquisgrane*, a well known Town in *Germany*" (2:112). While there for "the benefit of those *Baths*," Donne writes, "I found my self in a house, which was divided into many families, and indeed so large as it might have been a little Parish, or, at least, a great lim of a great one" (2:112). Yet, as he explains, it was not a parish but a whole community of Anabaptists, floor after floor (each containing a family) above Donne's room. Donne proceeded to inquire "in what room they met, for the exercise of their Religion" only to be informed they never met,

> for, though they were all *Anabaptists*, yet for some collaterall differences, they detested one another, and, though many of them, were near in bloud, and alliance to one another, yet the son would excommunicate the father, in the room above him, and the Nephew the Uncle. (2:112)

As a result, Donne immediately left the house, and the reason he offers is that "I began to think, how many roofs, how many floores of separation, were made between God and my prayers in that house" (2:113). It was not the sectarian difference between himself and the Anabaptists that caused him to quit the house; instead, it was the division among those who should be able to

> ministerie; the irkesome deformities whereby through endles and senseles effusions of indigested prayers they oftentimes disgrace in most unsufferable manner the worthyest parte of Christian dutie towardes God, who herein are subject to no certaine order but pray both what and how they list; to him I say which waigheth dulie all these thinges the reasons cannot be obscure, why God doth in publique prayer so much respect the solemnitie of places where, thautoritie and callinge of persons by whome, and the precise appointment even with what wordes or sentenses his name should be called on amongst his people. (*The Folger Library Edition of the Works of Richard Hooker*, II:116–17)

live in accord that Donne fears will keep him from God. Prayer exists for Donne, when properly exercised within its higher common expression, as a manifestation of the unity of the Church.

As a consequence of these communal implications for prayer, Donne first states in one of his St. Paul's sermons, "True love and charity is to doe the most that we can, all that we can for the good of others" (5:278), and then he entreats his auditors:

> And something there is which every man may doe; There are Armies, in the levying whereof, every man is an absolute Prince, and needs no Commission, there are Forces, in which every man is his owne Muster-master, The force which we spoke of before, out of *Tertullian*, the force of prayer; . . . Charity is to doe all to all; and the poorest of us all can doe this to any. (5:279)

Prayer is the act of religion that defines the believer's relationship with God, for as Donne states, "When we leave praying, God leaves us" (8:339). Thus, through prayer Donne believes God manifests himself within us through our words. Prayer is incarnational in this respect. Prayerful utterances, according to Donne, are as "lineaments and apparel upon our Devotions" (8:338); they are a revelation of God, who communicates himself to humankind as the Word made flesh.

Finally, it should not be surprising that so much of what Donne says about prayer, in the *Sermons* specifically, occurs within the context of the Psalms. Of the eleven sermons in which prayer is the central focus, only two use verses as sermon texts that are not from the Psalms, and six of the eleven are homilies upon Psalm 6.[22] This connection between the Psalms and prayer reflects the Prayer Book, which orders the Psalter so that it is read in its entirety each month during the course of the Morning and Evening Prayers.[23]

PRESCRIBED BY THY SON

Beyond the teaching and tradition of the Church, Donne also looks to the example of prayer found in Christ. The most obvious place to begin is the Lord's Prayer. As a priest in the Church of England, Donne was well-acquainted with the prominence of this prayer in the liturgy. The Lord's Prayer, as prescribed in the Prayer Book, was recited aloud following the General Confession of sin by the congregation and the minister's statement of absolution during Morning Prayers. It is also the Lord's Prayer that was

---

[22] The eleven sermons, cited here by volume and sermon number in the Simpson and Potter edition, use the following texts: Luke 23:24 (5:12), I Cor. 15:29 (7:6), Psalm 6:1 (5:16), Psalm 6:2, 3 (5:17), Psalm 6:4, 5 (5:18, 19), Psalm 6:6, 7 (8:8), Psalm 6:8–10 (6:1), Psalm 32:6 (9:14), Psalm 38:9 (2:6), and Psalm 90:14 (5:14).

[23] See John Booty, ed., *The Book of Common Prayer, 1559*, which contains "The Table for the Order of the Psalms to Be Said at Morning and Evening Prayer" (p. 24).

proclaimed at the opening not only of the Evening prayers, but also of the Service of Holy Communion.

Donne's own statements in the *Sermons* concerning the Lord's Prayer, however, are rather conventional, and they are often included within passages that comment upon other formulaic statements of faith and doctrine, such as the Ten Commandments and the Apostles' Creed. One of the few instances in which Donne discusses the particulars of the Lord's Prayer appears in his sermon on Psalm 6:2, 3. The context for the reference centers on Donne's insistence that no matter how imperfect or weak our prayers might be, "yet still if it be a prayer, it hath a *Quia*, a Reason, upon which it is grounded," for "that prayer is very farre from faith, which is not made so much as with reason" (5:345). Donne then illustrates this idea by noting that within the Lord's Prayer the injunctions "Thy Kingdom come" and "Hallowed be thy name" and the requests for daily bread and forgiveness of sins are grounded upon the reasons that "God hath a Kingdome here," that he desires "to be glorified by us," and that the ability to provide sustenance and forgiveness are "in his power," respectively (5:345–46).

In spite of its obvious applications as a model of and for devout petition, the Lord's Prayer is not the prayer of Christ's to which Donne most often calls attention in the *Sermons*. Instead, it is Christ's entreaty in the Garden of Gethsemane, where he pleads three times to be spared from crucifixion and in his agony sweats drops of blood (Mt. 26:36–46; Lk. 22:39–46), that Donne refers to with regularity in his preaching. On several occasions this prayer serves as an example of the need to be persistent in prayer, "to repeat often the same prayer in the same words," for as Donne notes, "Our Saviour did so; he prayed a third time, and in the same words" (5:286). Christ's prayer in Gethsemane is also used in a sermon on the final three verses of Psalm 6 to illustrate two important principles in prayer. Donne begins the third part of the sermon by explaining that the Old Testament definition for clean animals was that they have a divided hoof and that they chew the cud, and by analogy he suggests that all resolutions made in prayer must have similar marks:

> they must divide the hoofe, they must make a double impression, they must be directed upon Gods glory, and upon our good, and they must passe a rumination, a chawing of the cud, a second examination, whether that prayer were so conditioned or no. (6:52)

Alluding then to the incident in Gethsemane, Donne notes, "Christ brought his own Prayer, *Si possibile, If it be possible &c.* through such a rumination, *Veruntamen, yet not my will &c.*" (6:52).

Most commonly, however, Donne refers to Christ's prayer in the garden as an example of one who in the midst of his affliction seeks earnestly for release, but who ultimately relinquishes himself, as Christ did, in humble conformity to God's will. In concluding his sermon on Psalm 38:9 ("Lord all my desire is before thee, and my groaning is not hid from thee"), Donne applies the verse "to Christs prayer in his Agony in the garden" (2:161) and reiterates that our prayers for deliverance from our sufferings are accomplished in God's time and not in ours. In the final paragraph of his final sermon, *Deaths Duell,* Donne alludes again to this prayer of Christ's, as he urges his listeners to a humble reconciliation with God:

> In that *time* and in those *prayers* was [Christ's] *agony* and *bloody sweat.* I will *hope* that thou didst *pray,* but not *every ordinary* and *customary prayer,* but *prayer actually* accompanied with *shedding of teares,* and *dispositively* in a readines to *shed blood* for *his glory* in *necessary cases,* puts thee into a *conformity* with him. (10:246)

It is within this struggle of the believer to conform the will with God's that Donne finally understands and defines prayer.

MY PARTICULAR NECESSITIES

Donne's orthodox views of prayer, especially in relation to the teachings of the Church and the models of Christ, reveal his personal struggles with regard to the act of prayer as a central expression of Christian faith. The "particular necessities" of Donne's idea of prayer, therefore, include reconciling the duty of prayer with the unavoidable distractions Christians experience, and the importunity God himself urges with Donne's own inclination toward what he calls "impudency."

In a sermon preached on Candlemas Day, Donne asserts to his congregation that they have two great debts to God – the first is the debt of glory and praise and the second is prayer – and then explains by way of a paradox, "we grow best out of debt, by growing farther in debt; by praying for more, we pay our former debt" (4:309). In the same sermon Donne comments further that "God will not be paid, with money of our owne coyning, (with sudden, extemporall, inconsiderate prayer)," but rather, Donne insists, "with currant money, that beares the Kings Image, and inscription; The Church of God, by his Ordinance, hath set his stampe, upon a Liturgie and Service, for his house" (4:310). The economic terms employed in these passages are common to the New Testament, and in using them Donne is attempting to illustrate the obligation believers have to God and to one another because of Christ.

The duty to pray, in particular, stems from the implications Donne perceives in identifying the Church as the body of Christ, who is the Word made flesh. In a Lenten sermon at Whitehall, Donne preaches, "God came to us *in verbo,* In the word," and then urges, "Let us, that are Christians, go to God so, too" (8:338), and in his fifth Prebend sermon he reiterates, "Christ is *Verbum, The Word,* and that excludes silence. . . . *Dicite, Say,* sayes *David,*

Delight to speake of God, and with God, and for God; *Dicite*, say something" (8:119). For Donne the words of prayer are, as Herbert describes them in his lyric "Prayer"(I), "Gods breath in man returning to his birth" (l. 2).[24] Prayer is the palpable connection between God and his people, and their collective breathing "unto the nostrils of God *a savour of rest*" (8:197) is the necessary response of God's Church in the world.

In spite of the acute sense of duty to prayer that Donne espouses throughout the *Sermons*, there arise distractions of slumber, of deviation, of vain repetition, of ignorance, of negligence and error, and of wantonness and misinterpretation (cf. 10:56–57). The distractions are those related to the limitations and corruptions of the flesh, so that Donne always imagines prayer as the struggle of the body and soul. In this context, prayer itself is understood as a typological expression of the Incarnation, as the Word is recreated through the words of prayer in order to reestablish the relationship of God and his creatures that has been severed because of original and habitual sin.

One of the more memorable passages concerning the distractions to prayer appears in the funeral sermon preached for Sir William Cokayne, in which Donne delineates a variety of distractions with particular poignancy:

> But when we consider with a religious seriousnesse the manifold weaknesses of the strongest devotions in time of Prayer, it is a sad consideration. I throw my selfe downe in my Chamber, and I call in, and invite God, and his Angels thither, and when they are there, I neglect God and his Angels, for the noise of a Flie, for the ratling of a Coach, for the whining of a doore; I talke on, in the same posture of praying; Eyes lifted up; knees bowed downe; as though I prayed to God; and, if God, or his Angels should aske me, when I thought last of God in that prayer, I cannot tell: Something I finde that I had forgot what I was about, but when I began to forget it, I cannot tell. A memory of yesterdays pleasures, a feare of to morrows dangers, a straw under my knee, a noise in mine eare, a light in mine eye, an any thing, a nothing, a fancy, a Chimera in my braine, troubles me in my prayer. (7:264–65)

These distractions cause one to forget. The struggle here is the struggle to remember, to recall the promises of God and the mercies of God, even in the midst of the whirl of this life. In fact, one of the functions of structured and repeated prayers in the liturgy of the Church is to arouse the memory. As he concludes his sermon on Psalm 6:2, 3, Donne states, "*Pray*, and *Stay*, are two blessed Monosyllables; To ascend to God, To attend Gods descent to us, is the Motion, and the Rest of a Christian" (5:363). Within this context, it is clear that the benefit of prayer is for those who pray, for those who thereby complete the double motion of the relationship between the divine and the

---

[24] Herbert, *The Works of George Herbert*, p. 51.

human, and the purpose of prayer is to remind the faithful of the preeminence of attaining God's rest.[25]

Because of the human propensity to forget and, therefore, to become susceptible to sin, Donne pleads for steadfastness in prayer. Again, in the sermon preached for the funeral of Sir William Cokayne, Donne reminds those present of the biblical precedent for importunity in prayer as he calls to mind the parable of the person seeking bread at midnight (Lk. 11:5–8), the parable of the unjust judge and the persistent widow (Lk. 18:1–6), and the account of the woman from Canaan who pleaded with Christ to heal her daughter (Mt. 15:21–28), concluding, "It is not enough to have prayed once; Christ does not onely excuse, but enjoine Importunity" (7:269).

Even beyond persistence, Donne expresses the need to pursue what he calls a "religious impudency," as he asserts in the opening paragraph of his sermon on Psalm 6:4, 5:

> Prayer hath the nature of Impudency; Wee threaten God in Prayer; . . . And God suffers this Impudency, and more. Prayer hath the nature of Violence; In the publique Prayers of the Congregation, we besiege God, saies *Tertullian*, and we take God Prisoner, and bring God to our Conditions; and God is glad to be straitned by us in that siege. (5:364)

In the *Sermons* Donne is fond of the metaphor so commonly found in his religious verse of prayer as warfare, in which one engages God in violent struggle. Nevertheless, Donne always describes the battle not as one enacted against God, but with God; it is a contest God himself encourages. By way of illustrating his point that one may confront God in prayer boldly, and even brazenly, Donne notes that God "grudges not to be chidden and disputed with, by Job" (Job 6:4, 12), nor to be "directed and counselled by *Jonas*" (Jon. 4:2, 9), nor to be "threatned and neglected by *Moses*" (Ex. 32:32) (5:232–33). Furthermore, "Prayer is the way," Donne insists, "which God hath given us to batter Heaven," whether in the public congregation where "we besiege God with our prayers," or in our private chambers where "we wrastle with him hand to hand" (5:223). In fact, Donne contends that unless a prayer is undertaken with reason, "with a serious purpose to pray," such prayers "are but false fires without shot, they batter not heaven" (5:345), a metaphor that

---

[25] Describing the ascent of the mind in prayer, Donne writes,

S. Bernard makes certaine gradations, and steps, and ascensions of the soule in prayer, and intimates thus much, That by the grace of Gods Spirit inanimating and quickning him, (without which grace he can have no motion at all) a sinner may come *Ad supplicationes*, which is *S. Pauls* first step, To supplications, . . . he may come *Ad orationes*, which are *Oris rationes*, The particular expressing of his necessities, with his mouth; . . . he may come farther; *Ad Intercessiones*, to an Intercession, . . . And to a farther step then these, which the Apostle may intend in that last, *Ad gratiarum actiones*, to a continuall Thanksgiving. (5:341)

brings to mind again a line from Herbert's "Prayer" (I) that prayer is an "Engine against th' Almightie" (l. 5).[26]

While a number of critics have discussed Donne's religious verse, and especially the *Holy Sonnets*, as prayerful utterances, only a few have explored the rhetorical implications of this connection. Heather Asals analyzes "The Grammar of Redemption" in the *Holy Sonnets* as an imitation of "God's primary idiom, imperative command, and his secondary idiom, the hortatory 'let'" and concludes that these poems are "essentially explorations in and examinations of the possibilities of language as reflections of God's promises in his Word."[27] In an article centering on Donne's "holy importunitie" and "pious impudencie,"[28] Raymond-Jean Frontain demonstrates that "the *Holy Sonnets* seem scripted to produce a divine reply that would at least resolve the speaker's uncertainty about his condition, if not actually provoke God to intervene and extend to the speaker the prevenient grace he so desperately desires."[29] The orthodoxy of this prayerful struggle in Donne's religious verse, to procure the assurance of salvation, not only echoes the language of the Psalms, but also suggests a public dimension for these poems as devotional models. In an article in which he notes that "as prayers, both the Penitential Psalms and the 'Holy Sonnets' primarily adopt the dramatic pose of the sinner addressing God directly," Roman Dubinski concludes by asserting the plausibility "that in sending his 'Holy Sonnets' to his friends, Donne would expect them to complement the Penitential Psalms as part of their evening penitential devotions."[30] In spite of the rather private implications of Donne's *Holy Sonnets*, at least the first six were sent to the Earl of Dorset with a dedicatory sonnet. In addition, Donne's two poetic examples of liturgical prayer, "La Corona" and "A Litanie," both reflect devotional intentions; the former was most likely sent with a letter and prefatory sonnet to Lady Magdalen Herbert,[31] and the latter was intended, as Donne himself specifies in a letter to Goodyere, "for lesser Chappels, which are my friends."[32] The nature of the spiritual struggle Donne dramatizes in the *Divine Poems* stems from his orthodox, yet nonetheless troubling, recognition both of his own sinfulness and his dependence on God, who alone can forgive.

---

[26] Herbert, *The Works of George Herbert*, p. 51.

[27] Asals, "John Donne and the Grammar of Redemption," pp. 134, 136.

[28] These phrases appear in the opening lines of the tenth expostulation of Donne's *Devotions*, in which he alludes to the sister of Gregory of Nazianzus, Saint Gorgonia, who prayed to God in this manner. Although Donne then states, "I dare not doe so" (p. 52), his tenth prayer, as I explain below, is a witty example of "religious impudency."

[29] Frontain, "'With Holy Importunitie, with a Pious Impudencie': John Donne's Attempts to Provoke Election," p. 99.

[30] Dubinski, "Donne's Holy Sonnets and the Seven Penitential Psalms," pp. 209, 215.

[31] See the commentary on this prefatory sonnet by Helen Gardner, ed., *John Donne: The Divine Poems*, pp. 55–56 and also the explanatory note by John Shawcross, ed., *The Complete Poetry of John Donne*, p. 408.

[32] *Letters to Severall Persons of Honour (1651)*, p. 33.

Although this tension defines the prayerful action of the *Holy Sonnets*, it is within his religious occasional verse that Donne resolves his struggle, but nowhere more successfully than in the hymns, in which Donne couches his private concerns in a distinctly public genre. In particular, the imperatives found throughout the three hymns culminate in an expressed conformity to the body of Christ. Following the first two stanzas which question the extent of God's forgiveness, "A Hymne to God the Father" concludes as Donne insists that God continue to confirm his salvation: "Sweare by thy selfe, that at my death thy Sunne/ Shall shine as it shines now, and heretofore" (ll. 15–16). The resolution, "Thou haste done,/ I have no more" (ll. 17–18), occurs in response to this promise that Donne has been fully incorporated – past, present and future – within the light of Christ. In "Hymne to God my God, in my sicknesse," Donne resolves his command "Looke Lord, and finde both *Adams* met in me" (l. 23) specifically within the crucified body of Christ. The final stanza implores God to receive him in Christ's "purple wrapp'd" (l. 26) and to be given not Christ's crown of thorns but "his other Crowne" (l. 27). The reason for this petition is that Donne, in his physical illness, accepts that salvation is possible only to the extent that he realizes the sufferings of his own body in those of Christ's. Finally, in "A Hymne to Christ, at the Authors last going into Germany," Donne reads the occasion of his journey as an emblem for his relationship with Christ, which he defines in the final sentence of the poem: "Churches are best for Prayer, that have least light:/ To see God only, I goe out of sight:/ And to scape stormy dayes, I chuse an Everlasting night" (ll. 26–28). As he struggles in this poem to divorce himself from the false mistresses of his youth (fame, wit and hope) and know only "th'Eternall root of true Love" (l. 14), the defiant and sinful individuality of Donne disappears from sight as he conforms himself through the "religious impudency" of his prayer to Christ's body, the Church.[33]

One of Donne's favorite biblical figures in the *Sermons* for illustrating typologically this battering of heaven is Jacob. In the second part of his sermon on Genesis 18:25 ("Shall not the judge of all the earth do right?"), Donne states his general point "That God admits, even expostulation, from his servants" and then alludes to the account of Jacob wrestling with God (Gen. 32:24–28), noting, "God would have gone from *Iacob* when he *wrestled*, and *Iacob would not let him go*, and that prevailed with God" (3:145). Further in the same paragraph, following other examples of Old Testament figures who confronted, rebuked, and even chided God, Donne contrasts the reaction of God to this behavior with that of earthly rulers:

what Prince would not (and justly) conceive an indignation against such a petitioner? which of us that heard him, would not pronounce him to be mad,

---

[33] This hymn is discussed in its historical context in chapter 4 in the section "Gold in the Washes."

to ease him of a heavier imputation? And yet our long suffering, and our patient God, (must we say, our humble and obedient God?) endures all this.

(3:146)

The point here is that God, in the vulnerability of his desire to commune with humankind, not only encourages this type of effrontery in prayer, but also rewards it. After all, Jacob secures a blessing from God, which is highlighted by God's renaming of Jacob ("supplanter") as Israel ("God strives").

Even though Jacob's contest with God is the model of "religious impudency" in prayer, Donne consistently reiterates that such brazen approaches must be undertaken above all else for the glory of God. Referring again to this wrestling match, Donne cautions, "Yea, God was so far, from giving [Jacob] present meanes of deliverance, that he made him worse able to deliver himselfe, he wrastled with him, and lam'd him" (3:199). Jacob struggled with God and prevailed, but it came at a price; it involved a sacrifice. While Donne urges believers to strive aggressively to procure God's favor, he never overlooks the fact that the goal of prayer is reconciliation with God and the Church, which involves an acknowledgment of Christ as "a stone of rest and security to our selves" (2:186), as well as a true and sorrowful confession of one's sinfulness. Jacob being lamed by God is the emblem for this humble intent in approaching God. Certainly for Donne, prayer is a warring with God, and yet, as he explains in another paradox, "warre is a degree of peace, as it is the way of peace; and these colluctations and wrestlings with God, bring a man to peace with him" (2:186). John Booty's discussion in his edition of the Prayer Book complements this pattern for approaching God that Donne finds in the example of Jacob, noting that "the rhythm of penitence and praise, penitence rising to praise, praise falling back into penitence and then rising again to praise, [is] the rhythm of the Christian life," and that, in fact, "all of the Prayer Book can be regarded in terms of this repetition of penitence and praise."[34] While Donne adds his own idiosyncratic and personal "impudency" to this pattern, the pattern itself is entirely orthodox and liturgical.

FASTING AND PRAYER

The importance Donne places on prayer, and its significance for defining Christian faith and practice, is illustrated in a sermon he offered before Charles I, the headnote for which reads, "Preached to the King at White-hall, upon the occasion of the Fast, April 5, 1628" (8:192).[35] Although the headnote

---

[34] Booty, ed., *The Book of Common Prayer, 1559*, p. 379.

[35] P. G. Stanwood ("Donne's Earliest Sermons and the Penitential Tradition") argues that although the heading for the sermon is undoubtedly correct, he believes that "the sermon was not composed specially for this time; for the first sixty-four lines (in Potter and Simpson's edition) and the final forty lines are all that make the sermon distinctive for this

specifically draws attention to the fast Charles ordered because of recent military defeats,[36] what Donne actually offers is a homily on prayer, which serves, during this time of national suffering, as a doctrinal corrective to the King, who is to live up to his role as spiritual model for his subjects. The unity Donne desired for the Church of England at this time could be achieved not through simple bodily abstinence, but only in the pursuit of communal prayer.

The historical record at the time of this sermon, preached just one year prior to Charles' dissolution of Parliarment, reveals that England was threatened as much by the infighting of its own leaders as it was by the continuing warfare with Spain and then France. The tone for the initial years of Charles' reign was set at his first calling of Parliament and the need for the new king to contend with the failure of military expeditions to the Palatinate and the aborted assault on the Spanish treasure ships at Cadiz. In fact, the military preparations for the first four years of Charles' reign were, according to Conrad Russell, "undertaken on a greater scale (and at greater cost) than anything since 1588," yet the result, which Russell adds, "ranged from the laughable to the lamentable,"[37] exposed the open wound of the financial problems that became increasingly worse during those war years. The historian Kevin Sharpe contends that the military failures addressed in Charles' opening session with Parliament, and the subsequent debates about them, "initiated what was to become the recurrent dialogue of the next few years."[38] On the one hand, the House of Commons came to view the ill-supplied military expeditions of the mid-1620s as an inevitable consequence of the corruptions at court, and, as a result, the failures of these ventures from 1625–28, according to Sharpe, "progressively proved the incompentence of royal counsels and the need to remove the king's favourite [Buckingham]."[39] On the other hand, Charles became increasingly frustrated because of the bungling surrounding the procurement, appropriation, and delivery of military supplies that only served, again as Sharpe relates, to heighten Charles' "personal guilt at the nation's betrayal of his trusted friend the duke and the public shame of defeat."[40]

---

occasion" (p. 369). This fact, however, makes this sermon no less poignant or applicable for this historical moment.

[36] Conrad Russell (*Parliaments and English Politics, 1621–1629*) records Delbridge's comments from the *1625 Debates* that show the regular practice of national fasts during this period:

> Heretofore we had hopes and expectations wherewith to please the country, though we gave away their money. Now there are nothing but discouragements, pardons to Jesuits, the news from Rochelle, for which town we have heretofore had public fasting; the interruption of the fishing trade, the losses by pirates; so that, whereas we returned the last time with fasting and prayer, now we may return with sackcloth and ashes. (p. 249)

[37] Ibid., p. 323.

[38] Sharpe, *The Personal Rule of Charles I*, p. 8.

[39] Ibid., p. 8.

[40] Ibid., p. 8.

The continued struggle to uncover sources of revenue for equipping and executing military expeditions, as well as the ongoing political fingerpointing and infighting between Charles and Parliament that only exacerbated the financial difficulties, culminated in the naval tragedies that occurred during the latter half of 1627 and the early months of 1628. In the summer of 1627 Buckingham gathered men and supplies at Portsmouth for an expedition intended to bring relief to the Protestants of La Rochelle who were being attacked by Richelieu's troops. During this time, the financial debt for naval expenditures alone had reached such proportions that Charles was compelled to write his Treasurer Marlborough in August 1627, stating, "If Buckingham should not be supplied, it were an immeasurable shame to the king and the nation."[41]

The navigation of the La Rochelle harbor was controlled by the two islands of Oleron and Rhé, and because he realized it would be impossible to provide effective naval assistance without gaining control of one of these, Buckingham landed on the Île de Rhé on 10 July 1627. The English losses were considerable not only because the fort of St. Martin was particularly well fortified, but also because, as Godfrey Davies reports, the Rochellese were "very unwilling to cast in their lot with their would-be deliverers, so that only a few score joined Buckingham's force."[42] The initial assaults on the fort proved so thoroughly ineffective that the Duke was forced to attempt a blockade; however, Russell points out that "it was precisely this type of warfare, in which the ultimate weapon was time, which gave the biggest advantage to the side with the longest purse."[43] Buckingham, whose resources were quickly depleted, departed on 30 October 1627 and returned to England, as one contemporary described it, "with no little dishonour to our nation, excessive charge to our treasury, and great slaughter of our men."[44]

In spite of the obvious waste of human life and resources, the disaster at Île de Rhé only served to fix more completely the obstinancy of both Charles, who stated of Louis XIII that he "is determined to destroy La Rochelle, and I am no less resolved to support it," and Buckingham, who added, "as long as this punctilio exists, it is useless to think or speak of peace."[45] As a result, a

---

[41] Quoted from Sharpe, *The Personal Rule of Charles I*, p. 44. With respect to the national debt, Sharpe states that by the end of 1627 "arrears due to the navy exceeded a quarter of a million pounds and, it was estimated, £110,000 was needed to fit out fifty sails for the next spring" (p. 14).

[42] Davies, *The Early Stuarts, 1603–1660*, p. 66.

[43] Russell, *Parliaments and English Politics, 1621–1629*, p. 329.

[44] Quoted from Davies, *The Early Stuarts, 1603–1660*, p. 66.

[45] Ibid., p. 66. With regard to the loss of life, Russell (*Parliaments and English Politics, 1621–1629*) notes, "Less, and perhaps much less, than half the English force returned to Plymouth and Portsmouth" (p. 330), and on the financial side, Sharpe (*The Personal Rule of Charles I*) states, "the cost of the soldiers and seamen raised for the defeated Rhé expedition alone amounted to £200,000 and an estimated £600,000 was required to prepare another fleet" (p. 20).

new expedition to La Rochelle was made ready in the last months of 1627 and sailed in March 1628 under the command of Denbigh. Not surprisingly, a lack of funds, along with Richelieu's strengthened fortifications, condemned this expedition to failure. Sir Henry Slingsby records in his diary that when Charles learned of the loss of Denbigh's ships, the king claimed he was "never so dishonoured."[46]

In addition to the warfare directed against the French Catholics, the divisive quarrelling between Protestants in England grew more severe as the continuing military defeats threatened the nation's sense of security. Peter White asserts that "'Arminianism' did become an issue in the Parliament of 1628," as he explains, "after its definition had been further widened to include not merely 'popery,' but also 'a plot to introduce arbitrary government.'"[47] There were a small number of MPs who, sharing John Pym's concern for "the incipient disappearance of true religion in England," were willing, as Russell contends, to make "Arminianism one of the leading issues of the [1628] Parliament."[48] The contentions between Charles and the House of Commons, especially the Calvinist MPs, had been building since, according to Fincham and Lake, "the king's religious preferences were made quite clear with his appointment of Laud and Neile to the Privy Council in April 1627 and his preferment of Richard Montagu to first a chaplaincy and then a bishopric in the face of Parliamentary criticism."[49] The fast Charles ordered in the spring of 1628 only added to the religious/political quagmire that, soiling the relations between the King and Parliament and England's foreign policy, Donne sought to address in his sermon preached at Whitehall on 5 April 1628.

The sermon text consists of two verses from Psalm 6, one of six sermons he preached on this particular Psalm ("I am weary with my groaning; all the night make I my bed to swim, I water my couch with my teares. Mine eye is consumed because of griefe; it waxeth old, because of all mine enemies," vs. 6–7), and these words would have undoubtedly resonated with Charles who was feeling beset by his enemies both at home and abroad. The rather extensive introduction to the sermon opens by referring directly to the text ("This is *Davids* humiliation"), and then Donne abruptly declares, "And yet here is no Fast; It is true; No Fast named" (8:192). From the outset Donne makes clear to his sovereign that the sermon will not address the occasion of the fast that had been ordered. Although he acknowledges the benefits of fasting, noting, "At all times, Religion feeds upon fasting, and feasts upon fasting, and grows the stronger for fasting" (8:193), Donne nevertheless finds

---

[46] Sharpe, *The Personal Rule of Charles I*, p. 45. Charles' sense of loss, however, would become even worse for him personally when Buckingham was assassinated in August 1628 as he was preparing yet another attempt on La Rochelle.

[47] White, *Predestination, Policy and Polemic*, p. 248.

[48] Russell, *Parliaments and English Politics, 1621–1629*, p. 345.

[49] Kenneth Fincham and Peter Lake, "The Ecclesiastical Policies of James I and Charles I," p. 37.

in the example of David reason for caution: "thrice in the Psalmes does *David* speake of his fasting, and in all three places, it was misinterpreted, and reproachfully mis-interpreted" (8:192). Donne's warning to Charles centers on his concern that because fasting is "the body that carries, and declares" (8:194), it is susceptible to the misinterpretation of all explicitly outward acts. As a result, Donne adds that "the soule that inanimates, and quickens all, is prayer; and therefore this whole Psalme is a prayer" (8:194). In this sermon, Donne chooses to instruct Charles on the theological necessity for prayer to precede and inform fasting, and he does so not because the King is irreligious. On the contrary, Kevin Sharpe makes the case for the devotional nature of Charles' faith:

> From the very day of his coronation – the day of purification of St. Mary the Virgin, on which the king wore white rather than imperial purple – Charles attended assiduously to his devotions. In his bedchamber he surrounded himself with devotional paintings and kept by his side the gospels and the apocalypse. Unlike his father, he joined in prayers every Sunday at royal chapel, which was adorned with religious hangings and a crucifix.[50]

Donne's sermon on this occasion serves as a theological fine-tuning for his royal auditor, and illustrates what Jeanne Shami sees as a general principle, that Donne seeks to instruct, "not through a sudden blaze of understanding, but through a progressive clearing and sharpening of human vision to its highest potential."[51] Donne further clarifies in the introduction that, in so far as the sermon text is a two-part prayer, "both parts of the prayer are (as all prayer must be) grounded upon reasons" (8:194), namely what David did for the present and what he will do for the future. These reasons are, according to Donne, rooted in the doctrine of the Trinity and his communal understanding of the godhead:

> God works not alone in heaven, nor man lives not alone upon earth, but there is a Conversation, and a Correspondence, and a Commerce betweene God and Man, and Conditions, and Contracts, and Covenants, and Stipulations between them, and so a mutuall interest in one another. (8:194)

As part of the commerce between Creator and creatures, Donne makes it abundantly clear to Charles that he is to view David as a model of religious faith and practice; Donne asks his royal auditor to ponder "What *David* did, and what we are to doe" (8:195). Donne, in fact, is fond of using the figure of David in this way, for, as he states of David in another of his sermons,

> His example is so comprehensive, so generall, that as a well made, and well placed Picture in a Gallery looks upon all that stand in severall places of the

---

[50] Sharpe, *The Personal Rule of Charles I*, pp. 280–81.
[51] Shami, "Anatomy and Progress," p. 228.

Gallery, in severall lines, in severall angles, so doth *Davids* history concerne and embrace all. For his Person includes all states, betweene a shepherd and a King, and his sinne includes all sinne. (5:299)

This sermon, therefore, provides yet another instance of Shami's general contention that throughout the *Sermons* Donne attempts "to illuminate the Image of God in each regenerate Christian, . . . not in terms of ideal types and hyperbolically dramatized examples, but usually in terms of imperfect and struggling examples," and that, as a result, David is "one of those rectified but imperfect men whom Donne loves to consider."[52]

In the first of the two parts of the sermon, Donne analyzes the manifestation of David's prayer, in which he "first *gemmuit*, he came to *groane*, to sigh" (8:195). Donne explains that such an action is an outward sign of God's mark on David that is comparable, he explains, to the letter *taw* (the last in the Hebrew alphabet) that forms the sign of the cross imprinted on the forehead in baptism:

so God imprinted upon them, that sighed, and mourned, that *Tau*, that letter, which had the forme of the Crosse, that it might be an evidence, that all their crosses shall be swallowed in his Crosse, their sighs in his sighs, and their agonies in his. (8:198)

This assurance of the "Conditions, and Contracts, and Covenants" between God and humankind affords the humble penitent the ability to perceive tribulations as judgments of God that restore one's soul to health. The example of David's sighing and groaning, therefore, teaches that there can be no rest, no peace, as long as former sins and the inclination to future sins press on the conscience. Warning against ignoring one's own sins and against half efforts in repentance, Donne unfolds for Charles that this type of prayerful petition, when humbly and sincerely offered, is physic. Donne then concludes the first part by directly applying David's situation to that of Charles when he asks, "Who were his [David's] enemies?" and then responds, "It is of best use to pursue the spirituall sense of this Psalme, and so his enemies were his sins" (8:208). Donne overtly instructs his sovereign to be less concerned with the French and with certain MPs than he is with his own spiritual health and example. Donne's point here is that Charles is not merely to react to his circumstances, but to lead by his actions.

Donne's focus in the second part is the lesson of affliction; one must learn from adversity and not simply seek relief from it, for tribulation opens the way for divine comfort:

There is no person to whom we can say, that Gods Corrections are Punishments, any otherwise then Medicinall, and such, as he may receive amendment

---

[52] Shami, "Donne's Protestant Casuistry," pp. 56, 59. For further discussion of David's "middle nature," see Shami's "Donne on Discretion."

by, that receives them; Neither does it become any of us in any case, to say God layes this upon him, because he is so ill, but because he may be better. (8:211)

Yet, such an argument, Donne acknowledges, opens the problematic issue of what he calls "after-afflictions" (8:215) – the question of whether God has actually pardoned one's sins if the tribulations continue after one has sincerely repented. The conclusion Donne articulates to Charles, who is grieving because of all his enemies, is that such "after-afflictions" are not the result of the former sins, but a preventative to keep one from future sins, or, in other words, they are not the consequence of the initial lapse, but part of the commerce between God and fallen humanity against a relapse. Reminding his auditors again of the twofold reason of David's example in this prayer (that "which *David* did for the present, and that which he promised he would doe for the future" – 8:216), Donne closes the body of the sermon by articulating the dialogic nature of prayer offered in response to afflictions, "by which God intends to establish us in that spirituall health, to which our repentance, by his grace, hath brought us" (8:216).

Donne concludes the sermon by reiterating to Charles that through prayer (rather than fasting), "thou hast past the signet, that thou hast found the signature of Gods hand and seale, in a manifestation, that the marks of his Grace are upon thee," and with this assurance Donne urges the King to "plead that seale to the Church, (which is Gods Tribunall, and judgement seat upon earth) in a holy life, and works of example to others" (8:217). The individual groaning of repentance Donne has called for throughout the sermon must finally be discovered "in a holy life, and works of example to others" and thereby become part of the common prayer of the Church. In an article discussing the drama of conversion throughout the *Sermons*, Shami argues that Donne engages his auditors in "processes of doubt and reassurance, to move them emotionally towards a reconciliation to their own circumstances" and that his auditors "are induced to engage in this drama with David and to experience, with him, a sense that even in adversity God never abandons those who seek 'commerce' with him."[53] As an example of this pattern, Donne presents Charles with a reminder of his role in the dialogic interplay between God and the Church, noting that because Charles is answerable to the King of Kings, he himself must be a proper example to his own subjects.[54]

In the midst of Charles' anguish over his enemies at home and abroad, and in direct response to the King's ordered fast, Donne instructs and comforts his sovereign with a sermon on prayer. Specifically, Donne counsels Charles

---

[53] Shami, "Anatomy and Progress," pp. 234, 230.
[54] In her "Kings and Desperate Men," Jeanne Shami argues convincingly that Donne's "court sermons abound with comparisons to Christ," and that "this strategy allows Donne to remind Kings of their humanity, and so to limit their absolutist claims, at the same time as it flatters" (pp. 11–12).

that David provides a theologically sound model for attaining the peace that is only possible through the communal exchange between God and self and then self and others. It is this same process that so clearly informs the *Devotions upon Emergent Occasions*, in which Donne attempts to move his readers from his own afflictions to prayerful repentance through the example of his own life, and in this process Donne redefines his relationship to the Church, which itself ideally reflects the divine community.

DEVOTIONS UPON EMERGENT OCCASIONS

Although Donne's views on prayer are most clearly articulated in the *Sermons*, he enacts those ideas in his published prayers, and none so completely as the twenty-three that appear in the *Devotions*. In her article focusing on the last sentences of the final prayer in the *Devotions*, Sharon Seelig questions what readers are to make of Donne's seemingly divided self. In the concluding sentence, in particular, Seelig describes that the very structure of the statement expresses not affirmation for his return to health, but anxiety concerning the possibility of a relapse. Such a concern is "not a sudden failure of nerve" or "an inability to accept good fortune," but rather, as Seelig concludes, an understanding that

> to be lowered here is to be raised in heaven, to see that what in human terms is a victory, a return to health, is in theological terms a postponement of the goal, and that fear of relapsing, contrary to our first impression of the matter, may be taken as a sign of hope and of health.[55]

As this statement makes clear, Donne imagines prayer and the Christian life as a contest between human weakness and divine faithfulness, as a coming to terms with one's own propensity to sin in relation to the grace and mercy of God. Because he is acutely aware of the temptations of the flesh and the failings of the will, Donne not only relies upon, but also demands God's own promises of mercy. In fact, Donne believes it necessary and appropriate both to remind and to bind God to such promises as a way to guarantee them. Referring directly to the first half of his text from Psalm 90:14 ("O satisfy us early with thy mercy"), Donne explains that "this is a Prayer of limitation even upon God himselfe, That our way may be his, and that his way may be the way of *mercy*" (5:274).

The "religious impudency" Donne exhibits throughout the *Devotions* is clearly illustrated in the final lines of the tenth prayer as he recalls God's nature and limits Him in terms of it:

> And since sinne in the nature of it, retaines still so much of the author of it, that it is a *Serpent*, insensibly insinuating it selfe, into my *Soule*, let thy *brazen*

---

[55] Seelig, "In Sickness and In Health," pp. 104, 112.

Serpent, (the contemplation of thy *Sonne* crucified for me) be evermore present to me, for my recovery against the sting of the first *Serpent*; That so, as I have a *Lyon* against a *Lyon*, *The Lyon of the Tribe of Judah*, against that *Lyon, that seekes whom hee may devoure*, so I may have a *Serpent* against a *Serpent*, the *Wisedome of the Serpent*, against the *Malice of the Serpent*, And, both against that *Lyon*, and *Serpent*, forcible, and subtill tentations, Thy *Dove* with thy *Olive*, in thy *Arke*, *Humilitie*, and *Peace*, and *Reconciliation* to thee, by the *ordinances* of thy *Church. Amen.*[56]

As he struggles in this prayer with his own sinful nature, Donne commissions God to employ His serpent and His lion against those of Satan. Donne wrestles with God in this way, not to usurp Him, but in order, as Jacob did, to extract His blessing. His impudency toward God is tempered, however, as he is lamed by the memory of his fallen nature. Nevertheless, only by means of humbling himself and remembering who he is in relation to God is Donne able to find peace and reconciliation.

The thirteenth prayer of the *Devotions* models all the elements Donne finds necessary for addressing God. Before examining the prayer, however, a brief overview of this section of the *Devotions* is necessary, the English heading for which reads, "The Sickness declares the infection and malignity thereof by spots" (p. 67). The thirteenth meditation opens as Donne espouses that the human condition consists more of misery than of happiness, and that while "All men call *Misery, Misery*," yet "*Happinesse* changes the name, by the taste of man" (p. 67). As Donne then contemplates the spots that have appeared on his body, he cannot decide whether they portend ill or good, and then concludes the meditation by stating that happiness can only be understood in comparison to misery, that he must suffer in order to receive and appreciate healing.

In the expostulation Donne offers himself to God as a sacrifice, but he immediately laments that his self-offering will be unacceptable since it is a spotted one. Quickly shifting his argument, however, Donne questions why his spottedness should disqualify his sacrifice and keep him from God. In a brilliantly witty passage Donne remembers the promises of God and turns them to his own advantage: his body, spotted as it may be, is not only the dwelling place of Christ, but also the temple of the Holy Spirit; Christ himself, "who hath al our stains, & deformities in him" (p. 69), is spotted; and the spouse of Christ, the Church, is itself tainted in that "every particular *soule* in that *Church* is full of staines, and spots" (p. 69). Donne concludes, therefore, that the only spots, the only deformities on the body and the soul, that God despises are those one attempts to hide from Him. As a result, Donne urges his readers to confess and repent of their sins, for, as he writes, "When I open my *spotts*, I doe but present him with that which is *His*, and till I do so, I

---

[56] *Devotions upon Emergent Occasions*, p. 55. All subsequent references are cited in the text by page numbers.

detaine, & withhold *his right*" (p. 70). It is only by presenting one's sinful, spotted self to God that one may be reconciled to Him and incorporated fully within the body of Christ.

The thirteenth prayer, which plays upon the paradox of sickness and health addressed in the meditation and expostulation, opens by acknowledging the generosity of God and by binding God to His mercy:

> eternall, and most gratious *God*, who as thou givest all for *nothing*, if we consider any precedent Merit in us, so giv'st *Nothing*, for *Nothing*, if we consider the *acknowledgement*, & *thankefullnesse*, which thou lookest for, after, accept my humble thankes, both for thy *Mercy*, and for this particular *Mercie*, that in thy *Judgement* I can discerne thy *Mercie*, and find *comfort* in thy *corrections*. (p. 70)

In humbling himself to God by acknowledging his own weakness, Donne insists, nevertheless, on reminding God of His divinity so that, as Donne states in a wonderful example of chiasmus, "in thy *Judgement* I can discerne thy *Mercie*, and find *comfort* in thy *corrections*." This opening sentence, as well as the remainder of the prayer, portrays Donne as a type of Jacob, in whom affliction becomes the sign and seal of God's blessing. It is by means of God touching Donne, as it were, on the thigh and laming him that Donne is assured of his reconciliation to God and his fellowship within the Church:

> I know, O *Lord*, the ordinary *discomfort* that accompanies that phrase, *That the house is visited*, And that, *that thy markes, and thy tokens are upon the patient*; But what a wretched, and disconsolate *Hermitage* is that *House*, which is not visited by thee, and what a *Wayve*, and *Stray* is that *Man*, that hath not thy *Markes* upon him? These heates, O *Lord*, which thou hast broght upon this *body*, are but thy chafing of the *wax*, that thou mightest *seale* me to thee; These *spots* are but the *letters*, in which thou hast written thine owne *Name*, and conveyed thy selfe to mee; whether for a *present possession*, by taking me now, or for a future *reversion*, by glorifying thy selfe in my stay here, I limit not, I condition not, I choose not, I wish not, no more then the house, or land that passeth by any *Civill* conveyance. (p. 70)

Donne reminds God, and thereby comforts himself, that his body and soul belong to God and that his present spotted condition is a visible sign of his salvation. Suffering within the body and in imitation of Christ's suffering conforms one to Christ. As a result, Donne insists that God has an obligation to claim this diseased body since it is actually a part of the body of God's own Son. Prayer thirteen concludes by affirming Donne's desire to conform himself to his Lord:

> Onely be thou ever present to me, O *my God*, and this *bed-chamber*, & thy bed-chamber shal be all one roome, and the closing of these bodily *Eyes* here, and the opening of the *Eyes* of my *Soule*, there, all one *Act*. (p. 70)

Donne's plea in this petition is not exclusively self-interested, for throughout the *Devotions* Donne holds himself up as an example of the corporate body of Christ and, in doing so, reiterates the essential relationship between seeing, knowing and loving.

In his discussion of the *Devotions*, Terry Sherwood writes that Donne's "double consciousness of self and its shared awareness of community precludes a separation of the self from its Calling in the Body."[57] Prayer brings the individual into community, not only with God, but also with the Church, both Militant and Triumphant. As Donne meditates in his *Devotions* upon the tolling of a bell, he speaks to God in the seventeenth prayer concerning one who has recently died:

> When thy *Sonne* cried out upon the *Crosse*, *My God, my God, Why hast thou forsaken me?* he spake not so much in his *owne Person*, as in the person of the *Church*, and of his afflicted *members*, who in deep distresses might feare thy *forsaking*. This *patient*, O most blessed *God*, is one of them; . . . unite *him & us* in one *Communion of Saints*. Amen. (p. 90)

In this prayer Donne cannot imagine himself and his own fears and sufferings except in the communal context of Christ's passion and his afflicted body, the Church, which Donne particularizes here in the death of the individual for whom he prays.

*

In defining the place of prayer in the Christian life, Donne availed himself of a wide spectrum of sources in the Church, relying on teachings from Roman Catholic and Protestant theologians, for he was well aware that prayer had not in fact given rise to significant partisan debate either in the Reformation or in the Christian tradition as a whole. Further, Donne reads in New Testament accounts of Christ at prayer a model not only for persistence in making his requests known to God, but also for conforming himself to God by humbly submitting to His will. It is, finally, within these orthodox contexts that Donne argues for "religious impudency" in prayer, the body of Christ wrestling with God to secure the divine blessing. The mannered use of paradox and typological analogy as figures for the act of prayer, mannerisms which themselves define Donne's style, sit comfortably alongside traditional teachings about the centrality of prayer and its constitutive function for the Christian community. Donne could therefore remain, as usual, at his most public when he was at his most private, as illustrated in the hymns and the *Devotions*, in which the prayers stemming from Donne's personal suffering also articulate the petitions of and for the common body of Christ.

---

[57] Sherwood, *Fulfilling the Circle*, p. 185.

Chapter Three

THROUGH HIS OWN RED GLASSE

WHITEHALL PALACE

USING language that echoes section seventeen of the *Devotions*, Donne opens his sermon preached on 29 February 1627 by questioning,

> Is there any man, that in his chamber hears a bell toll for another man, and does not kneel down to pray for that dying man? and then when his charity breaths out upon another man, does he not also reflect upon himself, and dispose himself as if he were in the state of that dying man? (8:174)

This Lenten sermon was presented at Whitehall Palace, where Donne was typically commissioned to preach this time of year,[1] and in it he insists, "He that will dy with Christ upon Good-Friday, must hear his own bell toll all Lent" and, furthermore, must "begin to hear Christs bell now" (8:174).

The text for the sermon, Acts 7:60 ("And when he had said this, he fell asleep"), alludes to the dying words of St. Stephen, whom Donne describes as "a poor bell-man" whose death is "our example," and "what he suffered, what he did, what he said" is "our preparation for death" (8:175). Donne presents this figure to his auditors as "Christs earliest witness, his Proto-Martyr" (8:175), as an emblem of holy dying: "*Stephen* had a pattern, and he is a pattern; Christ was his, and he is our Example" (8:187). In fact, the entire sermon is an extended meditation on the necessity for appropriating examples and images by which to guide and measure one's life and death.

At one point in the sermon Donne even includes a summary of Pliny's history of "al the great Masters in the art of painting," about whom he concludes, "This is still that that dignifies all their works, that they wrought so, as that posterity was not only delighted, but improv'd and better'd in that art by their works" (8:178). By analogy Donne asks the members of Court in

---

[1] Bald (*John Donne: A Life*) briefly notes, in the context of two sermons Donne preached at court in 1617 and 1618, it was at Whitehall where "he preached his usual Lenten and April sermons" (p. 329); and Izaak Walton (*The Lives of John Donne, Sir Henry Wotton, Richard Hooker, George Herbert, and Robert Sanderson*) writes of Donne, in the context of *Deaths Duell*, "before that month ended, he was appointed to preach upon his old constant day, the first *Friday* in *Lent*" (p. 74).

attendance to offer their lives as paintings to be read,[2] and as such each individual "must actuate it self, dilate, extend and propagate it self according to the dimensions of the place, by filling it in the execution of the duties of it" (8:178). The actions of such a person, Donne notes while shifting the metaphor, becomes a perfume, breathing in all directions "an improvement of the present, and an Instruction and a Catechisme to future times" (8:179).

Such an approach, in which Donne looks to images and emblems in the fashioning of one's life as an object worthy of religious instruction and imitation, is not surprising from someone who surrounded himself in and with works of art. Among all of his possessions that he found valuable enough to enumerate and discuss in his will, Donne took great care concerning the works of art that graced his residence at St. Paul's, which housed a collection that Ernest Gilman states "was surely large enough to have filled nearly every corner of Donne's little world with imagery."[3] The subject matter of these "pictures" (as Donne calls them), both secular and religious, included representations, among others, of King James, Mary Magdalene,[4] Adam and Eve, and "Christe in his Toombe."[5] Fourteen paintings were bequeathed in his will to twelve separate individuals and an unspecified number of works (including "the fower large Pictures of the fower greate Prophett*es*" and the "large Picture of auncient Churcheworke"[6]) were willed to remain where they hung in the hall of the rectory, in the lobby leading to his bedchamber, and in the garden.[7] The painting Donne willed to his friend Robert Ker, "that Picture of myne w[ch] is taken in Shaddowes and was made very many yeares before I was of this profession,"[8] reminds us also of the images of Donne's own self-fashioning, namely, the 1591 engraving of the young Donne grasping a sword, the mid-1590s Lothian portrait in the pose of a melancholy lover (the one presumably willed to Ker), the 1616 miniature by Isaac Oliver, the 1620 roundel portrait in the Deanery of St. Paul's, and the now lost sketch of Donne wrapped in his funeral shroud,

---

[2] In a complementary metaphor, Donne urges his auditors in another sermon, "He that desires to *Print* a book, should much more desire, *to be* a book; to do some such exemplar things, as men might read, and relate, and profit by" (7:410).

[3] Gilman, *Iconoclasm and Poetry in the English Reformation*, p. 121.

[4] Milgate ("Dr. Donne's Art Gallery") explains that this painting "would have come into Donne's possession upon [Christopher] Brooke's death in 1628; and it is no doubt this painting of Mary Magdalene that we find Donne bequeathing in turn to George Gerrard" (p. 318).

[5] Bald, *John Donne: A Life*, p. 565.

[6] Ibid., p. 564.

[7] In his discussion of Donne's art collection, Gilman (*Iconoclasm and Poetry in the English Reformation*) speculates that "there may have been twenty-five to thirty pictures in all, not counting the hanging maps one would like to have supposed were also in Donne's possession – for maps are prominent in the inventories of other private holdings and, as a source of imagery, nearly inevitable in Donne's writings" (p. 120).

[8] Bald, *John Donne: A Life*, p. 567.

which served as the model both for the engraving Martin Droeshout used as frontispiece for *Deaths Duell* (1632) and for the Nicolas Stone sculpture in St. Paul's. Donne is well aware of the power to create meaning through the reading of those images he offered of himself, as well as those defining the space where he lived and entertained others.

In addition to the tangible representations that fill the eye, Donne is equally aware of the power that images created in the spoken and written word have on the mind's eye. The sermon noted above marking the beginning of the 1627 Lenten season, and delivered from the very pulpit at Whitehall Palace where three years later Donne would preach what Izaak Walton describes as "*his own Funeral Sermon,*"[9] focuses the attention of Donne's auditors on the image of St. Stephen's death. The pattern Donne establishes in this sermon is the same as that in the *Devotions*, in which he holds up a single individual as an example of and for the members of the Church being united by sharing in the sufferings of Christ. Explaining that "Gods suffering for man was the Nadir, the lowest point of Gods humiliation" and that "mans suffering for God is the Zenith, the highest point of mans exaltation" (8:185), Donne then openly asserts the commerce, established through suffering, between God and humankind: "That as man needed God, and God would suffer for man, so God should need man, and man should suffer for God" (8:185). As a result, Donne declares, in response to St. Stephen's example, "I will give God a Cup, a cup of my blood" so that the gospel will be "the better accepted, because the seal of my blood is set to it" (8:185). To avoid any misunderstanding, Donne adds that his desire to fulfill the sufferings of Christ and to be offered up for the Church is "not for the purchasing of it," but instead "for the fencing of it, though not by way of satisfaction as [Christ] was, but by way of example and imitation as [Christ] was too" (8:185–86).

In the era in which he lived, seized as it was by ecclesiastical battles over the use of external objects in worship, Donne never succumbs to the characteristically Puritan suspicion of the eye and the ease with which it is led to idolatry.[10] On the contrary, he persistently argues for a use of pictures and images, both those created by human hands and those painted in the mind that, when properly applied, serve to aid one's spiritual vision. Donne concludes the body of his 1627 Lenten sermon at Whitehall by drawing "two pictures in little: two pictures of dying men" (8:188), one who in his rejection of God presents a picture "that hath been Nothing, that hath done

---

[9] Walton, *The Lives of John Donne, Sir Henry Wotton, Richard Hooker, George Herbert and Robert Sanderson*, p. 75.

[10] For an overview of this controversy during Donne's lifetime, see John Phillips, *The Reformation of Images*, chaps 6–8; and for an overview of Donne's views on this issue, see Ernest Gilman, "'To adore, or scorne an image': Donne and the Iconoclastic Controversy," in which he argues, "Donne's poetry, written during the brief repose of the Anglican compromise epitomized in his sermons, is nonetheless strongly charged by the iconoclastic controversy" (p. 63).

nothing, that hath proposed no *Stephen*" (8:189), and the other whose life Donne compares to a copper engraving:

> So this Picture of that dying Man, that dies in Christ, that dies the death of the Righteous, that embraces Death as a Sleepe, was graving all his life; All his publique actions were the lights, and all his private the shadowes of this Picture. (8:190)

As articulated in the opening chapter of this study, Donne's theology is based on the communal interplay of the Trinity and the commerce the godhead desires with the Church. From this theological foundation, Donne propagates the use of a whole range of visual representation, from the tangible to the imagined, as a means for fostering the redemptive relationship with God that Donne believes is completed through participating in the sufferings of Christ.

VAE IDOLOLATRIS, VAE ICONOCLASTIS

Strictly speaking, Donne relegates the use of external pictures and images as a formal element of worship to the category of "things indifferent." In the conclusion to an intriguing sermon he preached at Paul's Cross (6 May 1627), Donne spells out his mediating position in the final paragraph:

> in some cases, it may bee some want, to bee without some *Pictures in the Church.* So farre as they may conduce to a reverend *adorning* of the place, so farre as they may conduce to a familiar *instructing* of unlettered people, it may be a losse to lack them. (7:431–32)

The words "some" and "may" in this passage reveal his conciliatory approach to this controversy, an approach he further balances by then referring to Calvin, who in the *Institutes* (I.xi.7)[11] permits the use of pictures for the uneducated, yet laments that even the uneducated would be better served, as Donne quotes, "*if those things which were delivered in picture, to their eyes, were delivered in Sermons to their eares*" (7:432).

Although Donne confirms in response to Calvin "that where there is a frequent preaching, there is *no necessity* of pictures" (7:432), he, nevertheless, pushes the matter further:

> but will not every man adde this, That if the true use of Pictures bee preached unto them, there is *no danger* of an abuse; and so, *as Remembrancers* of that which hath been taught in the Pulpit, they may be retained; And that was one office of the Holy Ghost himselfe, *That he should bring to their remembrance* those things, which had been formerly taught them. And since, by being taught

[11] *Institutes of the Christian Religion* (I.xi.7), in which he states "that pictures are the books of the uneducated" (I:106) and "that today there are not a few who are unable to do without such 'books'" (I:107).

the right use of these pictures, in our preaching, no man amongst us, is any more enclined, or endangered to worship a picture in a Wall or Window of the Church, then if he saw it in a Gallery, were it onely for a reverent adorning of the place, they may bee retained here, as they are in the greatest part of the *Reformed* Church, and in all that, that is *properly Protestant.* (7:432)

In defining here all that he believes is "properly Protestant," Donne defends a use of pictures by implying that they are crucial for salvation, since he links the work of the Holy Spirit and the memory, that very interaction of the divine and human which he describes elsewhere as "the art of salvation" (2:73). Beyond this implication of necessity, Donne cites two of the 1559 injunctions from Elizabeth, the one against the extolling of images and the other invoking the destruction of such images. Concerning the former, Donne explains that the injunction does not mean "that they shall not *set them up*," but instead that "*They shall declare the abuse thereof*," and for the latter, he contends, "it is limited to such *things*, and *such pictures, as are monuments of feigned miracles*" (7:432).[12]

The sermon as a whole culminates with Donne's warning:

> *Vae Idololatris*, woe to such advancers of Images, as would throw down Christ, rather then his Image: But *Vae Iconoclastis* too, woe to such peremptory abhorrers of Pictures, and to such uncharitable condemners of all those who admit any use of them, as had rather throw down a Church, then let a Picture stand. (7:433)

By way of explanation, Donne then calls initially upon the warning of St. Jerome, in relation to "the Commination of this Text" (Hosea 3:4), against being "without those Sacrifices, those Ephods, those Images, as they are *outward helps* of devotion" (7:433). Donne, however, does not end the matter with St. Jerome, but calls finally upon "*Christ* himselfe, who is the God of love, and peace, and unity," under whom falls "a heavy, and insupportable *Vae*, to violate the peace of the Church, for things which concern it not fundamentally" (7:433). Although Donne clearly sides with St. Jerome, to whom he gives the first word for a proper use of pictures, the last word is given to Christ, through whom Donne pleads for the unity of the Church.

In spite of Donne's plea for unity in this controversy over the use of external objects in worship, it is difficult to ignore the distinct imagery Donne presents to his auditors' minds at the opening of this Paul's Cross sermon. Comparing the discovery of Christ's mercies to a sea voyage, Donne asserts that for the journey "let *this text be our Mappe*" (7:415), and then in the *divisio* he adds, "Consider our text then, as a *whole Globe*, as an *intire Spheare*, and

---

[12] Gilman ("'To adore, or scorne an image'") asserts that "the Elizabethan injunctions Donne alludes to had sought to ban offensive images secreted for private use as well as those on public display" and that "the construction Donne puts on this point of the law, however, virtually reverses its original thrust" (p. 67).

then our *two Hemispheares* of this Globe, our *two parts* of this text" (7:416). The spectacle Donne imagines here is further enhanced by Millar MacLure's description of the location and arrangement of preacher and audience at Paul's Cross: "if we look at the scene as a whole, it reminds us of the Elizabethan theatre: groundlings and notables, pit and galleries, and, in the midst, the pulpit as a stage. Indeed it was a theatre."[13] If the use of external objects in worship is for Donne "not fundamental," then why does he go to such lengths to defend their use, or, to approach the issue from another perspective, why does he place so much importance, not just in the *Sermons* but throughout his writings, on the eye and sight?

Among the plethora of examples found throughout the *Sermons*, Donne identifies, to begin with, God himself as "all eye, an universall eye, that pierceth into every darke corner" (6:47), posits viewing the scene of Christ weeping for Lazarus "through this glasse of his owne teares" (4:326), and compares the eye of Christ to "the eye of the Ostrich," who with a look of that eye "is said to hatch her young ones, without sitting" (7:152). In addition, Donne enumerates the variety of aids to one's vision, including nature ("Man hath a natural way to come to God, by the eie, by the creature" – 6:217), scripture ("The Scriptures are as a room wainscotted with looking-glass, we see all at once" – 3:57),[14] the sacraments (Christ "speakes to thine eye, (and so to thy soule by that) in the exhibition of his Sacraments" – 6:79), and the conscience ("every man hath a glasse in himself, where he may see himselfe, and the Image of God" – 8:352). By contrast, Donne professes, "The love of the world, is but a smoke" that "putts out our eyes" (3:51) and, referring to the worldly man who has lost his soul, states, "nothing weakens the eyes more then vomiting; when this worldly man lost his honey, he hath lost his sight" (3:237–38). Donne also proposes a whole range of exemplary objects for vision and models of seeing, such as when he writes, first, "the sight of God is Heaven, and to be banisht from the sight of God, is Hell in the World to come" (7:366); then, "God makes his Ministers *speculatores*" (2:164); next, "Who would wish to be sharper sighted then the Eagle? And his strength of sight is in this, that he lookes to the Sun" (7:204); and last,

> We call *Noah, Ianus*, because hee had two faces, in this respect, That hee looked into the former, and into the later world, he saw the times before, and after the flood. *David* in this Text, is a *Ianus* too; He looks two wayes, he hath a Prospect, and a Retrospect, he looks backward and forward, what God had done, and what God would doe. (8:112)

Donne often reminds his auditors that "The sight is so much the Noblest of all the senses, as that it is all the senses" (8:221) and that "All things concur to

---

[13] MacLure, *The Paul's Cross Sermons, 1534–1642*, p. 4.

[14] In a complementary way, Donne asserts in another sermon "That prophecies till they come to be fulfilled, are but clouds in the eyes, and riddles in the understanding of men" (8:302).

this Seeing, and therefore in all the works of your senses, and in all your other faculties, See ye the Lord" (7:346). The relation of Christian faith and practice to the eye and sight, represented by this small sampling, is depicted everywhere in the *Sermons*. While Donne identifies the use of pictures and images in worship as a matter of "things indifferent," the proliferation of visual representation in his preaching speaks to the theological significance he ascribes to vision, beginning with his views on the sacrament of baptism.

GOD'S WARDROBE

In his sermon to the Earl of Exeter, preached at the Earl's chapel on 13 June 1624, Donne articulates three ways God has sealed himself to humankind:

> First, God sealed us, in imprinting his *Image* in our soules, and in the powers thereof, at our *creation*; . . . But then we were all sealed againe, sealed in our *very flesh*, our mortall flesh, when the image of the invisible God, *Christ Jesus*, the onely Sonne of God, tooke our nature: . . . [and] He sets another seale upon us, when, though *we* know not of it, yet the *world*, the *congregation* does, in the Sacrament of *Baptisme*, when the seale of his *Crosse*, is a testimony, not that Christ was *borne*, (as the former seale was) but that also he *dyed* for us; there we receive that seale upon the *forehead*, that we should conforme our selves to him, who is so sealed to us. (6:158–60)

This passage, which Donne considers in a paragraph highlighting "the accessiblenesse, the communicablenesse, the conversation of our good, and gracious *God* to us" (6:158), reaffirms Donne's theological foundation of the communal interplay God establishes with humankind, whose souls bear the image of the creator. In other passages throughout the *Sermons*, Donne explains that the tripartite soul reflects the image of God as "the picture of Father, Sonne, and Holy Ghost too" (6:296), yet through sin individuals "deface that leafe in which the Authors picture, the Image of God is expressed" (9:373). As a result, Donne elsewhere imagines the children of God as "the *Marble*, and the *Ivory*" on which God works in order "to re-engrave, and restore his Image" (3:193).

The selection above from the sermon to the Earl of Exeter also confirms God's "accessiblenesse," "communicablenesse" and "conversation" to humankind in the person of Christ, initially through his incarnation and finally through his crucifixion, in which one participates through the sacrament of baptism. As prescribed by the Prayer Book and as discussed and practiced by Donne himself, the administration of baptism provides for Donne a visible seal of and for the visible Church being conformed to Christ.

The Prayer Book specifies that the sacrament of public baptism be administered on a Sunday or holy day immediately following the last lesson at either Morning or Evening Prayers. The priest performs the christening by dipping the child into the baptismal font and saying, in the words commanded by Christ (Mt. 28:19), "I baptize thee in the name of the Father, and of the Son, and of the Holy Ghost." Afterwards he makes the sign of the cross on the child's forehead, thus sealing the child to the Church with the emblem of Christ's death.[15] In the closing prayer, the priest expresses to God that these things have been done "to incorporate him [the child] into thy holy congregation."[16] Although the Prayer Book includes a liturgy for private christenings, it reinforces the intended communal implications of this sacrament by specifying that private baptisms should only occur "in time of necessity." Finally, parishioners are encouraged to attend to the sacrament in a timely manner: "the pastors and curates shall oft admonish the people that they defer not the baptism of infants any longer than the Sunday or other holy day next after the child be born, unless upon a great and reasonable cause."[17]

As a priest of the Church of England, Donne acknowledges in the *Sermons* what by his time had become a rather widely accepted Protestant recognition of the Lord's Supper and baptism as the only two sacraments.[18] Donne's general statement of the benefit of the sacraments, that "In the Sacraments our eyes see his [God's] salvation" (7:296), is comparable to the sense of Hooker's less epigrammatic explanation from his *Ecclesiastical Polity*, that

> sith God in him selfe is invisible and cannot by us be discerned workinge, therefore when it seemeth good in the eyes of his heavenly wisdom, that men for some speciall intente and purpose should take notize of his glorious presence, he giveth them some plaine and sensible token whereby to knowe what they cannot see (V.lvii.3)[19]

---

[15] This signing of the cross at baptism was a genuine point of contention during Donne's lifetime, as evidenced, for example, with the Millenary Petitions presented to James during his progress from Scotland to London and with the subsequent discussions at the Hampton Court Conference and its aftermath. See, G. W. Bromiley, *Baptism and the Anglican Reformers*, pp. 152–59; Horton Davies, *Worship and Theology in England*, II:333–37; Kenneth Hylson-Smith, *The Churches in England from Elizabeth I to Elizabeth II*, I:94–96; and Kenneth Fincham, "Ramifications of the Hampton Court Conference in the Dioceses, 1603–1609."

[16] *The Book of Common Prayer, 1559*, ed. John Booty, p. 275.

[17] Ibid., p. 277.

[18] Peter White ("The *via media* in the Early Stuart Church") notes that one of the outcomes of the Hampton Court Conference was "the addition of a section on the sacraments to the Prayer Book catechism," specifically:

> It taught that two sacraments only, those of baptism and the Lord's Supper, were "generally necessary to salvation." The inward and spiritual grace received in baptism was defined as "a death unto sin, and a new-birth unto righteousness: for being by nature born in sin, and the children of wrath, we are hereby made the children of grace" (pp. 219–20).

White makes these comments in the larger context of noting the error of those who believe that in Hooker's emphasis on the sacraments he was "attacking Calvinist piety," for as White explains, "Calvin too had a strong doctrine of the sacraments" (p. 219).

[19] *The Folger Library Edition of the Works of Richard Hooker*, II:246. See also Donne's statement that "As we cannot see the *Essence* of God, but must see him in his *glasses*, in his *Images*, in his

as well as to Calvin's rather surprising analogy that a sacrament "represents God's promises as painted in a picture and sets them before our sight, portrayed graphically and in the manner of images" (IV.xiv.6).[20] As a corollary to the benefits of the sacraments for sight, Donne describes baptism itself as "*Collyrium, an Eye-salve* to all, by which they may mend their eye-sight" (5:85).

The most clearly detailed expression of Donne's views on baptism appear in his four extant christening sermons, and all of them discuss baptism within the context of Donne's theology of communal participation and its relation to visual representation.[21] In the first, Donne repeats the word "conversation" six times in the opening paragraph in order to drive home the point that "*Our conversation is in heaven*" (5:96) and that, as a result, the community of believers "are all of a knot, and such a knot as nothing shall unty, as inseparably united to one another, as that God, with whom they are made one Spirit, is inseparable in himself" (5:97). The second begins in a complementary manner when Donne asserts, "Almighty God ever loved *unity*, but he never loved *singularity*," for God "was never *singular*, there was never any time, when there were not *three persons* in heaven" (5:113). He then completes this initial paragraph by focusing on human relationships in what he refers to as the three relations of creation: "the first relation was between *Prince* and *Subject*, . . . the second relation was between *husband* and *wife*, . . . and the third relation was between *parents* and *children*" (5:113–14), concerning which he adds, "The general duty, that goes through all these three relations, is expressed, *Subditi estote invicem, Submit your selves to one another, in the feare of God*" (5:114). In the last two of his christening sermons, Donne derives a communal emphasis from their respective scripture texts. The third of the series uses as its text I John 5:7, 8 ("For there are three which beare record in heaven; the Father, the Word, and the Holy Ghost; and these three are one: and there are three which beare record in the earth; the spirit, and the water, and the bloud; and these three agree in one"), from which Donne enumerates that the witnesses of heaven "are the *Trinity*" and those of earth "are the *sacraments* and *seales* of the Church" (5:139), namely "*Preaching*, and *Baptisme* and *Communion*" (5:149). In fact, the entire sermon draws explicit connections between the sacrament of

Creatures, so we cannot see the decrees of God, but must see them in their *duplicats*, in their *exemplification*, in the *sacraments*" (5:161).

[20] *Institutes of the Christian Religion*, II:1281.

[21] All four appear in volume 5 of the Simpson and Potter edition of the *Sermons* (numbers 4–7). In their introduction to the volume, the editors explain that "the four baptismal sermons afford no clues to when and where they were preached, and they are therefore printed here in the order in which they occur in the Folio of 1649" (5:10). Further, they speculate that the curious absence of any names on these sermons, first printed in the 1649 edition of *Fifty Sermons* (the year of Charles I's execution), was due to John Donne, Jr. who "was actively engaged in trying to curry favour with the Parliamentarians who were now the dominant party" (5:7).

baptism and the doctrine of the Trinity. In the final christening sermon, preached on Galatians 3:27 ("For, all yee that are baptized into Christ, have put on Christ"), Donne associates the putting on of Christ with the Parable of the Prodigal Son, whose father "clothed him intirely, and all at once; he put a *robe* upon him, to cover all his defects" (5:154), and Donne then concludes that in baptism God "hath sealed a Covenant *to them, and their seed*," a surety discovered "in the unity, and in the bosome of the Church" (5:166).

This communal framework is reinforced through Donne's claim that "they that are led to baptisme, *any other way then by the Church*, they are misled" (5:108). After all, Donne acknowledges the common doctrine that baptism is an act of initiation into the Church – "This Sacrament of Baptisme is the first; It is the Sacrament of *inchoation*, of *Initiation*" (5:127) – , and this doctrine was visually reinforced in the Church of England by placing the baptismal font at the west entry of the church so that all who entered passed by it.[22] As a consequence, therefore, Donne asserts, "we argue with an invincible certainty, that because this Sacrament belongs generally to the Church as the *initiatory* Sacrament, it belongs to *children*, who are a part, and for the most part, the most innocent part of the Church" (5:129). Given Donne's obvious acceptance of the doctrine of original sin, this insistence on infant baptism comes as no surprise.

Furthermore, Donne sees infant baptism as a practice that by and large has unified Christendom:

> All Churches, *Greek*, and *Russian*, and *Ethiopique*, howsoever they differ in the *body* of the Church, yet they meet, they agree in the *porch, in Limine Ecclesiæ*, in the *Sacrament* of *baptisme*, and acknowledge that it is communicable to *all children*, and to *all Men*. (5:101)

Donne makes this statement in response to what he calls the errors of the Anabaptists, who deny infant baptism, and those of "the *Arrians*, and the *Donatists*" who "did *rebaptize* those who were baptized by the true Christians, whom they counted *Heretiques*" (5:101). Reacting then to the Anabaptist practice of believer baptism,[23] which would of course exclude infant baptism, Donne challenges,

> Let him that will contentiously say, that there are *some* children, that take no profit by baptisme, shew me *which* is one of them, and *qui testatur de scientia, testetur de modo scientiæ*; If he say he knowes it, let him tell us *how* he knowes that which the Church of God doth not know. (5:101)

---

[22] Milton, *Catholic and Reformed*, p. 216. See also Horton Davies, *Worship and Theology in England*, in which he notes, "the font was most awkwardly placed, if it was intended that the congregation should share in the sacrament of initiation, for they had to turn round" (II:9, n10).

[23] For overviews of this practice, see Horton Davies, *Worship and Theology in England*, II:337–43; and G. W. Bromiley, *Baptism and the Anglican Reformers*, pp. 91–101.

In the fourth of his christening sermons, Donne further asserts the necessity of infant baptism when he addresses the problems of churches offering the sacrament only on a few occasions during the year, of infants not being given the sacrament until they were older, and of parents and clergy neglecting the sacrament altogether.[24] Such acts Donne boldly labels "spirituall Murder," and to those responsible he declares that "God imputes this as such a murder to them, who endangered the child, as farre as they could, by neglecting his ordinance of baptisme" (5:163).[25] Finally, and as a sidenote to this discussion, Donne interjects in the third of his christening sermons that "we cannot baptize our selves" (5:131) because such a practice undermines, in a manner analogous to neglecting the public rite of infant baptism, the communal nature of God as manifest in the Church.[26]

In fact, Donne emphatically expresses the communal significance of baptism when he asserts that in order to guarantee a righteous life "you must find your selves to be the *Sonnes of God*; And you can prove that, by no other way to your selves, but because you are *baptized into Christ*" (5:151). Baptism is the seal of adoption that establishes one as a child of God, and the public and visible emblem of that seal is the signing of the cross on the infant's forehead. Although Hooker relegates this signing of the cross to "matters indifferent" (V.lxv.1–21),[27] Donne insists on the action, for baptism imprints "a *crosse* upon us, that we should not be ashamed of *Christs crosse*, that we should not be afraid of our *owne crosses*, yet by all these waters, by all these *Crosse ways*, we goe directly to the eternall life, the kingdome of heaven" (5:110).

This passage, with an eye towards pursuing "these *Crosse ways*," is reminiscent of Donne's lyric "The Cross," which begins by asking, "Since Christ embrac'd the Crosse it selfe, dare I/ His image, th'image of his Crosse deny?". In the poem Donne writes that nothing, specifically "no Pulpit, nor

---

[24] Judith Maltby ("'By this Book': Parishioners, the Prayer Book and the Established Church") cites a variety of examples in local parishes of the types of problems Donne addresses (cf. pp. 122–24). For additional examples, see F. G. Emmison, *Elizabethan Life*, pp. 139–42.

[25] The severity of Donne's language here is reflected in Hooker's *Ecclesiastical Polity* (V.lx.7) when he states that the Church suffers "from guiltines of blood, if thorough hir superfluous scrupulosities lettes and impedimentes of lesse regard, should cause a grace of so greate moment to be withheld" (*The Folger Library Edition of the Works of Richard Hooker*, II:262).

[26] Kenneth Hylson-Smith (*The Churches in England from Elizabeth I to Elizabeth II*) narrates the account of Separatist leader John Smyth who in 1609 baptized himself and his friend Helwys as a rejection of their infant baptisms and in order to establish their own Separatist congregation. Smyth was severely criticized for this act and, Hylson-Smith notes, "was dubbed the Se-Baptist, or Self-baptizer" (I:111).

[27] *The Folger Library Edition of the Works of Richard Hooker*, II:302; however, he does argue that the ceremony of the cross should not be despised (V.lxv.6),

> especiallie seinge that by this meane where nature doth earnestlie implore aid, religion yeeldeth hir that readie assistance then which there can be no helpe more forcible servinge only to relieve memorie and to bringe to our cogitation that which should most make ashamed of sinne (II:306).

misgrounded law,/ Nor scandall" (ll. 9–10), can remove this cross, "for, the losse/ Of this Crosse, were to mee another Crosse" (ll. 11–12).[28] Donne then refers directly to the sacrament of baptism and asks, "Who can blot out the Crosse, which th'instrument/ Of God, dew'd on mee in the Sacrament?" (ll. 15–16). Later in the poem he explains that allowing crosses establishes in the believer not just the image of Christ, but Christ himself (cf. ll. 35–36), and to emphasize the proliferation of crossing imagery throughout the poem (including the arms of a swimmer, birds in flight, a mast, and the meridians and parallels on a map), he writes, "But most the eye needs crossing" (l. 49). In the closing lines, Donne alludes to the communal implications of christening infants as a sacrament of initiation into the Church, which itself contains images for worship:

> Then doth the Cross of Christ worke fruitfully
> Within our hearts, when wee love harmlessly
> That Crosses pictures much, and with more care
> That Crosses children, which our Crosses are.

As Donne's poem and the christening sermons make clear, the baptismal ceremony directly relates the action signified by crossing to the effect of conforming the Church to Christ, for, Donne argues, "the *sacraments* are never without *Grace*, whether it be accepted or no, there it is" (5:147).[29] Several places in the christening sermons Donne speaks against a Separatist view of baptism as nothing more than an outward sign or figure.[30] In doing so, he reiterates that "baptisme doth truly, and without collusion, offer grace *to all*; and nothing but baptisme, by an ordinary institution, and as an ordinary meanes, doth so" and that "if we speake of reall salvation by it, baptisme is more then a figure" (5:163). By "an ordinary institution" and "an ordinary meanes," Donne surely intends the administration of the sacrament as directed in the Prayer Book, including the signing of the cross, and it is in this public rite that the Church discovers "reall salvation."

---

[28] P. M. Oliver (*Donne's Religious Writing*) dates the poem, and therefore reads it, in the context of the Hampton Court Conference and the Puritan objection to the signing of the cross in baptism (cf. pp. 67–80).

[29] In his discussion of "The Cross," Oliver (*Donne's Religious Writing*) insists that "the idea of a living, deathless martyrdom is central to the poem's thinking" (p. 78) and fails as a poetic comment on the debate of crossing in "deftly moving the debate away from the question of a ritual gesture's significance and by suggesting that metaphorical crosses constitute a route to salvation" (p. 80). However, the poem must fail in these ways because Donne's point resides elsewhere, specifically, as I have argued throughout this section, in addressing the theological necessity of crosses in bringing the Church to participate (sacramentally, not simply metaphorically) in the sufferings of Christ.

[30] Both Calvin and Hooker argue for the sacraments as necessary for salvation and, therefore, against the view that they are merely signs or tokens (*Institutes*, IV.xv.1, and *Ecclesiastical Polity*, V.lvii.5, respectively).

For Donne the sacrament of baptism signifies a conforming of the Church to Christ, which he imagines throughout the fourth of his christening sermons as a putting on of Christ. Explicating his scripture text (Gal. 3:27), Donne clarifies that "*to be baptized is to put on Christ*" so that through this sacrament "we are translated even into the nature of God, By his pretious promises we are made *partakers of the Divine nature*" (5:153). Later Donne considers the twofold aspect of *Induere* (to be cloathed): "1. *Vestem*, put on a garment; 2. *Personam*, put on a person" (5:158), or as he states in another of his sermons, "We need clothing; Baptisme is Gods Wardrobe" (2:66), and concludes:

> from this (which is *Induere vestem*,) from this putting on Christ as a garment, we shall grow up to that perfection, as that we shall *Induere personam*, put on *him*, his person; That is, we shall so appear before the Father, as that he shall take us for his owne Christ; we shall beare his name and person; and we shall every one be so accepted, as if every one of us were *all Mankind*; yea, as if we were *he* himselfe. He shall find in all our bodies his *woundes*, in all our mindes, his *Agonies*; in all our hearts, and actions his *obedience*. (5:159–60)

Therefore, the sacrament of baptism is necessary Donne contends precisely because it "signifies our dying, and buriall with Christ" (5:161); it is "our Crosse, and our passion, and our buriall; that is, in that, we are conformed to Christ as he suffered, dyed, and was buried" (5:165).[31] This is precisely the mystery of the sacrament, that in the ritual of baptism there is a conjoining of the visible and the invisible.

---

[31] In the context of explaining "the case of *infants*, that might be in danger of dying without baptisme" (5:162), Donne argues that baptism is "not absolutely necessary, but necessary by Gods ordinary institution," adding, "I speake not this, as though the state of *children* that died without baptisme were desperate; God forbid, for who shall shorten the Arme of the Lord?" (5:163). A similar distinction is made by Hooker in his *Ecclesiastical Polity* (V.lx.6):

> Touchinge infantes which dye unbaptised, sith they neither have the sacrament it selfe nor any sense or conceipt thereof, the judgment of many hath gone hard against them. But yeat seinge grace is not absolutely tyed unto sacramentes, and besides such is the lenitie of God that unto thinges altogether impossible he bindeth no man, but where wee cannot doe what is injoyned us accepteth our will to doe in stead of the deed it selfe; againe for as much as there is in theire Christian parentes and in the Church of God a presumed desire that the sacrament of baptisme might be given them yea a purpose also that it shalbe given, remorse of equitie hath moved divers of the schooledevines in these considerations ingenuouslie to graunt, that God almercifull to such as are not in them selves able to desire baptisme imputeth the secret desire that others have in theire behalfe and accepteth the same as theires rather then casteth away theire soules for that which no man is able to helpe. (*The Folger Library Edition of the Works of Richard Hooker*, II:259–60)

SUCH *GLASSES* AND SUCH *IMAGES*

Donne's arguments for visual representation in the Church and the preference he affords the sense of sight is, in the strictest sense of the term,
theological, for they grow out of his understanding of God's nature. "God
himselfe," Donne reminded his auditors at the Spittle on Easter Monday
1622, "works by Patterns, by Examples" (4:93) so that from the beginning of
time God possessed "an internal pattern, an *Idæa*, a preconception, a form in
himself, according to which he produc'd every Creature" (4:98).[32] Continuing
this line of thought, Donne asks that if God proceeds in this manner, then
how "shall we adventure to do, or to say any thing in his service
unpremeditately, extemporally?" (4:99). Because "It is not Gods way" to
act without preconceiving and following a pattern, Donne further questions,
"Who shall be our Example?" (4:99). This question underlies, as discussed
above, his understanding of the sacrament of baptism, and his insistence on
crossing, for in it the Church participates in the pattern and example of
Christ's passion. This question also leads to another, one that Donne raises in
the context of speaking against those in the Church with separatist inclina-
tions: "What greater injustice, then to propose no Image, no pattern to they
selfe to imitate; and yet propose thy selfe for a pattern, for an Image to be
adored?" (9:75).

For Donne, it is individuals of a "middle nature," such as St. Stephen,
David, and St. Paul, who provide good patterns, and by means of con-
templating and imitating such examples in the mind's eye, Donne seeks to
transform his auditors into becoming fit patterns for others.[33] It is this two-
way mirror of one seeing proper patterns of imitation even as that person is
being seen as a pattern that Donne often holds up through his use of the
common Renaissance trope *theatrum mundi*. In a 1620 Lenten sermon to
James, preached in the intimate outdoor setting of the Sermon Court at
Whitehall, Donne refers directly to I Corinthians 4:9 ("We are made a
spectacle to men and angels") and, noting that in this verse St. Jerome
translates "spectacle" as "theatrum," concludes, "And therefore let us be
careful to play those parts well, which even the *Angels* desire to see well acted"
(3:218). However, as Donne makes clear later in the same paragraph, the eye
with which one should be most concerned is God's, which "is always open,
and always upon thee" (3:218), and, as a result, he warns his congregation at

---

[32] Hooker, *Ecclesiastical Polity*, I:58–63; those sections in Hooker's *Ecclesiastical Polity* (I.ii.1–6)
that define God's eternal law as that "which hath bene the patterne to make, and is the card to
guide the world by" (*The Folger Library Edition of the Works of Richard Hooker*, I:62) are
echoed by Donne's language.

[33] For a discussion of Donne's homiletic use of men of a "middle nature," see Shami, "Anatomy
and Progress."

St. Dunstan's, "Make account that this world is your Scene, your Theatre, and that God himself sits to see the combat, the wrestling" (6:108).

The second part of Donne's second Prebend Sermon powerfully articulates the need for the Church to proceed by pattern and example. In it Donne reiterates that every purpose and action of a person ought to be carried out according to a rule or example and that the precedent of the Creator is the one to follow "Because God hath already gone this way" (7:60). Explaining that "from the meanest artificer, through the wisest Philosopher, to God himselfe," Donne states, "all that is well done, or wisely undertaken, is undertaken and done according to pre-conceptions, fore-imaginations, designes, and patterns proposed to our selves beforehand" (7:60). These ideas, Donne insists, contain "so much truth, and so much power" that "without acknowledging them, no man can acknowledge God," for the very nature of God reveals itself through "Counsaile, and Wisdome, and delibera-tion in his Actions" (7:60). To deny this is, for Donne, to deny the existence of God. Therefore, the pattern for working according to patterns is God, who created humankind "*Faciamus hominem*," through "a concurrence of the whole Trinity" (7:61). Again, reacting against Separatist practices of extem-poral prayer and preaching, which he argues lead to an extemporal religion that would necessitate an extemporal heaven, Donne explains that religion, prayer and preaching have been formulated through a concurrence of the former patterns and ancient beliefs belonging to the Church universal.

In this second Prebend Sermon, Donne reveals through these powerful personal statements his theological foundation not only for the use of external objects in worship, but also for understanding one's position both as viewer and as object in the reflexive act of religious self-fashioning. Donne's 1622 sermon on the anniversary of the Gunpowder Plot goes beyond his funda-mental claim that "Of all things that are, there *was* an *Idea* in God" to express "but of Monarchy, of Kingdome, God, who is but one, *is* the *Idea*; God himself, in his Unity, *is* the Modell, He *is* the Type of *Monarchy*" (4:240).[34] Passages from the *Sermons* such as this have produced a great deal of critical debate concerning the extent to which Donne's views, both politically and theologically, can be considered absolutist.

There is little doubt that Donne is fond of reminding both James and, especially, Charles that "Kings are Images of God" (9:59), that "*Kings* are pictures of God" (7:422). However, Jeanne Shami ably argues, in an article discussing what she labels "The Absolutist Politics of Quotation," that critics such as John Carey and Debora Shuger have reached their conclusion of Donne as absolutist by means of mining the *Sermons* for choice passages that are quoted as uncontextualized fragments.[35] My own point in calling

[34] There are no substantive differences in this passage between the Simpson and Potter edition (quoted here) and the transcription of Shami's edition of this sermon (cf. p. 63, ll. 198–208).

[35] Shami, "Donne's Sermons and the Absolutist Politics of Quotation." In particular, she campaigns, and rightly so, against the manner in which Carey buries his support from the

attention to this critical debate is that Donne's analogies between God and king involve James and Charles in a reflexive act of religious self-fashioning. When properly read in their contexts, the passages typically quoted in isolation reveal Donne reminding his monarch, whether James or Charles, of his humanity and challenging his auditors, including the King, to compare the ideal with the real.[36]

For example, Donne's assertion that "Kings are Images of God," from the first of his two sermons on Genesis 1:26, is immediately followed by the statement, "such Images of God, as have eares, and can heare; and hands, and can strike" (9:59), distinctly human attributes with which Donne humbles Charles even as he praises him. In addition, although Donne states, "*Kings* are pictures of God," he makes the claim in order to demonstrate that they must, therefore, be careful of portraying an image that leads the nation into error, for "when they turn upon new *gods*, they turn to new pictures of God too, and with a forein *Religion*, invest a forein *Allegiance*" (7:422). Further, in a passage in which Donne asks royal subjects to look on the King with "little and dark spectacles" so that his "errors are to appeare little, and excusable to them," he continues by noting the enormity of the King's responsibilities to his subjects and to God:

> Gods perspective glasse, his spectacle is the whole world; he looks not upon the Sun, in his spheare onely, but as he works upon the whole earth: And he looks upon Kings, not onely what harme they doe at home, but what harme they occasion abroad; and through that spectacle, the faults of Princes, in Gods eye, are multiplyed, farre above those of private men. (6:172)

Finally, in a paragraph that begins "Long life is a blessing, as it is an image of eternity: Kings are blessings, because they are images of God," Donne boldly adds, because "*Finite* and *Infinite* have no proportion to one another," a king "hath no proportion at all to God, . . . the King is *nothing* to God" (7:357). Donne explains that his purpose in stating these ideas is not only "to assist the Kings Religious humiliation of himself in the presence of God," but also to remind his auditors that "we need such *Glasses* and such *Images*, as God shews us himself in the King" (7:357). Although Donne certainly believes in the monarchy, it is also apparent from a careful reading of the *Sermons* that he uses these analogies between God and king both to strengthen royal authority *and* to restrict the King's authority and define his responsibilities as an image of God for his subjects.[37]

In one Lenten sermon in which he implores his auditors to raise their hands

---

Sermons in footnotes that are distinguished by their imprecision, an act of criticism Shami describes as "the *arcana imperii* or mysteries of state of sermon scholarship" (p. 386), as well as Shuger's form of critical follow-the-leader, basing her views on "footnotes to Carey's footnotes and isolated comments taken from the sermons at large" (p. 406 n12).

[36] See Shami's "Kings and Desperate Men."

[37] For an excellent discussion of this idea, see David Nicholls, "Divine Analogy."

when they pray, Donne recreates in their minds an emblem of the Emperor Constantine in prayer. Noting that "Other Emperours were coyned Triumphing, in Chariots, or preparing for Triumphs, in Battailes, and Victories," and yet by contrast Constantine was coined "in that posture, Kneeling, Praying" (9:220), Donne explains:

> He knew his coyn would passe through every family; and to every family he desired to be an example of piety; Every peece of single money was a Catechisme, and testified to every Subject all this, surely he will graciously receive my Petition, and look graciously upon me, when I kneele, for, behold he kneels to, and he exhibits petitions to that God, from whom he acknowledges, that he needs as much as I can from him. And yet this Symbolicall, and Catechisticall coyn of *Constantines*, was not so convincing, nor so irrefragable a testimony of his piety, (for *Constantine* might be coyned praying, and yet never pray) as when we see as great a Prince as he, actually, really, personally, daily, duly at prayer with us. (9:220)

This passage appears in a sermon Donne preached before Charles I in 1630. It is just this type of appeal to the mind's eye that Donne uses in the *Sermons* to illustrate for his auditors, including princes and patrons, that participating in the Church necessarily involves fashioning themselves as images of righteousness even as they look to find themselves reflected in the spectacle of Christ's passion.

HANWORTH, 1622[38]

In the summer of 1622, Donne was invited to Hanworth, a royal manor bordering Hampton Court, to participate in the lavish entertainment and hospitality that James, Lord Hay (who within three weeks was made Earl of Carlisle) extended to the Earl of Northumberland (Henry Percy), his father-in-law. The occasion for the festivities was the opportunity for Hay to honor Percy, who, having been wrongly accused and sentenced as a conspirator in the Gunpowder Plot, had recently been released from his extended imprisonment in the Tower (1605–21), and Percy's presence at Hanworth, as R. C. Bald notes, "seems to have marked his reconciliation " with his son-in-law.[39] The poignancy of the Hanworth sermon is revealed in the degree to which Donne personalized his homily to fit the circumstances of these two aristocratic patrons. Donne's affiliation with the Percy family originated in the early 1580s and marked, according to Dennis Flynn, "the beginning of

---

[38] A version of this section appeared as my article "Spectacle, Patronage, and Donne's Sermon at Hanworth, 1622."

[39] Bald, *John Donne: A Life*, pp. 432–33, who in the context of the festivities at Hanworth speculates that "the occasion to which Donne was invited was probably the first time Doncaster had been able to show hospitality to his father-in-law, the Earl of Northumberland, since his release from the Tower" (p. 432).

Donne's lifelong friendship with Henry Percy, ninth Earl of Northumberland."[40] That friendship certainly manifested itself in February 1601 when, in the account by Izaak Walton, the Earl served as the messenger for the letter informing Sir George More of Donne's clandestine marriage to More's daughter, Ann.[41] Further, while Donne assuredly visited his patron in prison, it seems likely, as Flynn surmises, that given their history "Donne may well have been among the many gentlemen and scholars who regularly dined with the Earl during his confinement in the Tower beginning in 1606."[42] As for Hay, he was a handsome Scotsman who, as a young man having come south with James VI, rose quickly in the Jacobean court and became an influential admirer and supporter of Donne, to whom Hay described himself in a letter as the one who "first begat in you the purpose to employ your extraordinarie excellent parts in the affairs of another world,"[43] namely the priesthood. In 1619, Hay (then Viscount Doncaster) requested that Donne be appointed chaplain for the embassy he led to Germany, during which Hay certainly heard Donne preach at Heidelburg and The Hague, as well as before and after this trip at Lincoln's Inn and St. Paul's.

As a result of the relationships Donne had with both of these aristocrats, it is not surprising that Hay would request that Donne prepare a sermon for this celebratory occasion at Hanworth. What is worthy of attention, however, is Donne's decision to focus his message on the theological significance of sight and its preeminence among the human senses. It is my contention that Donne's Hanworth sermon reaffirms his views regarding the iconoclastic controversy of his time by providing a compelling reading of the private lives of Hay and Percy. To be precise, Donne uses the occasion of his 1622 sermon at Hanworth to correct and to dilate, through biblical exegesis and allusion, the spiritual vision of his chief auditors so that they might attain the right and godly use of vision discovered in the spectacle of Christ crucified.

The contrasting sensibilities of Northumberland and Doncaster reveal the demands confronting Donne in the Hanworth sermon. A recent article by Stephen Clucas argues that during his imprisonment in the Tower, Henry Percy turned to natural philosophy for solace, seeking the Stoic ideal "of achieving tranquillity of the soul and freedom from the ravages of the passions, by maintaining a rational equanimity and neutrality before the assaults of fortune and the grim facts of mortality."[44] Donne's knowledge of Northumberland's turn toward a Stoic brand of natural philosophy while in

---

[40] Flynn, *John Donne and the Ancient Catholic Nobility*, p. 16. Flynn conjectures that in June 1585 Donne may have been in Paris with Henry Percy and his brothers, and if this is true, then "this would help explain the lifelong friendship of Donne and Northumberland" (p. 159).

[41] Walton, *The Lives of John Donne, Sir Henry Wotton, Richard Hooker, George Herbert, and Robert Sanderson*, p. 28.

[42] Flynn, "Donne's *Ignatius His Conclave* and Other Libels on Robert Cecil," p. 170.

[43] Bald, *John Donne: A Life*, p. 304.

[44] Clucas, "'Noble virtue in extremes,'" p. 267.

the Tower can be established in two ways. First, Percy (known also as the "Wizard Earl") was patron to the mathematician Thomas Hariot, himself a student of natural philosophy, whom Bald establishes as a friend of Donne's and who was also "a frequent visitor to the Tower of London, where the Earl was deep in his alchemical studies."[45] It seems quite likely, therefore, that these two friends would have at some time been together in visiting their imprisoned patron and would have broached the subject of natural philosophy during those visits. Second, Flynn points out that in February 1611 Percy purchased a copy of the Latin edition of Donne's *Ignatius His Conclave* and concludes that "Northumberland would have been personally interested in *Ignatius His Conclave*, if only because it was connected to his own conversations with Donne and Hariot in the Tower."[46] Flynn conjectures further that because of the similarity between the topics addressed in *Ignatius His Conclave* and the list of volumes in Northumberland's library – Continental works on theology, astronomy, medicine, voyages of exploration, and Italian literature –, Donne may have, in fact, used his patron's library in writing his work of satire.[47] If Flynn is correct, then Donne would have been well-acquainted with Northumberland's readings. Therefore, the Stoic lens through which Percy viewed the natural world defines, as Clucas summarizes at the conclusion of his article, his self-fashioned philosophical outlook at the time of his release from the Tower:

> The earl's reading in prison of stoic texts, and the stoic sentiments of his client's dedicated texts are an excellent example of the way in which humanistic reading-practices could help to shape both aristocratic self-image and political conduct in the Jacobean period, [and that] denied the capacity to act in the political sphere, the earl's adoption of stoic consolation was both therapeutic and an act of political resistance.[48]

The mind's quiet Henry Percy sought through Stoic resignation offers for Donne a challenging contrast to the prodigality of the Earl's son-in-law. Even by the standards of excess in the Jacobean court, James Hay was, as G. P. V. Akrigg describes him, a "magnificent profligate" who excelled in "parvenu ostentation";[49] he was one who, having "spent in a very jovial life above £400,000,"[50] earned the reputation, according to Bald, as "the greatest dandy of the court."[51] During his early years at court, Akrigg recounts, Hay was

---

[45] Bald, *John Donne: A Life*, p. 229. In conjunction with "Northumberland's alleged complicity in the Gunpowder Plot," Bald describes lists that were being compiled of the names of Percy's "most intimate friends and associates," including that of Thomas Hariot, and then notes, "all those whose names were mentioned were friends of Donne" (p. 190).

[46] Flynn, "Donne's *Ignatius His Conclave*," p. 173.

[47] Ibid., p. 171.

[48] Clucas, "'Noble virtue in extremes,'" p. 291.

[49] Akrigg, *Jacobean Pageant*, p. 49.

[50] *The Sermons of John Donne*, eds. Evelyn Simpson and George Potter, 4:12.

[51] Bald, *John Donne: A Life*, p. 161.

made Master of the Wardrobe, but soon after, because of his wasteful expenditures, "was persuaded to resign in return for £20,000 paid to him out of the Exchequer."[52] Lawrence Stone relates that some time later, while on embassy to Paris, Hay had his horse shod with silver shoes so that "as he rode to Court, wherever he wished to make an impression he would make his horse cavort, with the result that the shoes flew off to be fought over by the mob."[53] Hay's most notorious extravagances, however, were culinary in nature. John Chamberlain details in his letters that at one feast for the French Ambassador at Essex House in January, 1621 (which cost a total of £3,300) Hay employed 100 cooks for 8 days to prepare upwards of 1,600 dishes, including one dish consisting of 12 pheasants, another of 144 larks, and two others of two swans and two pigs each, as well as a half dozen Russian salmon, all at least six feet in length.[54] It was also Hay, as described by another contemporary of his, who introduced to London society that emblem of conspicuous consumption known as the ante-supper:

> The manner of which was, to have the board covered, at the first entrance of the ghests, with dishes, as high as a tall man could well reach, filled with the choycest and dearest viands sea or land could afford: And all this once seen, and having feasted the eyes of the invited, was in a manner throwne away, and fresh set on to the same height, having only this advantage of the other, that it was hot.[55]

Amidst the immoderate display that Hay undoubtedly exhibited for his father-in-law at Hanworth and the contrasting philosophical consolation Percy had cultivated during his years in the Tower, Donne presents his sermon, preached on 25 August 1622, and offers his patrons "this supreme cordiall, of bringing God into the eyes of man" (4:164). Donne's purpose in this sermon is "to dilate" the vision of his chief auditors so that they might see beyond their own circumstances to the God who is "afar off," which Donne insists, "is not a phrase of diminution . . . ; it is a power of seeing him so, as wheresoever I am, or wheresoever God is, I can see him at any distance" (4:175). From the equally obscuring distances of Doncaster's prodigality and Northumberland's Stoic resignation, the sermon at Hanworth offers correctives to both patrons. Specifically, while Hay's pursuit of outward extravagance and ceremony keeps him from the error of iconoclasm, and while Percy's attraction to a Stoic tranquillity of mind tempers the idolatrous trappings of material prosperity, Donne insists that the former's indulgence in worldly magnificence and the latter's negation of his passions in a type of inner iconoclasm must both be moderated through the spectacle of Christ crucified.

[52] Akrigg, *Jacobean Pageant*, p. 99.
[53] Stone, *The Crisis of the Aristocracy, 1558–1641*, p. 566.
[54] *The Chamberlain Letters*, pp. 277–78.
[55] Quoted in Bald, *John Donne: A Life*, p. 432.

The text for the Hanworth sermon is Job 36:25, "Every man may see it, man may behold it afar off." These are the words of Elihu, whom Donne initially identifies as "one of *Jobs* friends, and a meer *natural* man" and then goes on to describe as someone who is

> not fettered, not enthralled, in any *particular forme* of Religion, . . . not macerated with the *fear of God*; not infatuated with any preconceptions, . . . not dejected, not suppled, not matured, not entedred, with *crosses* in this world, and so made apt to receive any impressions, or follow any *opinions* of *other men.*
>
> (4:163)

Donne here draws obvious parallels between Elihu, who even "in the meer use of meer *naturall reason*" (4:163) is able to perceive the Creator in the creation, and Northumberland, who in his readings of natural philosophy has a similar lens through which to catch a rudimentary, and therefore limiting, glimpse of God. Yet, this sermon also seeks to adjust the pomp and circumstance filling the sight of Hay, of whom Donne asks, "How many times go we to Comedies, to Masques, to places of great and noble resort, nay even to Church onely to see the company?" (4:176).

In the *divisio* Donne summarizes the two halves of the scripture text: "The first part is a discovery, a manifestation of God to man; . . . and the other will be a tacite answer, to a likely objection, is not God *far off*, and can man see at that distance?" (4:164). Donne explains further that although "God is the subject of both parts; *God alone*; one God," yet "in both parts there is a Trinity too; three branches in each part; for in each, there is an *object*, something to be apprehended; there is a *meanes* of apprehending it, it is to *be seene*; [and] there is a *person* enabled to see it" (4:164). Donne concludes the *divisio* by differentiating the three branches of each part, namely, God first in the creation and then in glory, seeing with the eyes here (that is knowing) versus beholding what is above, and the figures of Adam and Enoch, and all of these branches together form "those sticks of sweet wood," "those drops of sweet gums," which will "make up this present sacrifice" (4:165).

Although Donne explains that the object of both parts of the Hanworth sermon is God, he specifies that the object in the first half is God as discovered in the particulars of the creation: "a *worme*, a *weed*, thy *selfe*, thy *pulse*, thy *thought*, are all testimonies, that *All*, this *All* and all the parts thereof, are *Opus*, a *work made*, and *opus ejus*, his *work*, made by *God*" (4:167). The means, then, for apprehending the Creator is through the spectacle of seeing with bodily *eyes*, which leads to knowing, for as Donne states:

> Now the *sight* of God in this text, is the *knowledge* of God, to *see* God, is but to *know*, that there is a God. . . . So that our labour never lies in this, to prove to any man, that he *may* see God, but onely to remember him that he *hath* seen God: not to make him beleeve that there is a God, but to make him see, that he does beleeve it. (4:168, 169)

The "*person* indued with [this] faculty" (4:170), of being able to know God through the created world, is "*every man, even Adam*" (4:170).

In the second half, Donne responds to the question "Is not God in the highest heaven, *afar off?*" (4:170) by explaining at length the means for beholding God in the glory of eternity. Punning upon the word "spectacle," Donne states, "God made the Sun, and Moon, and Stars, glorious lights for man to see by; but mans infirmity requires *spectacles*; and affliction does that office" (4:171).[56] By articulating here that sufferings are eyeglasses enabling one to see God's glory, Donne prepares his chief auditors for the spectacle of Christ crucified and resurrected. In order for Percy to apprehend God more completely than in the imperfect glimpse afforded by natural philosophy, he must look through the lens of his own adversity to correct the Stoic suppression of his passions in the light of Christ's passion. So too, in order for Hay to perceive material magnificence properly as a reflection of God's splendor, he must color his worldly spectacles with the divine spectacle of Christ's blood. These are the eyeglasses Donne prescribes when he writes:

> But that man, who through his owne *red glasse*, can see Christ, in that colour too, through his own miseries, can see Christ Jesus in his blood, that through the calumnies that have been put upon himself, can see the revilings that were multiplyed upon Christ, that in his own imprisonment, can see Christ in the grave, and in his owne enlargement, Christ in his resurrection, this man, this *Enosh*, beholds God, and he beholds him *è longinquo*, which is another step in this branch, *he sees him afar off.* (4:174–75)

Of the four Hebrew names for humankind that Donne repeatedly draws attention to in the *Sermons*, two of them occur in this scripture text from Job, "Adam" in the first half (which "signifies nothing but *red earth*; Let it be earth red with blood, let it be earth red with blushing" – 2:200) and then "Enosh" in the second. While Donne's description of Enosh in the passage quoted above echoes those found throughout the *Sermons* as a name that "signifies nothing but *misery*" (2:79),[57] the use of the name in the Hanworth sermon creates additional possibilities of meaning when read as an allusion.

In the *divisio*, the text twice names Enoch, rather than Enosh, as "a miserable man, a man that hath tasted affliction, and calamity, for that man lookes after God in the next world, and as he feels God with a *rod* in his

---

[56] See Winfried Schleiner, *The Imagery of John Donne's Sermons*, pp. 144–49, in which he illustrates that "'multiplying glass' and 'spectacle' were Donne's favorite terms for expressing a concentration of spiritual vision" (p. 144), and that Donne's play upon "the phonetic and semantic similarity between *speculum* and *spectaculum*" (p. 148) allows him to use *spectacle* not only to suggest its more common meaning of "show" or "display," but also to indicate a lens.

[57] For similar descriptions of Enosh, see also 2:200–01; 9:62; and 9:140.

hand here, so he beholds God with a *crown* in his hand there" (4:165). Although in Hebrew the words for "Enosh" and "Enoch" derive from different roots, the two names become interchangable in the text of this sermon, and this confusion seems to be intentional on Donne's part. In addition to the canonical references to Enoch from Genesis 5:24 and the New Testament book of Jude, the primary message of which is to warn a Christian community against certain individuals who, as a result of their lasciviousness, have become "spots in your feasts of charity, when they feast with you, feeding themselves without fear" (v. 12), Donne may also be alluding to an apocryphal work, The Book of the Secrets of Enoch (or 2 Enoch, see especially 10:4–6), of which he was unquestionably aware.[58]

This non-canonical, though historically and theologically influential, work begins with a description of Enoch as "an eye-witness of the wise and great and inconceivable and immutable realm of God Almighty, of the very wonderful and glorious and bright and many-eyed station of the Lord's servants";[59] he is one who has seen the ineffable spectacle of God in heaven. The work is framed as a first person dream narrative in which Enoch recalls, "And when I was asleep, great distress came up into my heart, and I was weeping with my eyes in sleep, and I could not understand what this distress was, or what would happen to me."[60] Following a detailed description first of Enoch's vision of the various levels of heaven and then of the prophecies of judgment against the sinful, the book concludes by noting that after Enoch was taken to heaven, an assembly of his family and friends came together "and made a great feast, rejoicing and making merry three days, praising God, who had given them such a sign through Enoch."[61]

Although I have provided only a brief overview, this apocryphal work, along with the reference to Enoch in Jude's epistle, offers a compelling explanation for Donne's description of Enoch (rather than Enosh) as one who "feeles God with a *rod* in his hand here" and who "beholds God with a *crown* in his hand there" (4:165). Understood in this context, such an allusion serves to comment indirectly on Hay as one whose feasting and spectacle were for the purposes of securing the admiration of others, rather than for reflecting and promoting the greater community found in God. Although Donne would have obvious political reasons for not making such an accusation directly before his patron, he also has a theological justification for tempering such an analogy since the aim of the sermon is not to condemn, but instead to expand the vision of both Hay and Percy so that, as Donne delineates,

---

[58] Cf. 4:217–18 and 9:250.
[59] R. H. Charles, ed., *Apocrypha and Pseudepigrapha of the Old Testament*, II:431.
[60] Ibid., II:431.
[61] Ibid., II:469.

> I can see *both Hemispheres* at once, God in this, and God in the next world too. I can see him, in the *Zenith*, . . . and I can see him in the *Nadir*. . . . I can see him in the *East*, . . . see him in the *West*, . . . I can see him in the *South*, in a warme, and in the *North*, in a frosty fortune: I can see him in all angles, in all postures.
>
> (4:175)

Donne further clarifies this aim, of adjusting the sight of both patrons, in the conclusion of the sermon, in which he explains, "There is not another word, and yet there is another branch in the Text" (4:176). In relation to the vision of Enoch/Enosh, Donne first questions, "but what beholds he afarre off?", and then responds, "it is God in the glory, and assembly of his immortall Saints in heaven" (4:176). In one long sentence (eighteen lines in the Simpson and Potter edition), Donne articulates that to behold "this *Communion of Saints*, this fellowship of the faithfull," the child martyrs, the prophets and evangelists, the holy matrons and holy virgins, the princes and the subjects, the rich and the poor, the catholic Church, "not onely *Easterne* and *Westerne*, but *Militant* and *Triumphant*," to see all this Donne writes, "is worth all the paynes, that that sight costs us in this world" (4:177).

In the final paragraph of the sermon, Donne asks Hay and Percy to envision themselves and their contrasting circumstances in this context of the divinely unified community. Describing courts as "the place of *rising* and the place of *falling* too," Donne asks, "How then hath God doubled his mercies upon those persons to whom he hath afforded two great lights, a *Sunne to rule their day*, honour and prosperity, and a *Moone to rule their night*, humiliation and adversity" (4:177). Donne clearly expresses, in this metaphoric allusion to Genesis 1:16, that both Hay, whose fortunes in the court were still rising at this time, and Percy, whose misfortunes were known to all present, adjust their vision to see themselves as reflections of the divine spectacle of Christ's passion that makes possible the communion of saints. Donne then closes the sermon by asking, "for what picture of God would they have, that will neither have him in great, nor litle?" (4:177), a question touching both the extravagant indulgences of Hay and the Stoic resignation of Percy.

Such a question is asked again of Hay even after Donne's death. One painting from Donne's art collection, "the Picture of the blessed Virgin Marye wch hanges in the little Dynynge Chamber,"[62] was willed to James Hay and, though no longer extant, is believed to have been a work by Titian portraying Mary, Jesus and St. John.[63] It is impossible to know if Donne deliberately chose for Hay a work of art that hung in his dining chamber as an ironic lesson on spectacle. Nevertheless, this action made known in his will further

---

[62] Bald, *John Donne: A Life*, p. 563.

[63] Milgate ("Dr. Donne's Art Gallery"), who, quoting from a catalogue of Charles I's art treasures made in 1639 by Abraham Vanderdoort, states that this work by Titian "'was given heretofore to his Majesty by my Lord Carlisle, who had it of Dr Donn, *painted upon the right light*'" (p. 318).

illustrates Donne's understanding of his responsibility to his patrons, as he clarifies in another of his sermons:

> As the Minister is presented in the notion and quality of an *Eagle*, we require both an Open eye, and a Piercing eye; First, that he dare looke upon other mens sins, and be not faine to winke at their faults, because he is guilty of the same himselfe, and so, for feare of a recrimination, incurre a prevarication; And then, that he be not so dim-sighted, that he must be faine to see all through other mens spectacles, and so preach the purposes of great men, in a factious popularity, or the fancies of new men, in a Schismaticall singularity; but, with the Eagle, be able to looke to the Sun; to looke upon the constant truth of God in his Scriptures, through his Church; For this is *Vis speculatrix*, the open and the piercing eye of the Eagle. (8:42)

When considered in the context of the Hanworth sermon, the painting bequeathed to Hay is yet another example, as Shami contends, that "the discretion of choosing the means which will minister most effectively to the moral needs of his audience is everywhere Donne's greatest concern."[64] Within the circumstances of his command performance at Hanworth, Donne clarifies that his own theological justification for this sermon is to correct the spiritual vision of these patrons and their guests through the spectacle of Christ's sufferings and, thereby, to enlarge them to know the communion of God within the Church.

VISIONEM DEI, UNIONEM

In his magnificent Easter sermon of 1628, Donne implores the congregation of St. Paul's to employ the noblest of the senses, sight, upon the noblest object, stating, "see God in every thing, and then thou needst not take thine eye from Beauty, from Riches, from Honour, from any thing" (8:221). Filling the eye with the visible world finds its fulfillment in coming to know the Creator through that sight. Yet, Donne expresses in this homily on I Corinthians 13:12 ("For now we see through a glasse darkly, but then face to face; now I know in part, but then I shall know, even as also I am knowne") the desire, almost the obsession, to see not simply the reflected image in the creation, but the essence of God. While he is well aware that such a vision is not possible in this life, he is, nevertheless, resolved in the pursuit, for seeing God means being joined to God: "That which is our end, *salvation*, we use to expresse in Schooles by these two termes, we call it *visionem Dei*, the sight of God, and we call it *unionem*, an union with God; we shall *see* God, and we shall be *united* to God" (5:168). "In seeing God," Donne writes in one Candlemas Day sermon, "we shall see all that concernes us, and see it alwayes" (7:348); the seeing of God determines one's spiritual condition

---

[64] Shami, "Donne on Discretion," p. 48.

and defines who one is in relation to the Creator. In his Paul's Cross sermon preached on 22 November 1629, Donne states, "Blessednesse it selfe, is God himselfe; our blessednesse is our possession; our union with God" (9:127), and as he clarifies in the last of his St. Dunstan's sermons, "we place Blessednesse, *In visione*, in the sight of God" (10:228). However, while the sight of God is a blessing both in this life and in eternity, Donne finds more comfort in the assurance that God sees him.

In the first sermon he preached to Charles after the death of James, Donne quotes a string of biblical passages to make the point to his new king that "*Gods eyes are open upon all our wayes*; always open, and hee cannot chuse but see: So that, a wilfull shutting of the eye, a winking, a connivencie, is not an assimilation to *God*" (6:244). Although the all-seeing eye of God, as the passage above intimates, may be a source of fear, Donne urges that it is far worse to be out of God's sight, which is itself the very essence of hell, as he explains to James Hay and his company at Sion:

> this damnation, which consists in the losse of the sight and presence of God, [shall] be heavier to us then others, because God hath so graciously, and so evidently, and so diversly appeared to us, in his pillar of fire, in the light of prosperity, and in the pillar of the Cloud, in hiding himselfe for a while from us; we that have seene him in the Execution of all parts of this Commission [the sermon text Mk. 16:16], in his Word, in his Sacraments, and in good example, and not beleeved, shall be further removed from his sight, in the next world, then they to whom he never appeared in this. (5:267)

What Donne desires though is not just to be in God's line of vision, but more importantly to be in God's eye. As "the sharpest, and most sensible organ and instrument," the eye of God "soonest feeles, if any thing be amisse, and so inclines him quickly to rectifie us," and Donne is comforted in the fact that "Except the eye of God can be put out, we cannot be put out of his sight, and his care" (9:352).

Donne's lyric "Goodfriday, 1613" dramatically illustrates the desire to be united with, and recognized by, God in this way. As critics have been quick to point out, a good bit of the difficulty of this poem results from the tension created between outer and inner vision.[65] The sight, though not the eyes, of the persona is activated as his "Soules forme bends toward the East" (l. 10) and, in Augustinian fashion, his memory apprehends "That spectacle of too much weight" (l. 16). This westward rider is overwhelmed by the thought of physically seeing God die, specifically by beholding Christ's pierced hands and confronting that blood ("The seat of all our Soules," l. 26) and that flesh "rag'd, and torne" (l. 28), all of which, of course, is vividly present in his

---

[65] Noteworthy readings of "Goodfriday, 1613," as listed in the Bibliography, include those by Helen Brooks, A. B. Chambers (both essays), Donald Friedman, Frances Malpezzi, Patrick O'Connell, and Terry Sherwood (chapter 7).

memory. The speaker then wonders if he could fix his eye on the sorrow-filled countenance of Mary, who saw with her own eyes what he can hardly bear to imagine. Even as the speaker fixes his memory on these images, his attentions at the end of the poem are intent on focusing the gaze of Christ upon himself. The resolution of the poem and the resolve of the speaker are conditioned on conforming himself to the sufferings of Christ ("O thinke mee worth thine anger, punish mee, / Burne off my rusts, and my deformity," ll. 39–40) so that Christ will recognize the restored image.

The reciprocal exchange of vision, both seeing and being seen, that enacts the divine/human relationship in "Goodfriday, 1613" is clarified by Donne in the third and final part of his sermon on the eighth verse of Psalm 32, one of the penitential Psalms. Concentrating his attentions on the closing promise of the verse (*"That hee will guide us with his eye"*), Donne specifies that the guiding eye of God "we consider to be his particular care, and his personall providence upon us, in his Church" (9:367), the very place from which the westward rider on this holy day is removed. Donne reiterates in this sermon that the face of God is revealed in the Church service, in the preaching of the sermon, and in the administration of the sacraments, but he then adds, "there is an eye in that face," the eye of "a piercing and an operating Spirit, that lookes upon that soule, and foments and cherishes that soule, who by a good use of Gods former grace, is become fitter for his present" (9:367). As discussed in chapter one of this study, it is the Holy Spirit who for Donne fosters (primarily through "the art of memory") the commerce between the earthly community, especially in the Church, and the heavenly community, the Trinity. Donne moves on to explain that this work of the Spirit, guiding the Church with God's eye, manifests itself in the complementary effects of conversion to and union with God. Of the former, Donne writes, God's eye "turnes ours to look upon him," or, as he states a few lines later using a rather apt metaphor, "as a well made Picture doth alwaies looke upon him, that lookes upon it, this Image of God in our soule, is turned to him, by his turning to it" (9:367, 368). Of the latter, Donne eloquently states that God's eye not only "turnes us to himselfe," but finally "turnes us into himself" so that "we are not onely His, but He" (9:368, 369). These are precisely the effects found in "Goodfriday, 1613," in which the rider promises that he will turn (in the sense of repentance and conversion)[66] to face the gaze of Christ on the cross. Located as he is outside of the manifestation of God in the Church, the persona sees the spectacle of Christ in his memory and realizes that in order to be fully subsumed into and by the one who fills his inner vision, he must turn (that is return) to a participation in the sufferings of Christ afforded in the Word and the Sacraments.

---

[66] For discussions of this association with the word "turne," see Terry Sherwood, *Fulfilling the Circle*, pp. 158–72; and Helen Brooks, "Donne's 'Goodfriday, 1613. Riding Westward' and Augustine's Psychology of Time," pp. 297, 302–03 n19.

*

Book XI of Augustine's *De Trinitate* posits that traces of the Trinity can be discovered and understood in sight and vision. Initially in this book, Augustine explains that physical sight presents a type of trinitarian unity in the object that is seen, the impression of that object on the eye, and the will of the soul in directing the sensory organ. While Augustine admits that such sight is good "to that extent [that] it bears some resemblance, though very remote, to the highest good" (XI.v), it is imperfect, for he adds, "the rational soul lives disgracefully, when it lives according to the trinity of the outer man" (XI.iii).[67] However, a greater trinitarian vision arises, because between them "there is no longer any diversity of substance" (XI.iii), from the memory ("retaining the species which the soul absorbs into itself through the bodily sense"), inner vision ("when the eye of the mind is formed from that which the memory retains and absent bodies are conceived"), and the will ("in the act of remembering it causes the eye of the mind to turn back to the memory, in order that it may be formed by that which the memory retains, and that there may be a similar vision in thought" – XI.iii).[68]

The distinction Augustine makes between outer and inner vision offers a telling commentary on Donne's theological perspective of sight and spectacle. In general, the use of external objects as a formal element of worship corresponds to the vision of what Augustine refers to as the "outer man." Because physical sight is, according to Augustine, a less perfect means for instructing the soul, this may be the reason that Donne relegates the use of pictures and images in formal worship to the category of "things indifferent," even though he believes that they can be of genuine benefit when combined with instructive preaching. There seems to be no question, however, that the attention Donne directs to the eye and sight in the *Sermons*, as well as throughout his canon, depends on Augustine's trinity of inner vision and its reliance on the memory. Donne's proliferation of appeals to the eye of the mind is his method for engaging the memories of his auditors in "the art of salvation." The spectacle that Donne is most concerned to hold before the eye of the Church is that of Christ crucified, for it is that act that redeems the Church. As a result, the sacraments, not only the emblems of Christ's body and blood, but also the signing of the cross in baptism, are theologically necessary, for they are the spectacles that join the outer and inner eye in a single vision of the visible Church conforming itself to the sufferings of Christ.

[67] *The Trinity*, pp. 327, 322.
[68] Ibid., pp. 322, 323.

Chapter Four

VOICE OF THE TURTLE

ST. PAUL'S CROSS

DONNE received his first invitation to preach at Paul's Cross while he was still Reader at Lincoln's Inn, nearly five years prior to being installed as Dean of St. Paul's, yet not quite five months before his wife Ann would die from complications following the delivery of a still-born child. Preached on 24 March 1617, the sermon commemorates the anniversary of James' accession to the throne, and for this occasion Donne chose as his text Proverbs 22:11 ("He that loveth pureness of heart, for the grace of his lips, the king shall be his friend"). James himself was not present, having just left London for a trip to Scotland; however, the headnote to the sermon indicates that "the Lords of the Council, and other Honorable Persons" (1:183) were in attendance among the typically large audiences assembled for sermons at Paul's Cross that were comprised of people from every walk of life.[1] One witness of record was John Chamberlain who, in a letter dated five days after the event, describes for Dudley Carleton the audience, the sermon, and its reception:

> On Monday the 24th of this month, being the King's day, the Archbishop of Canterbury, the Lord Keeper, Lord Privy Seal, the Earl of Arundel, the Earl of Southampton, the Lord Hay, the Controller, Secretary Winwood, the Master of the Rolls, with diverse other great men, were at Paul's Cross, and heard Dr. Donne, who made there a dainty sermon upon the eleventh verse of the 22nd of Proverbs, and was exceedingly well liked generally, the rather for that he did Queen Elizabeth great right, and held himself close to the text without flattering the time too much.[2]

Simpson and Potter note in their introduction to the sermon that the epithet "daintie" seems "appropriate enough in its usual seventeeth-century sense of 'choice' or 'valuable'" (1:125).

The sermon, however, opens on an odd note, with an image that, while at

---

[1] See Millar MacLure, *The Paul's Cross Sermons*, especially chapter one, pp. 3–19.
[2] *The Letters of John Chamberlain*, p. 141.

first blush seems humorous, is followed by a stern comment on treason: "That Man that said it was possible to carve the faces of all good Kings that ever were, in a Cherry-stone, had a seditious, and a trayterous meaning in his words" (1:183). He quickly moves his auditors to the two pictures he will display from the sermon text, namely, "a good picture of a good King, and of a good subject," in order to establish that the subject who "proceeds sincerely in a lawful calling" God will seal with a blessing, "even that which is his own seal, his own image, the favor of the King" (1:183). Donne then anticipates the body of the sermon by stating that the mystery of the Trinity is "conveyed to our understanding, no other way, then so, as they have reference to one another *by Relation*," which Donne uses, not surprisingly, to explain that "As in Divinity, so in Humanity too, *Relations* constitute one another, King and subject come at once and together into consideration" (1:184).

The first half of this roughly two-hour sermon expatiates what William Proctor labeled in his own 1625 address as "the usuall subject" of Paul's Cross sermons, that is a rebuke of sin and an exhortation to the amendment of one's life.[3] In discussing at length the sins, both original and habitual, that keep one from a pureness of heart, Donne leads his auditors to the comfort of repentance, of which he writes, "that's the true, the proper Physick of the soul, it is the only means to recover thee" (1:196). A few pages later, Donne emphasizes that the only preservative for the pureness of heart acquired through repentance is the love communicated through the person of the Holy Spirit. In a passage that sounds remarkably like what the westward rider desires in the concluding lines of "Goodfriday, 1613," Donne writes of this love:

> It does not onely file off the rust of our hearts, in purging us of old habits, but proceeds to a daily polishing of the heart, in an exact watchfulness, and brings us to that brightness, *Ut ipse videas faciam in corde, & alii videant cor in facie*, That thou maist see thy face in thy heart, and the world may see thy heart in thy face; indeed, that to both, both heart and face may be all one: Thou shalt be a Looking-glass to thy self, and to others too. (1:199)

The notion here of repentance bringing one to a pureness of heart reflected to the benefit of oneself and of others leads to the central point of the sermon, which Donne draws from the phrase "the grace of lips."

Donne clarifies that his auditors are to apprehend "the grace of lips" not only in a literal sense in which "it signifies *speaking* onely," but primarily in a synecdochic manner "expressing a mans ability, to do service to that State in which God hath made his station; and by *lips*, and *fruits* of lips, is well understood the fruit of all his good labors and endeavors" (1:206). In the theater-like setting of Paul's Cross, itself a microcosm of the world, Donne asks his auditors to ponder their vocation: "Hath God made this World his

---

[3] MacLure, *The Paul's Cross Sermons*, p. 120.

Theatre, *ut exhibeatur ludus deorum*, that man may represent God in his conversation; and wilt thou play no part?" (1:207).

Throughout this middle section of the sermon, Donne repeats in a variety of ways the religious and civic duty every subject has to the King, both James and, more importantly, the King of Kings. Fulfilling one's responsibilities in this way is for Donne tied directly to his theology of communal participation, as elaborated in the opening chapter of this study. "In a word," Donne writes of those who do not commit their lives to this "grace of lips," "he that will be *nothing* in this world, shall be nothing in the next; nor shall he have the *Communion of Saints* there, that will not have the Communion of good men here" (1:209). This commerce between the king and his subjects, that itself finds its meaning for Donne in the relation of the persons of the Trinity, is both the benefit and the point of such a pursuit, which he describes when he writes,

> *Sociabit*, he [the king] shall associate them [the subjects] to him, and impart his consultations unto them: And *Sociabit* again, He shall go along with them, and accompany their labors, and their services, by the seal of his countenance, and ratification. (1:216)

Before bringing this section to an end, Donne emphasizes the particular responsibility of the King to follow the example of Christ, and to demand that his subjects enter into proper commerce with him by one of two doors, or as Donne corrects, "(indeed, not two *doors*, but a *gate*, and a *wicket*; a greater, and an inferior way) A *religious heart*, and *useful parts*" (1:215).

While James was not present because of his trip to Scotland, he had created before his departure Sir Francis Bacon Lord Keeper, and Bald speculates,

> in attending Donne's sermon Bacon was probably making his first public appearance since his new appointment, and it is obvious that many eyes must have been turned in his direction as Donne dilated on the pureness of heart and grace of lips of him whose friend the King would be.[4]

This sermon undoubtedly had a certain poignancy for Bacon, such as when Donne reiterates in the closing paragraph the obligation of all to God "not only to pay our *Rents*, (*spiritual* duties and services towards him)," but also to undertake "*reparations* too, to contribute our help to society, and such external duties as belong to the maintenance of this world, in which Almighty God hath chosen to be glorified" (1:222). The call to repentance that Donne sounds here links this particular sermon to the continuance of the ritual of public penance at Paul's Cross during his lifetime,[5] but it is also typical, in one form or another, of the pleas for repentance he makes in nearly all of his extant sermons.

[4] Bald, *John Donne: A Life*, p. 323.
[5] See MacLure, *The Paul's Cross Sermons*, pp. 15–18.

What this early sermon characterizes is the persistent attention Donne affords the doctrine of repentance, which restores the commerce within the Church, between Church and State, and between God and these human communities. The theological imperative of repentance is, therefore, an extension of Donne's communal understanding of the Trinity as a model for all relations. This first sermon of Donne's at Paul's Cross also characterizes, and personalizes, the connection he sees between repentance and calling, or vocation.[6] Thus, in addition to the applicability of this sermon for the changed circumstances of Bacon, Donne may very well have been preaching to himself.[7] Donne was a long time coming both to the Church of England and to the priesthood, and there are obvious indications that he struggled to feel confirmed in his vocation especially in moments of personal suffering, beginning, in the immediate context of this sermon, with the death of Ann and including the bouts of illness and moments of personal loss he would suffer over the next several years. Repentance for Donne, never simply a private matter between an individual and God, always finds its fulfillment in the community of the Church, as one glorifies the godhead in this world through "the grace of lips" that makes one useful to society.

AVERSIO & CONVERSIO

With regard to the doctrine of repentance, the *Sermons* reveal a clear connection in Donne's mind between the directives found in the New Testament (and as ordered in the Prayer Book) and his own sense of vocational duty as an Anglican priest. To begin with, Donne's assertion that "the Gospell is repentance, and remission of sinnes" (5:260) responds, of course, to Luke 24:47 and also echoes Calvin's statement that "the sum of the gospel is held to consist in repentance and forgiveness of sins" (III.iii.1).[8] Throughout the *Sermons*, Donne assumes the sinful nature of humankind, but while he acknowledges that we are all born into original sin, he reminds his auditors of the continual need both to repent and to avoid repeating habitual sins:

> This onely is true Repentance, *Plangere & plangenda non committere*, To bewayle our sins, and forbeare the sins we have bewayled. Neither alone will serve; which deludes many. Many thinke they doe enough if they repent, and

---

[6] For a wideranging overview of Donne's sense of calling, see William Mueller, *John Donne: Preacher*, pp. 35–84.

[7] See M. L. Donnelly ("Saving the King's Friend and Redeeming Appearances"), who reads this sermon primarily in order "to shed light on [Donne's] conception and rationalization of the patronage relationship," and who also asserts, "the language of grace and calling evoked by the text fits Donne's sense of his worldly situation and prospects, no less than it defines his spiritual condition" (p. 107).

[8] *Institutes of the Christian Religion*, I:592.

yet proceed in their sin; and many thinke they doe enough, if they forbeare their sin now, though they never repent that which is past; both are illusory, both deceitfull distempers. (9:325)[9]

This awareness of the fallen human condition and the biblically informed necessity of repentance speaks directly to Donne's own sense of clerical reponsibility. On 13 October 1622, Donne preached at St. Paul's the last of his three sermons on John 1:8 ("He was not the light, but came to bear witness to the light"), and in it he asserts in no uncertain terms the direct commands of God to his ministers: "Our Commission is to conform you to him, our Instructions are to doe that, that way, *By preaching the Baptisme of Repentance*, for the *remission of sinnes*" (4:229). Donne, however, goes further in this sermon. Beyond his obligation to preach, as well as his auditors' to repent, Donne elaborates on the notion of witness from his scripture text.[10] In particular, Donne explains that preaching the promises of the gospel and administering the Sacraments that seal those promises declare together the truth of Christ in the world, and that in response to the Word and the Sacraments, he enjoins his congregation, "witnesse to *others*, by thy *exemplar life*, and holy conversation" (4:234), or as he summarizes earlier in the sermon:

> This then is the chain; we *preach*, you *repent*; then we give you the *Seals*, the *Sacraments*, and you *plead* them, that is, declare them in a holy life; for, till that (*Sanctification*) come, *Preaching*, and *Repentance*, and *Seals*, are ineffectuall.
> (4:230)

The witness of holy living and holy conversation as requisite for true repentance again links this doctrine with Donne's understanding of the communal nature of God in the Trinity and the conversation that defines the creative activity of the godhead. It is this pattern that the Church of England sought to inscribe liturgically in its Prayer Book. The instructions for Morning and Evening Prayers begin with a montage of Old Testament passages attesting to the sinfulness of all and exhorting the need to repent, followed by a statement of general confession and the minister's pronouncement of absolution.[11] Further, as a preface to the service for Holy Communion, the Prayer Book mandates a penitent condition for those receiving the Sacrament, including the reconciliation of "those betwixt whom he [the curate] preceiveth malice and hatred to reign."[12] The service

---

[9] Donne's language here is similar to Hooker's (VI.iii.5), who explains that repentance is "a vertue, that hateth, bewayleth, and sheweth a purpose to amend sinne" (*The Folger Library Edition of the Works of Richard Hooker*, III:12).

[10] For an expanded discussion of the idea of witness in relation to this sermon, see Nancy Wright, "The *Figura* of the Martyr in John Donne's Sermons."

[11] Booty, ed., *The Book of Common Prayer, 1559*, pp. 49–51.

[12] Ibid., p. 247.

for the Lord's Supper itself includes, in a manner similar to that for Morning and Evening Prayer, a general confession and absolution.[13] Even in the Order for the Visitation of the Sick, the Prayer Book specifies that the minister is to request the afflicted person to "examine whether he be in charity with all the world, exhorting him to forgive from the bottom of his heart all persons that have offended him, and if he have offended other, to ask them forgiveness."[14]

Within the community of the Church, the Prayer Book requires individuals to enact their words of repentance publicly, and it is in this context that the variety of assertions and analogies Donne uses to articulate the doctrine of repentance can be properly understood. For example, in confirming his insistence on public, auricular confession, Donne cites Proverbs 18:21, "*Death and life are in the power of the tongue*" (2:210), and in a later sermon emphasizing the need to demonstrate the fruits of repentance, he writes, "And then are we reconciled by the blood of his Crosse, when having crucified our selves by a true repentance, we receive the seale of reconciliation, in his blood in the Sacrament" (4:300). Further, Donne describes repentance as "nothing but an Audit, a casting up of our accounts, a consideration, a survey, how it stands between God and our soule" (5:297), and, altering the comparison, it is "an everlasting Divorce from our beloved sin, and an everlasting Marriage and super-induction of our ever-living God" (7:163). These economic and domestic metaphors reinforce in relational terms that repentance inherently implies a condition requiring restoration and healing, such as when Donne writes, "but then is this Gods physick, and Gods Physician welcome unto you, if you be come to a remorsefull sense, and to an humble, and penitent acknowledgement, that you are sick" (2:94).[15] From his own perspective as a priest, Donne asserts, "The *reformation* of manners, and bringing men to *repentance*, is a miracle" (4:152), yet it is only so Donne believes when affirmed publicly in accord with the Church:

> Hast thou sought thy *Remission* at the Church, that is, in Gods Ordinances established in the Church? *In qua remittuntur, extra quam non remittuntur peccata*, In which Ordinances, there is an Infallibility of *Remission*, upon true repentance, and in a contempt or neglect of which Ordinances, all Repentance is illusory, and all Remission but imaginary. . . . Let no man say, I repent in secret; God sees that I repent; It was scarce in secret, that thou didst sin; and wilt thou repent but in secret? At least let us know thy repentance by the

[13] Booty, ed., *The Book of Common Prayer, 1559*, pp. 259–61.

[14] Ibid., p. 303.

[15] This analogy appears in a letter Donne wrote to Goodyer in March, 1608: "Of our souls sicknesses, which are sinnes, the knowledge is, to acknowledge, and that is her Physique, in which we are not dieted by drams and scruples, for we cannot take too much" (*Letters to Severall Persons of Honour, 1651*, p. 70). A similar metaphor also appears in Calvin's *Institutes* (III.iv.9), when he writes that the Lord "is the physician; therefore, let us lay bare our wounds to him" (I:634).

amendment of thy life, and wee shall not much presse the knowing of it any other way. (7:444)

With regard to the issues surrounding public versus private confession, Donne's views are distinct from those of Calvin and Hooker. From the outset, however, it is necessary to acknowledge that both Calvin and Hooker offer their discussions of repentance as a polemic to the Roman Catholic practice of sacramental confession. In the *Institutes*, Calvin condemns auricular confession to a priest not only because he believes it to be "useless and fruitless" (III.iv.19), but also because he believes it begs the question concerning "the power of the keys" (III.iv.20),[16] that priests through the apostolic succession of Peter (cf. Mt. 16:13–19) are the sole conduits through which one can receive the forgiveness of sins. In a similar vein, Hooker explains in his *Ecclesiastical Polity* that the Church Fathers from antiquity "did not gather by our Saviours words any such necessitie of seeking the Priests absolution from sinne, by secret, and (as they now terme it:) sacramentall Confession" (VI.iv.6).[17] One further note with respect to Hooker is that Book VI of his *Ecclesiastical Polity* was not published until 1648, although it obviously existed in manuscript prior to his death on 2 November 1600. Thus, it is questionable whether or not Donne had ever read Hooker's discussion of repentance.

With this said, and acknowledging the polemic intentions in their writings, it is nevertheless true that both Calvin and Hooker place much more emphasis on the efficacy of private, inner repentance than Donne. To begin with, both Calvin and Hooker cite Chrysostom in order to argue against the Roman Catholic sacrament of confession and for an internalized, private accounting of one's sins (III.iv.8 and VI.iv.16, respectively). Although both also allow for the practice of public confession, it is clear that both prefer, with respect to their own nuances of interpretation, the individual repenting before the Lord in secret. In particular, Calvin states that "he who will embrace this confession in his heart and before God will without doubt also have a tongue prepared for confession, when there is need to proclaim God's mercy among men" (III.iv.10) and further that because general, "ordinary confession has been commended by the Lord's mouth, no one of sound mind, who weighs its usefulness, can dare disapprove it" (III.iv.11).[18] As these passages indicate, Calvin is not forbidding the practice of public confession; however, it is also apparent in the phrases "whenever there is need" and who "can dare disapprove it" that only private confession is necessary for salvation.

Hooker concurs with Calvin in his assessment that "our way of reconciliation with him [God], is the inward secret repentance of the heart, which

---

[16] *Institutes of the Christian Religion*, I:645–47.
[17] *The Folger Library Edition of the Works of Richard Hooker*, III:24.
[18] *Institutes of the Christian Religion*, I:634, 635.

inward repentance alone sufficeth" (VI.iii.1), though to be fair he then adds, "unles some speciall thing in the qualitie of sinne committed, or in the partie that hath done amisse, require more" (VI.iii.1).[19] Further, while Hooker acknowledges that "the Ministers power to absolve is publickly taught and professed," he adds that "the Church of England hitherto hath thought it the safer way, to referre mens hidden crimes unto God and themselves only" (VI.iv.15) and that such supplication is to be made "if not with tongue, att the least with heart" (VI.iv.4).[20]

The closest Donne comes in the *Sermons* to a polemic on repentance appears in his exegesis of Psalm 32:5, a penitential psalm ("I acknowledged my sin unto thee, and mine iniquity have I not hid. I said, I will confesse my transgressions unto the Lord, and thou forgavest the iniquity of my sin"). Donne opens the sermon with the rather shocking contention that "This is the Sacrament of Confession" (9:296). Even though he immediately seeks to temper the assertion, noting, "So we may call it in a safe meaning; That is, The mystery of Confession: for true Confession is a mysterious Art" (9:296), he has, nevertheless, named confession as a sacrament. Whether he does so merely to seize the attention of his auditors or actually to challenge the accepted teachings of the Church of England is not entirely clear, primarily because he does not identify confession as sacramental in the strictest sense of a divinely ordained seal of God's promises.[21]

Instead, Donne repeats throughout the remainder of the opening paragraph that the sacramental nature of confession reveals itself in the divine wit and mystery "That no man comes thither, but in a sort as he is a notorious sinner," that "onely the Declaring, the Publishing, the Notifying, and Confessing of my sins, possesses me of the Kingdome of heaven," and that "Almighty God, love me the better, for knowing me to be such a sinner, then if I had not told him of it" (9:296–97). Using the example of David from the scripture text, Donne announces his intention to demonstrate in the body of the sermon that this mystery "is not delivered in one Rule, nor practiced in one Act" (9:297).

Donne departs in his analysis from the Scholastic tripartite division of repentance into contrition, confession, and satisfaction, and instead identifies two parts, David's preparation for repentance and the execution of his confession.[22] In the body of the sermon, Donne enumerates that the preparation itself consists of two parts, which he labels "*Notum feci*" and

---

[19] *Institutes of the Christian Religion*, I:6.

[20] Ibid., I:47–8, 19.

[21] See Calvin, *Institutes of the Christian Religion* (IV.xix.2), who defines a sacrament as "a seal by which God's covenant, or promise, is sealed" (II:1450).

[22] In the *Institutes*, Calvin rejects this three-part division as illogical (cf. III.iv.1) and instead offers a two-part division consisting of mortification and vivification (III.iii.3). By contrast, Hooker accepts the Scholastic division (cf. VI.iii.5–6), although he, of course, rejects the practice of penance as a sacrament.

"*Non operui.*" Of the former, Donne explains that "God by his Ordinance, executed by us, brings him to this *Notum feci*, into company with himself, into an acquaintance and conversation with himselfe" (9:300), and of the latter, that "That light of grace, by which a sinner disposes himselfe to confession, must discover every sinne, and hide none, suffer none to hide it selfe, nor lie hidden under others" (9:302).

The execution of David's repentance, as discovered in "This word, *Dixi, Amar, I said*" (9:303), consists of an interrelated three-part movement. *Dixi meditando* "implies first meditation, deliberation, considering" (9:303); then *Dixi statuendo* indicates that David "resolved too, for so the word signifies, Consideration, but Resolution upon it" (9:304); and finally, as an inseparable consequence of all, *Dixi confitebor*, "I considered, that my best way was to confesse, and I resolved to doe so, and I did it" (9:304). What Donne celebrates in this mystery of confession is "a sense of my reunion, and redintegration [sic] with God," for the glory of God arises not from the confession but "because he hath a straid soule, reunited to his Kingdome" (9:305). As one last point illustrating his decided preference for public confession, and in contrast to the prominence Calvin and Hooker afford private confession, Donne writes later in the sermon that "sinnes are not confessed, if they be not confessed to him [God]; and if they be confessed to him, in case of necessitie it will suffice, though they be confessed to no other" (9:309). In other words, Donne expresses here that a private confession of one's sins to God alone is to be considered the rare exception rather than the rule.

Donne returns to a communal point of emphasis in the concluding paragraph of the sermon, in which he states of David's example of repentance, "No man comes into the way, but by the illumination, and direction of God" and "The way is the Church; no man is cured out of the way; no man that separates himselfe from the Church; . . . except he conforme himself to that worship of God, and to those means of sanctification, which God hath instituted in his Church" (9:314). In the final sentence of the sermon, Donne grounds his insistence on repentance being fulfilled within the community of the Church on the theological foundation of the Trinity, delineating that prayer, preaching, and the Sacraments are "thy trinity upon earth, that must bring thee to the Trinity in heaven" (9:315).

In the midst of this sermon on Psalm 32:5, Donne introduces an intriguing image of an habitual sinner as one "that doth not stumble, but tumble, as a mighty stone downe a hill, in the wayes of his sin," and he then asks, "in his occasion, who can turne him?" (9:299). This idea of turning, an idea made evident in Donne's reading of Calvin and in his administration of the Church of England liturgy, captures for Donne the essence of repentance. Calvin recounts in the *Institutes* (III.iii.5–6) the etymology of "repentance," which in Hebrew is derived from "conversion" or "return" and in Greek from "change of mind" or "change of intention." "On this account," Calvin concludes, "in my judgment, repentance can thus be well defined: it is the true turning of our life to God."[23] Further, in the service for the Commination against Sinners, the Prayer Book instructs the minister to implore the offending person, "Turn you clean (saith the Lord) from all your wickedness, and your sin shall not be your destruction, . . . Turn you then and you shall live," and at the end of the service all of the people pray in unison, "Turn thou us, O good Lord, and so shall we be turned. Be favorable (O Lord) be favorable to thy people, which turn to thee in weeping, fasting, and praying; for thou art a merciful God, full of compassion, long-suffering, and of a great piety."[24]

Donne himself, in the context of renewing the image of God through repentance, calls the act of putting off the old man and putting on Christ *"Conversionem nostram, Encænia*, our turning to *God*, in a true repentance, or renewing, our dedication" (4:378). In a sermon explicating Psalm 6:8–10, he explains that the word from the text "*Convertantur*" is not "*Let them be overthrowne*, but *Let them returne*, let them be forced to returne" (6:59), and he then quotes Lamentations 5:1, "Turn us O Lord, and we shall be turned," which he explains "is, that we may be, that is, remaine turned, that we may continue fixed in that posture" (6:60). Donne's most clearly articulated passage on the idea of turning occurs in his sermon on Matthew 9:13, Christ's declaration that he calls not the righteous but sinners:

> Are ye to learn now what that is? He that cannot define Repentance, he that cannot spell it, may have it; and he that hath written whole books, great Volumes of it, may be without it. In one word, (one word will not do it, but in two words) it is *Aversio*, and *Conversio*; it is a turning from our sins, and a returning to our God. (7:162)

In pronouncing these words from the pulpit at Whitehall on 30 April 1626, Donne is fulfilling his duty to God to preach the gospel that is repentance. From Donne's vantage point of the one administering the liturgy, it is the public penance determined by God's ordinances (specifically in common prayer, in preaching, and in the Sacraments) that he sees as most efficacious for salvation, for public confession as such affirms the Church as a community of sanctified believers even as it reenacts the trinitarian unity of God.

THE CHURCHING OF WOMEN

Donne's two extant churching sermons, the one for Lady Doncaster (Lucy Percy) and the other for the Countess of Bridgewater (Frances Egerton), offer an intriguing historical, as well as liturgical, perspective from which to view Donne's application of his theology of communal participation to the

---

[23] Calvin, *Institutes of the Christian Religion*, I:597.
[24] Booty, ed., *The Book of Common Prayer, 1559*, pp. 319, 323.

doctrine of repentance. There is little doubt that the service for the churching of women, a practice carried over from the medieval church, was derived from the Old Testament laws of purification for women after childbirth. Leviticus 12 enumerates that a woman was considered unclean for seven days following the birth of a male child (fourteen for a female) and continued in "the days of her purifying," isolated from touching anything holy or from entering the sanctuary, for another thirty-three days (sixty-six if the child was female). After completing this period of purification, the new mother then brought to the priest a year old lamb for a burnt offering and a pigeon or turtledove for a sin offering, although if she could not afford a lamb, she could bring two pigeons or two turtledoves (one for each offering).

The Church of England Prayer Book service, a rather simple one, does not directly characterize the ceremony as one of purification, labeling it instead "The Thanksgiving of Women after Childbirth."[25] By custom, one undoubtedly influenced by the number of days of purification specified in Leviticus, the churching occurred roughly one month after the woman had given birth.[26] To begin the service, the woman was to kneel "in some convenient place nigh unto the place where the table standeth," although by Donne's day there was a pew designated for this purpose,[27] and the priest then expressed to the woman his gratitude that God "hath preserved you in the great danger of childbirth."[28] This pronouncement was followed by a reading of Psalm 121, a reciting of the Lord's Prayer, and finally a prayer by the priest, in which he again thanks God who "hast delivered this woman thy servant from the great pain and peril of childbirth."[29] The comments on the danger and pain of childbirth framing the churching service not only speak to the historical truth of the high mortality rate for both children and mothers during this period, but also allude to the curse Eve received because of the part she played in the Fall: "I will greatly multiply your pain in childbearing; in pain you shall bring forth children" (Gen. 3:16). Following the service, the woman was then instructed, again with an obvious parallel to the Old Testament laws, to provide an offering, which was a monetary one anywhere from 4d. to 11d., though if the child died it was typically 1d. to 2d.[30]

In his brief defense of the churching service from his *Ecclesiastical Polity* (V.lxxiv.1–4), Hooker asserts at the outset, "The fruit of mariage is birth, and the companion of birth travaile, the griefe whereof being so extreeme, and the daunger alwaies so great" that, he continues, "wee can never sufficientlie

---

[25] Ibid., p. 314.
[26] See Jeremy Boulton, *Neighborhood and Society*, p. 278; and William Coster, "Purity, Profanity, and Puritanism: The Churching of Women, 1500–1700," pp. 380, 385–86.
[27] See Coster, "Purity, Profanity, and Puritanism," pp. 382–83.
[28] Booty, ed., *The Book of Common Prayer, 1559*, p. 314.
[29] Ibid., p. 315.
[30] See Boulton, *Neighborhood and Society*, p. 277; and Christopher Hill, *Economic Problems of the Church*, p. 168.

praise him [the Lord] nor give him thankes for halfe those benefites for which this sacrifice were most due" (V.lxxiv.1).[31] Further, Hooker specifically addresses the one month period between the birth of the child and the churching service and notes, in response to popular belief and practice,[32] not only that canon law prescribes no such period, but more importantly that during this time of lying in, the woman "is not barred from thence in such sort as they interpret it, nor in respect of anie unholines forbidden entrance into the Church" (V.lxxiv.2).[33] Finally, Hooker defends the offering accompanying the churching of women by explaining that it is "a part of the ministers right" and that "as the life of the clergie is spent in the service of God, so it is susteined with his revenue" (V.lxxiv.4).[34]

There is a variety of historical evidence from the late sixteenth and early seventeenth centuries indicating the displeasure of some with the practice of churching, such as the objections raised by dissenting Puritans in *An Admonition to the Parliament* (1572):

> Churching of women after childbirthe, smelleth of Jewishe purification: theyr other rytes and customes in their lying in, & comming to church, is foolishe and superstitious, as it is used. She must lie in with a white sheete upon her bed, and come covered with a vayle, as ashamed of some folly. She must offer, but these are matters of custome, and not in the book. But this Psalme [Psalm 121] is childishly abused. . . . They pray that all men may be saved, & that they may be delivered from thundering & tempest, when no danger is nighe.[35]

As this passage indicates, a number of the complaints during this period focus overall on matters of custom that fall outside what is specified in the Prayer Book. The wearing of a white veil, in particular, was often insisted on by orthodox clergy, and there was even a legal judgment in the reign of James I upholding this stricture.[36] Additional complaints centered on the unscriptural nature of the ceremony and the clergy's demand for payment,[37] and the judicial records even indicate that women were prosecuted who, as briefly

---

[31] Hooker, *The Folger Library Edition of the Works of Richard Hooker*, II:406, 407.

[32] Boulton (*Neighborhood and Society*) notes that "associated with the element of purification ran a strong popular belief that women who died in childbed before being churched could not be given Christian burial" (p. 276). Further, Keith Thomas (*Religion and the Decline of Magic*) recounts that

> even at the end of the seventeenth century it was reported from parts of Wales that "the ordinary women are hardly brought to look upon churching otherwise than as a charm to prevent witchcraft, and think that grass will hardly ever grow where they tread before they are churched." (p. 39)

[33] *The Folger Library Edition of the Works of Richard Hooker*, II:408.

[34] Ibid., II:409.

[35] W. H. Frere and C. E. Douglas, eds., pp. 28–29.

[36] See both Boulton (*Neighborhood and Society*, p. 276) and Thomas (*Religion and the Decline of Magic*, pp. 59–60).

[37] Cf. Patricia Crawford, *Women and Religion in England, 1500–1720*, p. 55; and F. G. Emmison, *Elizabethan Life*, II: 159–61.

noted in one such entry, came "undecently and unwomanly without any woman with her."[38] By and large, however, records from the period indicate that the overwhelming majority of women complied with and even affirmed the practice. For example, Jeremy Boulton's study of the Boroughside district of St. Saviour's, Southwark (located on the south bank of the Thames between London Bridge and Lambeth Marsh), tabulates that upwards of 93% of those eligible were churched in a timely manner during the years 1619–25.[39] In addition, the historical work by F. G. Emmison and William Coster reveals not only that "refusing to go to be churched was not a common offense," but also that "the majority of women continued to acquiesce in, many actively to support, the ceremony as a social necessity."[40]

Taken together, what the scattered complaints and the widespread complicity of the women seem to signal is that by the time of Donne's clerical career the churching of women had become primarily social and ceremonial in purpose. Because of the isolation women endured during the months prior to and after delivering their children, the churching service had taken on the secular taint of something akin to a coming-out celebration, for as William Coster argues, "the ceremony of churching was the only means by which, after childbirth, a woman could return to the community of the Church, and indeed to society in general."[41] In spite of the fact that canon law actually specified that such isolation was not required, popular practice and belief dictated otherwise, and it is within the bounds of this cultural debate that Donne's two churching sermons reveal that he imagined this practice in the theological context of the need for communal repentance and, therefore, as an act of purification, not simply from the curse of travail and danger in childbirth, but principally from the taint of original and habitual sins.

Donne's sermon for the churching of the Countess of Bridgewater, which Simpson and Potter speculate was preached in 1621 or 1623,[42] is actually two sermons that explicate Micah 2:10 ("Arise and depart, for this is not your rest"). Dennis Flynn has recently demonstrated that Donne had known Frances Egerton from her early childhood while he served in the household of Henry Stanley,[43] yet in spite of his long-time association with Lady

---

[38] Ibid., II: 160.

[39] Boulton, *Neighborhood and Society*, pp. 277–78.

[40] Emmison, *Elizabethan Life*, II: 159; and Coster, "Purity, Profanity, and Puritanism," p. 386.

[41] Ibid., p. 377.

[42] In their introduction to this sermon, Simpson and Potter conjecture that although the Countess of Bridgewater had fifteen children, this sermon very likely "was preached after the birth of an heir, for most of the children were daughters" (5:14). They then note a letter from Chamberlain, dated 2 June 1621, recording the birth of a son who, unfortunately, died early in 1623; however, Chamberlain also records that the Countess was pregnant at this time and two months later, in June, she gave birth to another son, John, "who survived his father and became the second Earl of Bridgewater" (5:14).

[43] Flynn, *John Donne and the Ancient Catholic Nobility*, pp. 172, 177.

Bridgewater, the first of the two sermons is a lengthy and rather impersonal meditation from biblical history on the sinful, fallen condition of the Israelites. In their introduction to this sermon, Simpson and Potter express their belief that Donne divided what was initially one sermon into two only when he had written it out sometime after preaching it and, further, that "in the original sermon it is probable that the long disquisition on God's judgments on the Jews which occupies most of the first of these two sermons was compressed into a few paragraphs, as it would be very unsuitable for the churching of any lady" (5:14). While their conjecture that Donne lengthened the original text may be true, it is unnecessary to dismiss the material from the first of the two sermons simply on the question of its appropriateness. Just such an extended recounting of human sinfulness speaks directly to Donne's desire to raise this churching service above the secular context of the time in order to attend to the vocational responsibility he expresses throughout the *Sermons* of instilling in his auditors genuine contrition.

In reviewing the structural elements for both parts of his churching sermon for Frances Egerton, Donne demonstrates his intention to initiate the process of sanctification when he delineates the three-point explication of his scripture text:

> The first was a *Commination*, a departing without any Rest, propos'd to the Jewes; The second was a *Commonition*, a departing into a way towards Rest, proposed to repentant sinners; And this third is a *Consolation*, a departing into Rest it selfe, propos'd to us, that beleeve a Resurrection. (5:209)

This division, tracing as it does the necessary movement from fallenness to confession to consolation, articulates the doctrine of repentance as the remedy for human sin in general that Donne applies personally to Frances Egerton in the opening paragraph of the second sermon when he writes that the words "arise" and "depart"

> admit a just accommodation to this present occasion, God having rais'd his honorable servant, and hand-maid here present, to a sense of the *Curse*, that lyes upon *women*, for the transgression of the first woman, which is painfull, and dangerous *Child-birth*; and given her also, a sense of the last glorious resurrection, in having rais'd her, from that Bed of weaknesse, to the ability of coming into his presence, here in his house. (5:198)

The obvious allusion Donne makes to Genesis 3:16 in this passage links the churching of Lady Bridgewater, and for that matter of all women, not only to Eve and the sufferings of childbirth, but also to the genderless curse of original sin. Donne perceives Frances Egerton as a microcosm not simply of the female condition, but principally of the human condition, which he spells out later in this second part:

A Christian Mother does not conceive a Christian; onely the Christian Church conceives Christian Children. . . . The Parents may be up, and ready, but their issue abed, and in their bloud, till *Baptisme* have wash'd them, and till the spirit of Regeneration have rais'd them, from that bed, which the sins of their first Parents have laid them in, and their own continuing sins continued them in. This rising is first, from *Originall sin,* by baptism, and then from *actuall sin,* best, by withdrawing from the occasions of tentation to future sins, after repentance of former. (5:205)

In his religious imagination, Donne links the churching of women with baptism in the larger context of the doctrine of repentance, which fulfills the regenerative needs of all humanity in the publicly administered ordinances of the Church, for the Church alone "conceives Christian Children."

These same ideas on the doctrine of repentance are further elaborated in the sermon for the churching of Lady Doncaster, which is the earlier of the two and which Simpson and Potter date with certainty as being preached December, 1618.[44] The delivery and reception of this sermon must have taken place in an atmosphere of personal sadness. For Lord and Lady Hay this sadness resulted from the fact that their son, who was baptized Charles, lived only a few days and was buried in the churchyard of St. Clement Danes on 3 December 1618. Donne's own sadness stemmed not only from sharing in the grief of his friend and patron, but also, one would assume, from recalling his own loss sixteen months prior of his wife Ann, who was buried in the same churchyard.

The biblical text for Lucy Percy's churching sermon is Canticles 5:3 ("I have washed my feet, how shall I defile them?"), and in its explication Donne concentrates on the need for washing, not a physical cleansing, but a spiritual purification that is required of all, initially because of original sin and thereafter because of actual sins. The washing that Donne specifies as "absolutely, generally necessary" is that of baptism, and the washing that is "occasionally necessary" from habitual sins occurs in "the *bloud* of our Saviour in the *Sacrament*" (5:176). Both are necessary for salvation, and both, as communal acts of repentance, must be received in the Church, for Donne writes of these two Sacraments, "*fons in Ecclesia,* the whole *spring,* and river is in the Church, there is no *baptisme,* no *bloud* of Christ, but in the Church" (5:176). Donne notes further, however, that between these two there is another washing, "the water of *Contrite,* and *repentant teares,* in opening our selves to God, and shutting up of our selves against future tentations" (5:176). While Donne admits that this third type of washing can take place in an act of private repentance, he argues strongly for the efficacy of public

---

[44] In their introduction to this sermon, Simpson and Potter note that "the register of baptisms at St. Clement Danes Church, London, records for November 27, 1618, 'Charles Hay, Sonne to the Lord Hay, Viscount Doncaster, baptised in Essex House'" (5:12) and comment further that this was the only child Lady Doncaster, who was then nineteen, would bear.

repentance: "of this water, there is *Pelvis in Ecclesia*, the *Bason* is in the Church; for our best repentance (though this repentance be at home in our owne hearts) doth yet receive a Seale, from the *absolution* of Gods Ministers in the Church" (5:176). In emphasizing yet again the priority he ascribes to communal repentance, Donne comes very near in this passage to naming repentance as a sacrament by identifying it as a seal received from "Gods Ministers."[45] As in the sermon for the Countess of Bridgewater, this homily for Lady Doncaster is not a simplistic pronouncement of purification for and delivery from the pain and danger of childbirth, nor is it a fawning celebration for the return to society of this woman of society. Instead, Donne calls all those in attendance to a communal participation in the body of Christ. Noting the context of Christ's washing the feet of the Apostles at the Last Supper, Donne states in the sermon for Lucy Percy:

> If we come not to this washing of our feet, this preparatory washing by teares of *repentance*, we can have no part in him, that is, in the participation of his body, and his bloud; . . . let us often call our selves to account, implore the councell often, often accept the *absolution* of Gods Minister, and often settle our soules, in a true peace, by a worthy receiving of the seale thereof, in the Sacrament.
>
> (5:179)

In his article on the churching of women during the English Renaissance, William Coster states, "it would be easy to argue that the churching of women was not only religiously offensive, but personally insulting to these women,"[46] especially in the light of the forced isolation (both from the lying in and during the service itself), the association of the pains of childbirth with the curse of Eve, and the implication from the Old Testament purification laws of women's bodies as unclean vessels. Certainly from a late twentieth century perspective this liturgical practice seems offensive and insulting. Nevertheless, as Jeanne Shami rightly argues, "context is all" in reading the *Sermons*.[47] To the extent that Donne's individual sermons are rarely seen "as issuing from any specific context – generic, historical, theological, political, or cultural," Shami asserts that such fragmentary and uncontextualized readings are, more often than not, the result of critics seeking for "the confirmation of Donne's grasping, egotistical nature."[48] The churching sermons for Lady Doncaster and the Countess of Bridgewater, when properly contextualized, reveal Donne's theological and ministerial integrity in the midst of a cultural view of churching as merely ceremonial. The purification Donne prescribes in the sermons for these two aristocratic women, while associated with the bodily cleansing outlined in Leviticus, derives fundamentally from his own sense of

---

[45] See note 21 above.
[46] Coster, "Purity, Profanity, and Puritanism," p. 386.
[47] Shami, "The Absolutist Politics of Quotation," p. 383.
[48] Ibid., pp. 383, 389.

calling to preach the gospel that is repentance. In these sermons, he enlarges the need for purification to include all of fallen humanity; the churching of Frances Egerton and of Lucy Percy were for him particular occasions that touched the more universal condition of human sinfulness. Because of original sin, as well as the inevitability of actual sins, birth brings with it death, and as Donne makes clear in these churching sermons, the only way to life, the only way to seal one's repentance, is through a communal participation in the Word and Sacraments.

BAPTISMATE LACHRYMARUM

The churching sermon for Lady Doncaster, with the motif from its scripture text of water and washing, touches the pervasive association Donne makes throughout the *Sermons* between repentance and tears. To the extent that repentance is an act of purification for habitual sins, tears of contrition are for Donne the bodily emblem for that spiritual cleansing. Such tears are, Donne writes, "the Ambassadours of sorrow" and "the bloud of a wounded soule" (5:54), and because they testify to the divine promise that the sorrow necessitating them will be removed in heaven, Donne exclaims, "You must weepe these teares, teares of contrition, teares of mortification, before God will wipe all teares from your eyes" (4:45). Donne further urges his auditors to these penitent tears, especially those who believe themselves hardened beyond all possibility of weeping, when he reminds them that "A sinfull man, an obdurate man, a stony heart may weepe" (9:290), for "Not to mourn under the sense of evils, that may fall upon us, is a stony disposition; Nay, the hardest stone, marble, will weep towards foul weather" (3:183).

Tears of contrition are for Donne, most importantly, a theological complement to, and even a type for, the waters of baptism. "Christ and his Apostles," Donne writes, "had carried two Waters about his Church: The water of Baptisme [and] the water of contrite teares, and repentance" (9:329), and, as he specifies in another sermon, "he that comes washed with the water of Baptisme in his infancy, and he that comes washed with the teares of Repentance in his age, may receive health and cleannesse" (5:85). Therefore, repentance is for Donne "the second Baptism" (10:186), or as he states more fully in another sermon, the resurrection from sin "is begun, and well advanced in *Baptismate lachrymarum*, In the baptisme of true and repentant teares" (7:213). By drawing the tears of contrition into comparison with baptism, Donne once again comes very near to naming repentance as a sacrament that brings one to share in the sufferings of Christ within the community of the Church. Noting that God began the Christian Church with the sacramental water of baptism, Donne exhorts his auditors, "Pursue his Example; begin thy Regeneration with teares" (9:291), and in one of his christening sermons, he declares that all are to make their salvation sure by water and by blood:

> If thy heart, and bowels have not yet melted in compassion of his passion for thy soule, if thine eyes have not yet melted, in *teares of repentance* and contrition, he is not yet come by *water* into thee; If thou have suffered nothing for sinne, nor found in thy selfe, no resistance of Concupiscences, he that comes not to set peace, but to kindle this war, is not yet come into thee, by *bloud*.
>
> (5:137)

In a sermon preached at Whitehall the first Friday in Lent 1622, Donne reaffirms the necessity of repentance in his explication of John 11:35 ("Jesus wept"). Using a rather unique metaphor, Donne writes, "Every man is but a spunge, and but a spunge filled with teares," noting that such sponges will weep "Whether God lay his left hand [on them], temporall calamities, or his right hand, temporall prosperity" (4:337). Even though he asserts later in the sermon "I am farre from concluding all to be impenitent, that doe not actually weep and shed teares," he immediately adds, "And yet the worst Epithet, which the best Poet could fixe upon *Pluto* himselfe, was to call him *Illachrymabilis*, a person that could not weep" (4:339). In the concluding sentence of the sermon, Donne once again comes very near to naming repentance as a sacrament:

> Weep these teares truly, and God shall performe to thee, first that promise which he makes in *Esay, The Lord shall wipe all teares from thy face*, all that are fallen by any occasion of calamity here, in the militant Church; and he shall performe that promise which he makes in the Revelation, *The Lord shall wipe all teares from thine eyes*, that is, dry up the fountaine of teares; remove all occasion of teares hereafter, in the triumphant Church. (4:344)

Donne articulates in this passage that tears of repentance are the seals for the promises of God, as realized both now, in the Church Militant, and forever, in the Church Triumphant. Therefore, as he articulates in the opening paragraph of this Lenten sermon, Donne fulfills his clerical duty by preaching the gospel of repentance when he writes of Jesus weeping:

> My vicarage is to speake of his Compassion and his teares. Let me chafe the wax, and melt your soules in a bath of his Teares now, Let him set to the great Seale of his effectuall passion, in his blood, then. It is a Common place I know to speake of teares: I would you knew as well, it were a common practice, to shed them. (4:324)

The connection in Donne's imagination between the tears of contrition as a second baptism and his own sense of vocation underscores the sacramental overtones he ascribes to repentance, and this association between calling and penitent obedience is further demonstrated in the complementary hymn and sermon he wrote on the occasion of his last going into Germany.

GOLD IN THE WASHES[49]

Appointed by James I as chaplain for the embassy led by James Hay to mediate between Catholics and Protestants in Bohemia, Donne left England on 12 May 1619 apprehensive that he might never return. The hymn Donne wrote in conjunction with this trip has received not only less critical attention, but also less praiseworthy criticism than any of his major religious lyrics, particularly his other two hymns. Focusing primarily on the closing lines of the poem, critics tend to sum up, and thereby dismiss, "A Hymne to Christ, at the Authors last going into Germany" as another example of Donne's obsession with death. Helen Gardner concludes that "the close of the poem is a prayer for death, by which our divorce from the world is sealed or ratified,"[50] and R. C. Bald contends that, because Donne "seems to be weighed down by fears of shipwreck or drowning," the poem expresses little else than "the sick fancies of a troubled mind."[51] More recently, John Pollock surmises that the unusually dark mood of the poem "can be seen as the direct result of Donne's unrelieved guilt and fear of growing old."[52] While Arthur Marotti's discussion focuses upon "Donne's deep ambivalence about rejecting worldly values and ambitions," he, nevertheless, perceives in the hymn a "yearning for death."[53] The only reading more extreme than that provided by John Carey who, in his usual manner of exaggerated scorn, believes that "this is a poem about committing suicide,"[54] is that of David Aers and Gunther Kress who insist that Donne's approach in lines 9–12 is "actually that of a Moloch-worshipper."[55]

The singular voice of praise for the poem is that of Wilbur Sanders, who believes that "A Hymne to Christ" is "one of the greatest religious lyrics in the language."[56] Although I find this assessment overstated, the hymn is certainly a more engaging lyric than has generally been accepted. Throughout his discussion of the poem, Sanders insists that the hymn cannot be explained simply as a morbid longing for death, nor even as a convenient, and thereby vulgar, renunciation of the world in an attempt to receive "higher joys."[57] Sanders argues, instead, that the poem is one of discovery, one that is "instinct with wonder," as Donne "measures the preciousness of the faith

[49] A version of this section appeared as my article "Gold in the Washes: Donne's Last Going into Germany."

[50] Gardner, ed., *The Divine Poems of John Donne*, p. 107.

[51] Bald, *John Donne: A Life*, p. 343.

[52] Pollock, "A Hymne to Christ, at the Authors last going into Germany," pp. 21–22.

[53] Marotti, *John Donne, Coterie Poet*, p. 279.

[54] Carey, *John Donne: Life, Mind and Art*, p. 218.

[55] Aers and Kress, "Vexatious Contraries: A Reading of Donne's Poetry," p. 71.

[56] Sanders, *John Donne's Poetry*, p. 150.

[57] Ibid., p. 152.

by the costliness of the sacrifices he discovers himself already making for it."[58]
While I concur in general with Sanders, I contend that by reading the hymn in
the context of Donne's own Valediction Sermon that complements it, one
more clearly perceives the ingenuity of Donne as he celebrates the doctrine of
repentance. Within the adversities confronting him in the spring of 1619,
Donne discovers once again that suffering is the means for the power of God
to enter the world, for it is only by sharing in the sufferings of Christ that the
Church can be conformed to Christ.

When Donne was directed into the Church of England at the insistence of
James I, Izaak Walton would have us believe that Donne's acceptance of his
new vocation was immediate and complete:

> And now all his studies which had been occasionally diffused, were all
> concentred in Divinity. Now he had a new calling, new thoughts, and a new
> employment for his wit and eloquence: Now all his earthly affections were
> changed into divine love; and all the faculties of his own soul, were ingaged in
> the Conversion of others: In preaching the glad tidings of Remission to
> repenting Sinners, and peace to each troubled soul.[59]

However, as Helen Gardner points out in her discussion of "To Mr. Tilman
after he had taken orders," Donne was initially reluctant to enter the Church,
and, in fact, she argues that he "never speaks as if he ever felt any direct
inward call to the ministry."[60] The reason for such reluctance, on the one
hand, might stem from a sense of unworthiness in administering the
responsibilities of his new calling, for he must have been acutely aware, as
Bald points out, that taking orders "might seem rather shocking to some of
those who had known him formerly."[61] On the other hand, it is no secret that
prior to entering the Church, Donne had sought earnestly to procure a secular
position, first in Ireland, later in Virginia, and finally in Venice.

As a result of his difficulties in acquiring a secular preferment, it is curious
that when Donne was appointed early in 1619 as chaplain to Doncaster, he
was less than eager to involve himself in an activity of such obvious political
importance. In a letter addressed to Goodyer, Donne recounts some of his
reservations:

> I leave a scattered flock of wretched children, and I carry an infirm and
> valetudinary body, and I go into the mouth of such adversaries as I cannot

---

[58] Sanders, *John Donne's Poetry*, pp. 153, 152.

[59] Walton, *The Lives of John Donne, Sir Henry Wotton, Richard Hooker, George Herbert, and Robert Sanderson*, p. 48.

[60] Gardner, ed., *The Divine Poems of John Donne*, p. 131.

[61] Bald, *John Donne: A Life*, p. 305. Within this same context, Bald quotes from a letter Donne wrote to Henry Wotton and then comments, "there is a genuine humility of tone which contrasts quite sharply with the worldliness of some of the letters he had written a short time previously" (p. 305).

blame for hating me, the Jesuits, and yet I go. Though this be no service to my Lord, yet I shall never come nearer doing him a service, nor do anything liker a service than this.[62]

This passage offers a window to Donne's perceived limitations, both physical and spiritual. Following the death of his wife Ann eighteen months prior to his departure for Germany, Donne seems to have withdrawn from the world and, as a result, laments consigning his "scattered flock of wretched children" into the care of servants. Donne also confesses to Goodyer his hesitation to undertake this journey because of his "infirm and valetudinary body." It is clear from Walton's account and from Donne's letters and actions not only that Donne was in poor health, perhaps even as a result of his extended and intense grieving, but also that he felt his life might be drawing to a close. For a man in the seventeenth century who was forty-seven years of age and whose health was failing, these concerns are understandable, yet Donne seems to press the matter. In a letter to the Countess of Montgomery, who had requested a copy of one of his sermons, Donne alludes to his upcoming trip to Germany as "going out of the kingdom," and then adds parenthetically, "and perchance out of the world";[63] and for Robert Ker, with whom Donne appears to be in the process of putting his affairs in order, he provides a copy of *Biathanatos* and instructs his friend, "Reserve it for me if I live, and if I die I only forbid it the press and the fire."[64] Donne also admits to Goodyer his hesitancy to enter the realm of his adversaries, the Jesuits, whom he had satirized vehemently, especially in his prose works *Pseudo-Martyr* and *Ignatius His Conclave*.[65] Finally, Donne's own personal concerns were further colored at this time by the death of Queen Anne and the subsequent illness that nearly took the life of the King.

In spite of the tribulations affecting Donne during the spring of 1619, the hymn and the sermon he wrote at his last going into Germany are not morose, self-indulgent expressions in which he longs for death. There is a difference, after all, between feelings, however strong they may be, that death is near, and a desire to die, which is the sin of despair. The hymn, especially when read in conjunction with the Valediction Sermon, does not reveal the mind of a man who is seeking to escape from the difficulties of his life, but rather one who seems more concerned that his imminent trip to Germany will provide, as he expresses to Goodyer, "no service to my Lord."

The political occasion for Donne's trip to Germany accounts in part for the

---

[62] *Letters to Severall Persons of Honour, 1651*, pp. 174–75.

[63] Ibid., p. 25.

[64] Ibid., p. 22.

[65] Paul Sellin (*So Doth, So is Religion*) explains that because "more copies of the supposedly rare Continental *Conclave Ignati* have survived abroad than scholarship has generally realized" (p. 23), "one imagines that in Reformed courts such as the duke of Bouillon's at Amiens, the elector's at Heidelberg, or the States General's in The Hague, Donne had some name as a polemicist against the Jesuits when he arrived" (p. 22).

popularity among Donne's contemporaries not only for the hymn, but also for the Valediction Sermon.[66] However, the greater interest in the two works undoubtedly results from Donne's use of himself as an emblem of one who has been blessed with the mercies of God in the midst of his adversity. Within the public example of Donne's journey, it is impossible to overstate the importance of accounting for the audience of this sermon. Among the Benchers of Lincoln's Inn hearing this homily were those who knew Donne as a youth and who were also among Donne's closest friends, including Christopher Brooke. As a result, Donne sounds a personal and humble note in addressing his congregation, particularly in the conclusion of the sermon:

> Remember me, not my abilities, for when I consider my Apostleship to you, that I was sent to you, I am in St. Paules quorum, *quorum ego minimus*, I am the least of them that have been sent to you, and when I consider my infirmities (I know I might justly lay a heavier name upon them) I know I am in his other quorum, *quorum ego maximus*, sent to save sinners, of whom I am the cheifest. (2:388)

When Donne revised this passage for a later edition of the sermon,[67] he not only omitted the parenthetical statement, "I know I might justly lay a heavier name upon them [his infirmities]," but also, as the editors of Donne's *Sermons* remark, "toned the passage down into a more general acknowledgment of human infirmity" (2:34). One further example of this type occurs in the final sentence of the sermon, the earlier version of which states:

> To end, it is the Kingdome where we shall end, and yet begin but then, where we shall have continuall rest, and yet never grow lazy, where we shall have more strength and noe Enemyes, where we shall live and never die, where we shall meet and never part, but here we must. (2:390)

The later rendition omits the final four words ("but here we must") and, typifying the effect of the alterations existing throughout the later version, thereby removes the poignancy of Donne's personal farewell to his congrega-

---

[66] David Novarr (*The Disinterred Muse*) notes that "the widespread availability of the hymn in manuscript is an indication that Donne was not averse to its being known" (p. 130), and Simpson and Potter, in their introduction to the Valediction Sermon, state that its popularity "is evident from the fact that more manuscript copies of it have been preserved than of any other sermon" (2:33). In this context, Annabel Patterson questions if the popularity of this sermon, as well as the differences in the manuscript copies from the Folio edition, suggests that it was controversial, a question which she contends, "did not occur to Potter and Simpson, who printed the presumed original version for comparison's sake, but drew the innocuous conclusion that the revisions were *literary* in nature, performed by Donne himself and designed to prune and tighten the prose" ("Afterword," p. 226).

[67] The significant differences are revealed in the two versions Simpson and Potter print of this sermon; the later of the two appears as number 11 in Volume 2, and the earlier, which I quote from exclusively, is printed in the same volume as Appendix B.

tion, as he enjoins them to remember him, as he will remember them, within the fellowship of those who constitute the body of Christ.

The sermon itself explicates Ecclesiastes 12:1, "Remember now thy Creator in the daies of thy youth." While the sermon is, in fact, an exercise in remembering the mercies of God, the topic of the sermon is the virtue of repentance, which Donne likens to gold that is discovered, as he writes, "for the most part in the washes, . . . in the waters of Tribulation" (2:373). Following the introduction, which emphasizes that "the nearest way to bring man to God [is] by awaking his memory" (2:374), Donne divides the sermon into three parts. The first centers upon Donne's contention that the memory is a superior faculty to both the understanding and the will in bringing one to God. Altering St. Bernard's analogy that the memory is the stomach of the soul, Donne imagines the memory as the gallery of the soul, which is "hung with soe many, and so lively pictures of the goodnes and mercies of thy God to thee, as that every one of them may be a sufficient Catechisme to instruct thee in all thy particular dutyes to God for those mercies" (2:376). The second part, which begins with a discussion of the Offering of First Fruits, reinforces the urgency of remembering now, at this moment. An extended section of this second part is devoted to a recapitulation of the six days of Creation, which Donne, of course, reads typologically. In remembering the separate days of the Creation, Donne sees in the particulars of each, according to Gale Carrithers, "a typological allegory of 'our regeneration'"[68] through Christ and within the Church. The final division insists that the Creator is the object of the exercise of memory:

> Remember the Creator then, because thou canst remember nothing beyond him, and remember him soe too, that thou maist sticke upon nothing on this side of him, that soe neither height nor depth, nor any other creature may separate thee from God. (2:387)

It is by remembering the Creator and His faithfulness, Donne argues, that those who believe in Him receive comfort during the afflictions of this life.

In the conclusion of this sermon, Donne alters the Great Commandment, "Thou shalt love the Lord thy God with all thy heart, and with all thy soul, and with all thy mind [and] Thou shalt love thy neighbor as thyself" (Mt. 22:37, 39), when he implores his congregation, "as we remember God, soe for his sake and in him, let us remember one another" (2:388). As the personal interactions outlined within this injunction imply, Donne draws our attention in the conclusion to the circular structure both of this bit of instruction and of the sermon as a whole when he writes in the opening phrase of the final paragraph, "To shut up this Circle and to returne to the beginning . . ." (2:388). Further, the conclusion itself is punctuated with circular, and even

---

[68] Carrithers, *Donne at Sermons*, p. 139.

spherical, conceits that are scribed upon the memory, in a manner similar to a memory theatre.[69] Donne urges the Benchers of Lincoln's Inn to remember him in prayer, to remember him "in the eares of that God to whom the farthest East and the farthest West are but as the right and left eare in one of us" (2:388). A few lines later, Donne states that after he has departed from them, their eyes "shall meet every morning in looking upon the same sun, and meet every night in looking upon the same Moone" (2:389). Similarly, their hearts "may meet every morning and evening in that God who sees and heares alike in all distances," until finally, Donne assures them, "within the gates of heaven, I may meete you all, and there saie to my Saviour and your Saviour, that which he said to his Father and our Father, Of those whom thou gavest me have I not lost one" (2:389). As he bids farewell, Donne comforts his congregation, stating, "though we must saile through a Sea, yet it is the Sea of [Christ's] blood" (2:389), an image that repeats itself in the opening lines of the hymn. The conclusion to the Valediction Sermon culminates in an encircling act of remembrance that becomes, as Carrithers states, "a sacramental activity of self-creation in a context of charity and humility."[70]

Donne's "A Hymne to Christ," a complementary exercise in remembering God's mercies, echoes the same circular structure, in which Donne presents himself in a posture of humble repentance as he reads his trip to Germany typologically. In the opening stanza Donne reveals his anxieties about his ailing physical health as he embarks on this journey in a "torne ship," upon a sea that may "swallow" him, and beneath "clouds of anger" (ll. 1, 3, 5). In the midst of these adversities, however, Donne perceives not death and despair, but Christ. As in the Valediction Sermon, Donne finds gold in the washes; in the tribulations he associates with his impending journey, he finds the way to Christ through penitent obedience. The interface here between sermon and hymn plays upon the parallel that Renaissance alchemists frequently drew between the philosopher's stone and Christ, by whom the base matter of adversity is transformed into the precious metal of redemption.[71] In other words, the mercy and salvation offered by Christ are discovered through participating in his sufferings (cf. Phil. 3:8–11), an idea which Donne imagines in the hymn by aligning himself typologically with Noah and Moses.

The opening stanza resonates with biblical allusions. The ship and the sea, emblems for Donne of "thy Arke" and "thy blood" (ll. 2, 4), call to mind, of course, the story of Noah. Although Noah inhabited the ark, the salvation offered through it belong to God, for it was His idea and His design, and He was the one who also sealed the door (cf. Gen. 6–7). Furthermore, this event is understood in the New Testament as a type of baptism; through the ark

---

[69] See Francis Yates, *The Art of Memory*.

[70] Carrithers, *Donne at Sermons*, p. 143.

[71] See Allison Coudert, *Alchemy*, pp. 89–90, 96, and 104–06. I am indebted to Kate Frost for this citation.

that God provided, the eight members of Noah's family "were saved through water" (I Peter 3:20–21). Following the references to the Flood, the final three lines of the first stanza allude to two events recorded in Exodus. When Donne writes of the "clouds of anger" (l. 5) that disguise God's face and mask His eyes, it calls to mind Exodus 19 when God descended upon Mt. Sinai in a thick cloud, and the thunder and lightning emanating from the cloud frightened the people of Israel who were gathered at the base. However, it was during this time that Moses ascended the mountain, entered the cloud, and received from God the Ten Commandments. Later in Exodus Moses asks to see the glory of God, and Jehovah responds by saying that He will place Moses in the cleft of a rock and cover the prophet as He passes by so that Moses will be able to see God's back, but not His face (Exodus 33). This turning away by God is not, as alluded to in line 7 of Donne's hymn, an act of disdain, but instead one of revelation. The paradox here is similar to the one expressed in Henry Vaughan's "The Night," which praises "Wise *Nicodemus*," who "saw such light/ As made him know his God by night" (ll. 5–6).[72]

The next eighteen lines of the hymn portray Donne in a posture of humility as he turns, and thereby returns, to God in an act of repentance. In his poetic address to Christ, Donne determines to "sacrifice this Iland unto thee,/ And all whom I lov'd there, and who lov'd mee" (ll. 8–9); to "seeke the root below/ In winter, . . ./ Where none but thee, th'Eternall root of true Love I may know" (ll. 12–14); and, finally, to procure his "Divorce to All" (l. 22), especially the "false mistresses" of his youth, "Fame, Wit, Hopes" (l. 25). In response to these lines, Sanders eloquently states, "one may think one knows what is happening here, and that it is something of the kind usually understood by the word 'renunciation'"; what occurs, however, is "something more remarkable."[73] Renouncing the world and the things of the world are effects of repentance, but they are not the goals. Donne responds to Christ throughout this hymn by saying that he is jealous for the one who was first jealous for him. Donne is not so much giving up the world as he is giving in, and thereby giving himself over, to Christ. By allowing his Savior to defeat him, Donne, more than renouncing "the world," fills with Christ alone the void where "the world" once was.

In the final three lines, "A Hymne to Christ," like the sermon it complements, achieves a circular progress; it not only recalls its own beginning, but also moves the reader beyond a mere repetition of the opening allusions. Donne begins the final sentence of the poem by asserting, "Churches are best for Prayer, that have least light" (l. 26), a statement insisting upon the appropriateness of darkness, within the Church and for the purpose of prayer, for one to pursue relationship with God. The remaining

---

[72] *The Works of Henry Vaughan*, ed. L. C. Martin, p. 522.
[73] Sanders, *John Donne's Poetry*, p. 157.

two lines of the hymn must be read in terms of this claim, as well as in terms of the parallelism found in lines 26 and 27. By explaining that "to see God only" and "to scape stormy dayes" he goes "out of sight" and chooses "an Everlasting night," Donne returns the reader to the opening stanza. As the people of Israel cowered beneath the thunder, lightning, and smoke they perceived at the summit of Mt. Sinai, Moses, responding to God's command for him to ascend the mountain, "drew near unto the thick darkness where God was" (Exodus 20:21), and in a similar act of humble obedience, Noah and his family entered the ark and were saved during the Flood.

These final lines of "A Hymne to Christ" have caused difficulty primarily because critics have been misled by Donne's use of the word "Everlasting" and have believed, as a result, that he longs for his physical death. On the contrary, it is a sacramental death, through which he affirms his clerical vocation and finds life within the body of Christ, that Donne chooses here. His last going into Germany is a journey leading from the world and to God through the doctrinally orthodox path of Christ's sufferings, which poetically dramatizes a moment of calling analogous to Moses ascending to the darkness of Mt. Sinai where God was and to Noah descending into the bowels of the ark to escape the stormy days.[74] As a result, the very structure of the poem reinforces Donne's realization of the pervasiveness of Christ, whom Donne imagines in his life as both center and circumference, an image reflecting the alchemical symbol for gold.[75] Within the circle formed by the allusions that reveal Christ as antitype to Noah and Moses, the center of the poem is punctuated by Donne's expressed desire to know God's Son, whom he describes as "th'Eternall root of true Love" (l. 14). By prayerfully entering the Church in obedience to God's call, Donne (like Moses and Noah) (re)turns humbly to the one whose promises comfort him in the darkness of his "infirm and valetudinary body" as he enters "the mouth of such adversaries as I cannot blame for hating me, the Jesuits."[76]

---

[74] Donne may also be alluding here to Isaiah 60:19, which states, "The sun shall be no more the light by day; neither for brightness shall moon give light unto thee: but the Lord shall be unto thee an everlasting light, and thy god thy glory," and which is in contrast to verse two of this chapter: "For, behold, the darkness shall cover the earth, and gross darkness the people: but the Lord shall arise upon thee, and his glory shall be seen upon thee."

[75] See Michael Hall, "Circles and Circumvention in Donne's Sermons," who notes that "Donne was fond of recalling the Hermetic definition of God as a circle or sphere" and that "the creation is contained in that sphere and forms part of the perfect whole, though only the divinity himself is wholly perfect" (p. 202).

[76] See also John Shawcross' reading of this poem (*Intentionality and the New Traditionalism*), in which he notes that "the poem has been misclassified, mistitled; it is more correctly a prayer" and that "what the poem is about is the regeneration of spirit or self by the death of former spirit or former self, and the septenary (seven-foot line) that caps each of the four stanzas specifically points to mystic creation – the meaning of the number seven in numerology" (p. 71).

On 19 December 1619, Donne and the other members of the embassy led by Doncaster were in residence at The Hague where they awaited the end of their journey and their long-anticipated return to England. That day Donne preached on Matthew 4:18–20, which recounts the calling of Peter and his brother Andrew away from their fishing nets to become fishers of men. In response to the demands of his text, Donne fittingly emphasizes the obedience and humility necessary to fulfill one's calling and, thereby, to respond to Christ's command, "follow me." It is within this context that Donne answers the question he himself raises in the homily concerning how this humble obedience might be accomplished: ". . . you must goe *Iobs* way to Christs end. *Iob* hath beaten a path for us, to shew us all the way; A path that affliction walked in, and seemed to delight in" (2:299). Job's way is the path of tribulation, but Donne carefully explains that the afflictions of the godly are crosses to them; they are not the afflictions of the wicked that only "exasperate," "enrage," "stone and pave," and "obdurate and petrifie," but "doe not crucifie them" (2:300). The adversity that carries us to salvation, Donne insists, resides in the God-given corrections, that when willingly submitted to, conform one to Christ:

> so when my crosses have carried mee up to my Saviours Crosse, I put my hands into his hands, and hang upon his nailes, I put mine eyes upon his, and wash off all my former unchast looks, and receive a soveraigne tincture, and a lively verdure, and a new life into my dead teares, from his teares. I put my mouth upon his mouth, and it is I that say, *My God, my God, why hast thou forsaken me*? and it is I that recover againe, and say, *Into thy hands, O Lord, I commend my spirit*. Thus my afflictions are truly a crosse, when those afflictions doe truely crucifie me, and souple me, and mellow me, and knead me, and roll me out, to a conformity with Christ. (2:300)

This is the gold Donne finds in the washes. This is the gospel of repentance that he is called to preach and that he enacts typologically in the watery second baptism of the hymn marking his last going into Germany.

VOX TURTURIS

In the decidedly public genre of his "A Hymne to Christ," Donne sings the love of God in the midst of adversity and fear; it is a lyric in which Donne, placing himself poetically in the way and the calling of repentance, discovers divine song, such as when he explains in an early Lincoln's Inn sermon:

> in every *tentation*, and every *tribulation*, there is a *Catechisme*, and *Instruction*; nay, there is a *Canticle*, a *love-song*, an *Epithalamion*, a *mariage song* of God, to our souls, wrapped up, if wee would open it, and read it, and learn that new tune, that musique of God. (2:68)

Repentance is for Donne a conjoining of the human and the divine in a song of reconciliation, and in order to hear God properly, it is necessary to position oneself, as Donne does in his "A Hymne to Christ," in the Church.[77] Donne specifies in his Whitehall sermon of 4 March 1624 that "The Scriptures are Gods Voyce; The Church is his Eccho; a redoubling, a repeating of some particular syllables, and accents of the same voice" (6:223). Furthermore, Donne explains in his 1625 Easter sermon that "when God expresses his gathering of his Church, in this world, it is *Sibilabo & congregabo*, . . . He whispers in the voyce of the Spirit, and he speaks a little louder, in the voice of a man" (6:276).[78]

Donne understands his own sense of calling in the light of his responsibility of echoing God's voice in the Church. Specifically, Donne declares God's own desire that "his Minister shall be *Tuba*" (2:166), a trumpet, and as he contends in another of his sermons, "*The trumpet of God* is the loudest voice that we conceive God to speake in" (4:70). Donne's echoing voice is to become for his auditors "*musicum carmen*, a love-song in proposing the love of God to man," for he adds, "our musick is onely that salvation which is declared in the Gospel to all them, and to them onely, who take God by the right hand, as he delivers himself in Christ" (2:170). Donne warns, however, that there must be "musick in their preaching," as well as "musick in their example, in a holy conversation" (2:167). In other words, it is not enough simply for the minister to preach and the congregation to hear; they must also do and practice the gospel of repentance. In addition, it is not only in preaching that one should hear the echo of God's voice, for Donne reminds his auditors yet again that God's trumpet sounds its loudest call in "his publique Ordinance in the Church; Prayer, Preaching, and Sacraments; Heare him in these; In all these; come not to heare him in the Sermon alone, but come to him in Prayer, and in the Sacrament too" (4:71).

What Donne seeks, as a priest administering this liturgical call to repentance, is to evoke a response of penitent confession, for "*Silence* was a not Confessing, a not Repenting" (9:289). However, the unbridled wailings of sorrow for one's sins are unacceptable as well since, at the other end of the spectrum from silence, "*Roaring*, is not a voyce of Repentance" (9:288–89). The voice of repentance that for Donne is properly sounded is "*gemitus* not *rugitus*, a groaninge not a roaringe, the voice of the Turtle not of a Lyon" (2:154). In prayer and preaching and sacraments, Christ offers

---

[77] For a discussion of "the tuning metaphor" in Donne, see Frances Malpezzi ("Christian Poetics in Donne's 'Upon the Translation of the Psalmes'"), who states that "the end of both the preacher and the poet is the end of every Christian vocation, the edification of the body of Christ in love" (p. 223).

[78] Elsewhere Donne makes this same allusion to Zechariah 10:8, stating, "the Holy Ghost whispers to thy soule, as thou standest in the Congregation, in that voyce that he promises, *Sibilabo populum meum*, I will hisse, I will whisper to my people by soft and inward inspirations" (6:314).

himself to the Church, and in response the members of Christ's body are to voice their penitent confession and to rebaptize their souls in tears of contrition as an act that marks their peace and reconciliation with God (cf. 1:245). In his 1628 sermon on the occasion of the fast Charles I ordered, Donne expresses the full range of what he means by this voice of the turtle as not simply a sound of repentance but finally an act of repentance that defines one's life:

> To sigh, and turne backward, to repent, and relapse, is a wofull Condition: But to sigh, and turne forward, to turne upon God, and to pursue this sorrow for our sins, then, in such sighes, *The Spirit of man returnes to God that gave it*; As God breathed into man, so man breathes unto the nostrils of God *a savour of rest*, as it is said of *Noah*, an acceptable sacrifice, when he sighes for his sins. This sighing, this groaning, expressed in this word, *Anach, Gemitus*, is *Vox Turturis. Turtur gemit*; It is that voyce, that sound which the Turtle gives; And we learne by Authors of Naturall Story, and by experience, *Turturis gemitus indicium veris*, The voyce of the Turtle is an evidence of the Spring; When a sinner comes to this voyce, to this sighing, there is a Spring of grace begun in him; Then *Vox Turturis audita in terra nostra*, sayes Christ to his Spouse, *The voyce of the Turtle is heard in our Land*; And so he sayes to thy soule, This voyce of the Turtle, these sighs of thy penitent soul, are heard *in terra nostra*, in our Land, in the Kingdome of heaven. (8:197)

*

The voice of the turtledove, alluding as it does to Canticles 2:12, typifies Donne's understanding of the doctrine of repentance and his preaching of the gospel of repentance. Rather than with fire and brimstone, Donne searches the scriptures to echo God's voice with song, for "when God had given all the Law, he provided, as himself says, a safer way, which was to give them a heavenly Song of his owne making: for that Song, he sayes there, he was sure they would remember" (2:171). Donne offers this passage in the immediate context of the song of Christ's coming prophesied in Habakkuk 3 and the song of God's union with the Church in the Canticles. As a result, the doctrine of repentance reveals itself for Donne not just as a song, but specifically as the love song celebrating the reconciliation and communion of God and the Church.

Repentance is for Donne the necessary response to the severed relationship between God and humankind because of original and habitual sin. Repentance is, therefore, best accomplished, as both a voice and an action, in the communal prayer, preaching, and sacraments administered in the Church, and accompanied with genuine tears of contrition that seal the promises of God's forgiveness in this second baptism. It is little wonder then that Donne hedges throughout the *Sermons* toward a sacramental expression of repentance. Understood in this way, Donne's anxiety over his own calling seems to be less about a struggle over secular versus religious preferments than it is about living the gospel of repentance. The work of life, "the grace of lips" as it were, is turning to God, not in one moment alone, but in a continual, liturgical turning and returning that conforms one to Christ from within the community of the visible Church.

Chapter Five

O TASTE & SEE

DONNE AT HEIDELBERG

THE historical circumstances and the debate over the extant copy of the sermon Donne preached at the castle chapel at Heidelberg during his last going into Germany present a number of critical oddities. To begin with, the headnote for the printed sermon reads, "*Two Sermons, to the Prince and Princess Palatine, the Lady Elizabeth at Heydelberg, when I was commanded by the King to wait upon my L. of Doncaster in his Embassage to Germany,*" and the order and date of this single sermon are indicated as "*First Sermon as we went out, June 16. 1619*" (2:250). Although two sermons are specified in the headnote, no second sermon appears in any printed or manuscript source. Furthermore, Simpson and Potter note in their introduction to this text attributed to Donne's preaching at Heidelberg that "no reference to this particular occasion or to the Prince and Princess appears in the sermon itself" (2:36). In addition, these two editors draw attention to Donne's own comment in the opening paragraph that his biblical text (Romans 13:11) is one appropriated by the Church "for the celebration of the *Advent,* before the Feast of the Birth of our Saviour" (2:250),[1] to which they then add that taken together "these considerations lead a reader to wonder whether the heading may be wrongly placed before the particular sermon" (2:37). Nevertheless, Simpson and Potter accept the headnote and sermon as printed, "though with some misgivings," since as they state, "the burden of proof rests on any editor who believes the heading to be wrongly placed" and since "the present editors have no such proof and have no suggestion as to any other more probable date or occasion" (2:37).

R. C. Bald, however, thinks differently. In spite of what the headnote indicates, he believes that "the sermon does not seem to have survived" and laments it no longer being extant since, as he states, "Donne can hardly have been able to refer to the books he usually had in his study, so that the sermon probably had less patristic learning than those he preached in England."[2] Bald

---

[1] The Prayer Book in fact specifies Romans 13 as the Epistle reading for the First Sunday of Advent.

[2] Bald, *John Donne: A Life,* pp. 351, 352.

bases his conclusions that the extant copy is not the sermon Donne preached at Heidelberg on the internal evidence of lines 535–53 (2:265), which he argues,

> contain a direct confutation of Calvinistic doctrine, and it is incredible that Donne as an official member of an embassy would have been so tactless as to assail in this manner beliefs to which the Palatinate was still strongly sympathetic. It is therefore almost certain that the label or title-leaf of the two sermons preached at Heidelberg became detached and in the printed edition was prefixed to the wrong sermon.[3]

Paul Sellin, however, finds Bald's conclusions "equally incredible" and sees in them an illustration of "the loose way in which Donne scholars have drawn far-reaching conclusions regarding the Reformed churches and doctrine."[4] Citing passages from the Heidelberg Catechism (1563), the canons from the Synod of Dort (April 1619), and Calvin's *Institutes*, Sellin contends that in the passage highlighted by Bald, "Donne's remarks do little more than aptly, indeed ingeniously, describe something very like the traditional Reformed position on the assurance of salvation that the Holy Spirit imparts to believers."[5] In addition, Sellin quotes and refers to a variety of passages from the sermon and concludes that Donne's statements on the assurance of salvation in it are "at no variance whatever with Calvin himself or with the position expressed in the classical symbola of the Reformed churches."[6]

The sermon itself, preached within two months of the conclusion to the Synod of Dort, follows the lead of its biblical text ("For now is our salvation nearer then when we believed") to address the nature and means of salvation, and as such it is primarily a homily on grace. In particular, Donne declares to his royal auditors that "the knowledge which is to salvation, is by being in Gods house, in the Household of the Faithfull, in the Communion of Saints, and by having such a conversation in heaven in this life," which is conveyed "in an ordinary preaching of the Word, and an ordinary administration of the Sacraments" (2:253, 254). Later in the sermon, Donne explains further the communal implications for the conveyance of grace noting that its manifestation "is not only, (though especially) in the sacraments, but in other sacramental and ceremonial things, which God (as he speaks by his Church) hath ordained, as the cross in baptism, and adoration at the sacrament (I do not say, I am far from saying, adoration of the sacrament)" (2:258). Donne goes on to enumerate his ideas concerning prevenient and subsequent grace (cf. 2:261–62), as well as to unfold a rather ecclesiastical discussion of the manner in which faith and works produce an assurance of

---

[3] Bald, *John Donne: A Life*, p. 352 n1.
[4] Sellin, *John Donne and "Calvinist" Views of Grace*, p. 6.
[5] Ibid., p. 7.
[6] Ibid., p. 7.

salvation (cf. 2:264–66). It is difficult, especially without any genuinely convincing evidence to the contrary, not to read this sermon in the context specified in the headnote and in the wake of the Synod of Dort. Although there was extensive debate in England and abroad before, during and after the synod over the doctrine of predestination,[7] the theological issue at stake throughout this period was that of the Atonement and the distinctions being made regarding sacramental grace.[8] Therefore, the very subject matter of the Heidelberg sermon places it squarely in the environment of the theological debates occurring during 1619.

Sellin's reading of Donne's sermon at Heidelberg, along with that of the sermon Donne preached at The Hague on 19 December 1619,[9] leads him to conclude that "there are few grounds for believing that he [Donne] in substance differed with the official positions of his church in 1619, or extended them grudging acceptance only because it was his sovereign's will."[10] At this time, however, the theological positions of the Church of England, especially with regard to the doctrine of grace, had not been established in any definitive manner, and to a certain extent, then, Sellin's assessment of Donne's "Calvinist" views does not fully account for the religious and political complexities from which the canons of Dort were produced.

Peter White argues that "orthodox Calvinism in 1619 was dynamic and

---

[7] For overviews of these discussions at Oxford and Cambridge from 1590–1640, at the Hampton Court Conference, at Dort, and in tracts and sermons during the reigns of James I and Charles I, see Stewart Dippel, *A Study of Religious Thought at Oxford and Cambridge, 1590–1640*; V. C. Miller, *The Lambeth Articles*; Nicholas Tyacke, *Anti-Calvinists*; Dewey Wallace, *Puritans and Predestination*, pp. 29–104; and Peter White, *Predestination, Policy and Polemic*.

[8] For example, in his discussion of Richard Hooker, Peter White (*Predestination, Policy and Polemic*) notes that the doctrine of predestination was "far from being central to the *Ecclesiastical Polity*, which was above all a defence of the means of grace, of the necessity and efficacity of prayer and of the sacraments, and therefore of the theology implicit in the Book of Common Prayer" (p. 138). White adds later in this same study that "there is no evidence from what took place at Hampton Court to support the contention that either for James I or his bishops the doctrine of predestination was at all central to the Christian faith" and that "on the contrary, both the discussions of the first day and the subsequent reforms show how incomparably more important were issues to do with the doctrine and practice of baptism, and therefore of sacramental grace" (p. 152). Finally, White contends, first, that as the Synod of Dort drew near it was incumbent to distinguish "between fundamental doctrines necessary to salvation, and those matters of less importance about which conscientious differences of opinion were tolerable" and that James clearly "regarded the doctrine of predestination among the latter" (pp. 178–79), and second, that during the synod "at perhaps no point were the tensions within international Calvinism more acute than on the extent of the Atonement" (p. 187). See also, Peter Lake, "Calvinism and the English Church, 1570–1635," pp. 47–51.

[9] In 1630 Donne revised the notes of this sermon preached at The Hague, and when he did so, he divided his homily into two sermons, which appear in Volume 2 of the Simpson and Potter edition, numbers 13 and 14.

[10] Sellin, *John Donne and "Calvinist" Views of Grace*, p. 33.

variegated, encompassing a significant theological diversity," that "the decrees of Dort, while condemning the Remonstrants, took pains to obscure that diversity," and that "the decrees of the synod cannot, therefore, be assumed accurately to reflect the theology even of any particular Dutch delegation, still less that of any of the foreign contingents."[11] Citing at length from the *Collegiate Suffrage* that the British delegation presented to the synod on 9 March 1619,[12] White insists that the British delegates saw themselves as representatives of James, rather than as defenders of "Calvinist" orthodoxy, and as a result, believing that "the synod could be the foundation of renewed Protestant unity," they were "dismayed when they found themselves as it ended accessories in re-emphasized division."[13] The British contingent, White reveals, were surprised and appalled by a whole range of items that found their way into the final version of the documents produced from the synod, including the personal censure of the Remonstrants, which the British delegates refused to sign.[14] Although the British delegates did sign the canons, these were never officially ratified for England,[15] and furthermore, there are contrasting judgments, both then and now, as to what the canons represented for the Church of England. On the one hand, White describes, "some were convinced that they [the British delegates] had subscribed themselves, and committed their church, to extreme Calvinism," while on the other hand, "the extreme Calvinists themselves did not think so; on the contrary, they were liable to accuse them of being 'more than half Remonstrant.'"[16]

The complexities surrounding Donne's Heidelberg sermon and the implications of the proceedings at Dort exemplify the difficulties inherent in examining the doctrine of grace, both for the purpose of understanding Church of England theology during the period and in order to determine Donne's own views, specifically his articulation of the complementary interplay of prevenient and subsequent grace, the justification that comes through both faith and works, and the effectual means of grace provided together through the Word and Sacraments. While Paul Sellin and, more recently, Daniel Doerksen have made important contributions by establishing that

---

[11] White, *Predestination, Policy and Polemic*, p. 184.

[12] The British delegates included: George Carleton, Bishop of Llandaff; John Davenant, soon to be Bishop of Salisbury; Samuel Ward, Master of Sidney Sussex College, Cambridge; Walter Balcanqual, a Scotsman; and Joseph Hall, soon to be Bishop of Exeter, who after falling ill and returning to England was replaced by Thomas Goad, one of Archbishop Abbot's chaplains.

[13] Ibid., p. 180. See also, Lake, "Calvinism and the English Church, 1570–1635," pp. 51–60.

[14] White (*Predestination, Policy and Polemic*) notes that the British delegates were "certainly free of covert sympathy for the Remonstrants" (p. 180), and Tyacke (*Anti-Calvinists*) elaborates that "none of the British delegates at Dort, despite their doctrinal differences, can meaningfully be described as Arminian," and that in their anti-Arminian stand, "they had the backing both of the supreme governor, King James, and of Archbishop Abbot" (p. 100).

[15] See Tyacke, *Anti-Calvinists*, pp. 104–05.

[16] White, *Predestination, Policy and Polemic*, p. 201.

Donne was in no way hostile to the orthodox Calvinism that flavored the Church of England at this time,[17] it is one thing to assert that Donne was no enemy to Calvinism and quite another to claim that his theology is fundamentally Calvinist, especially when this determination is made, as is too often the case, by applying such secondary doctrines as those of election and predestination.[18] With respect to the doctrine of grace, the differences between Donne and Calvin are, on the one hand, never propounded by Donne with any vehemence. After all, Donne's is a theology of communal participation in the visible Church, and as such he is far more interested in discovering the broad path of unity through moderate conformity than he is with locating those straits of theological nit-picking that eventually tore apart the Church and State. On the other hand, those differences are, nevertheless, present in the *Sermons* and reveal themselves as a consequence of Donne's Trinitarian theology, centered as it is on the interrelational unity of the godhead that seeks to enfold humankind in its divine harmony. As a result, Donne's understanding of grace is that it requires a degree of human efforts in order to complete the relationship initiated by God, for with Donne grace culminates the reconciliation and assimilation of the human and divine, which he so often articulates by alluding to Psalm 34:8, "O taste and see that the Lord is good."

PREVENIENT AND SUBSEQUENT

In his understanding of the doctrine of grace, Donne insists on the necessity of prevenient grace operating in concert with subsequent grace,[19] and it is the complementary workings of both that he clarifies in the Heidelberg sermon and, to a lesser extent, in the sermon he preached at The Hague. To the Prince and Princess Palatine, Donne explains that "Grace does not grow out of nature," that "nature, and naturall reason do not produce grace," yet he adds that "grace can take root in no other thing but in the nature and reason of man" (2:261). Therefore, God's initial, prevenient grace "works upon our natural faculties, and grows there," while God's subsequent graces "grow out of his first grace, formerly given to us, and well employed by us" (2:261). In

---

[17] Paul Sellin, *John Donne and "Calvinist" Views of Grace*, and Daniel Doerksen, *Conforming to the Word* and "'Saint Pauls Puritan': John Donne's 'Puritan' Imagination in the *Sermons*."

[18] These doctrines are not even central ones for Calvin; neither one receives any detailed discussion until Book III of the *Institutes*. As I discuss in chapter 1 of this study, Calvin's theological first principle is the sovereignty of God and, as a necessary consequence, the depravity of humankind.

[19] This understanding of prevenient and subsequent grace is reflected in the Prayer Book collect for Easter Day: "Almighty God, which through thy only begotten Son Jesus Christ, hast overcome death, and opened unto us the gate of everlasting life: We humbly beseech thee, that as by thy special grace preventing us, thou dost put in our minds good desires, so by thy continual help, we may bring the same to good effect; through Jesus Christ our Lord, who liveth and reigneth, etc." (Booty, ed., pp. 152–53).

the next paragraph, Donne explains that neither a body alone, nor a soul alone constitutes a person, but as he asserts, "the union of these two makes up the man" (2:261), leading him to conclude:

> so in a regenerate man, a Christian man, his being born of Christian Parents, that gives him a body, that makes him of the body of the Covenant, it gives him a title, an interest in the Covenant, which is *jus ad rem*; thereby he may make his claim to the seal of the Covenant, to baptism, and it cannot be denied him: and then in his baptism, that Sacrament gives him a soul, a spiritual seal, *jus in re*, an actual possession of Grace; but yet, as there are spirits in us, which unite body and soul, so there must be subsequent acts, and works of the blessed spirit, that must unite and confirm all, and make up this spiritual man in the wayes of sanctification; for without that his body, that is, his being born within the Covenant, and his soul, that is, his having received Grace in baptism, do not make him up. (2:262)

In this passage, Donne employs the language of covenant theology for his Heidelberg auditors and includes the body/soul analogy in order to emphasize not only that grace is inherently prevenient as well as subsequent, but also that baptism in the visible Church provides the sacramental efficacy of "an actual possession of Grace."

Along similar lines, Donne asserts in his sermon at The Hague that "no man can renew himselfe, regenerate himselfe," and then explains that

> The desire and the actuall beginning is from the preventing grace of God, and the constant proceeding is from the concomitant, and subsequent, and continuall succeeding grace of God; for there is no conclusive, no consummative grace in this life; no such measure of grace given to any man, as that that man needs no more, or can lose or frustrate none of that. (2:305)

Donne is extremely careful in his discussions of grace to specify, as he does here, that the initiative for and the initial bestowing of grace belong to God alone, yet in urging his auditors to attend to the "continuall succeeding grace of God," Donne also expresses his contention that the grace of God can be resisted. In one of his sermons at Lincoln's Inn, another decidedly Calvinist congregation, Donne repeats this same idea: "first Gods preventinge grace prepares, enables us, and then he bends downe with a farther supply of concurringe grace, but that is to heere us. For yf we doe nothinge then, yf we speake not then, he departs from us" (2:157).

Before exploring the full implications of Donne's views regarding prevenient and subsequent grace, it is first necessary to discuss this issue of the irresistibility of God's grace, which is, of course, related to the doctrines of election and predestination and which was one of the hotly debated subjects at the Synod of Dort. Peter White, for example, reveals that in their explanation of prevenient grace in the *Collegiate Suffrage*, the British delegates stated that "far from being irresistible, the inward effects prior to conversion were often 'stifled and utterly extinguished by the fault of our rebellious will,'" and that "even in the 'very elect,' it could happen that they were resisted, and the grace of God thereby 'repelled' and 'choked,'" though they add that "'God doth urge them again and again, nor doth he cease to stir them forward, till he have thoroughly subdued them to his grace, and set them in a state of regenerate sons.'"[20] In debating this issue, it bears repeating that the British delegates were themselves upholders of Calvinism and that the synod sought to clarify the doctrines of orthodox Calvinism.

Donne's own statements in the *Sermons* show him to be in accord with the British delegates on this issue.[21] In the Lenten sermon he preached at Whitehall on 20 February 1617, Donne relegates the issue of irresistibility to matters indifferent, which would undoubtedly have pleased King James, by questioning, "Whether this grace, which God presents so, be resistible or no, whether man be not perverse enough to resist this grace, why should any perverse or ungracious man dispute?" (1:255). Donne explains to his auditors that all of them have felt temptations so strongly that no one could have kept them from the temptation, and that all have felt the grace of God so powerfully that they have concurred "without any resistance, any slackness" (1:255). In the light of this experiential confirmation of grace, Donne concludes:

> New fashions in men, make us doubt new manners; and new terms in Divinity were ever suspicious in the Church of God, that new Doctrines were hid under them. *Resistibility*, and *Irresistibility* of grace, which is every Artificers wearing now, was a stuff that our Fathers wore not, a language that pure antiquity spake not. (1:255)[22]

The point for Donne, beyond an avoidance of wrangling over what both he and James see as inessential, is that if subsequent grace is a continual response requiring human efforts, then Donne must logically ascribe, as he does, to the belief that God's grace, both prevenient and subsequent, can be resisted.

Although humankind can thwart the gracious intentions of God, no one but God alone, Donne makes clear, initiates the reconciliation that begins in prevenient grace. Donne is fond of portraying prevenient grace in terms of

---

[20] White, *Predestination, Policy and Polemic*, p. 193.

[21] In an early article, Randolph Daniel ("Reconciliation, Covenant and Election") correctly states that "Donne did not like the term irresistable [sic] grace and avoided it just as he avoided the terms effectual calling and perseverance of the saints" (p. 27), even though he does so within an article that wrongly asserts that "the core of Donne's theology is his doctrine of reconciliation in which he united a covenant theology taken from several traditions of covenant theology with the classical Protestant doctrine of justification by faith alone" (p. 26). Chapter 1 of this study establishes that Donne himself believes the core of his theology to be the doctrine of the Trinity, and Daniel's view that Donne believed in "justification by faith alone" is challenged below in the section "The Root and Fruit."

[22] For similar statements in the *Sermons*, see also 5:90 and 10:63.

light, such as when he writes, "without the light of Grace we dwell in darkness, and in the shadow of death" (1:248), and in another sermon, "So till this first beame of grace, which we consider here, strike upon the soule of a sinner, he lies in the mud and slime, in the dregs and lees, and tartar of his sinne," for "Hee cannot so much as wish, that that Sunne would shine upon him, he doth not so much as know, that there is such a Sunne, that hath that influence, and impression" (9:299). Further, in his sermon preached on Easter Monday, 1622, Donne interprets the light God first spoke into existence at the creation as the infusion of his prevenient grace:

> First, *He made light*. There was none before; so first, *He shines in our hearts*, by his preventing Grace; there was no light before; not of Nature, by which any man could see any means of salvation; not of foreseen Merits, that God should light his light at our Candle, give us Grace therefore, because he saw that we would use that Grace well. He made light, he infus'd Grace. (4:115)

Consistently and unambiguously throughout the *Sermons* Donne articulates that prevenient grace is dependent on nothing in or from humankind.

Subsequent grace, however, requires human efforts. In the second of his Prebend sermons, preached on 29 January 1625, Donne explains from his scripture text (Psalm 63:7) the two ways in which God has been his help: "first, That God hath not left me to my selfe, He hath come to my succour, He hath helped me; And then, That God hath not left out my selfe; He hath been my Helpe, but he hath left some thing for me to doe with him, and by his helpe," for he adds, "Helpe always presumes an endevour and co-operation in him that is helped" (7:63). By way of clarification, Donne immediately affirms, and then is careful to restate in the next paragraph, that "God infuses his first grace, the first way, meerly as a Giver; intirely, all himselfe," and only then does he add, "but his subsequent graces, as a helper; therefore we call them Auxiliant graces, Helping graces; and we always receive them, when we endevour to make use of his former grace" (7:63).

It is precisely this inclusion of human efforts in the action of grace that distinguishes Donne's understanding of the doctrine from that of Calvin's, whose own doctrine of total depravity espouses that humankind can bring nothing of good to the process of reconciliation. In the *Institutes*, Calvin expresses his displeasure with the division of what he calls "operating" and "co-operating" grace (or prevenient and subsequent) and with those who think that "we co-operate with the assisting grace of God, because it is our right either to render it ineffectual by spurning the first grace, or to confirm it by obediently following it" (II.ii.6).[23] However, in Donne's Whitehall sermon of 19 April 1618, he writes, "and in those men, in whom he [God] hath begun a regeneration, by his first grace, his grace proceeds not, without a

---

[23] Calvin, *Institutes of the Christian Religion*, I:263.

cooperation of those men" (1:272). Nevertheless, Donne is always careful not to overstate the extent of those human efforts, such as when he explains:

> When we speak of a *co-operation*, a joint working with the grace of God, or of a *post-operation*, an after working upon the virtue of a former grace, this *co-operation*, and this *post-operation* must be mollified with a good concurrent cause with that grace. So there is a good sense of *co-operation*, and *post-operation*, but *præoperation*, that we should work, *before* God work upon us, can admit no good interpretation. I could as soon beleeve that I had a being before *God* was, as that I had a *will* to good, before God moved it. (4:224)[24]

What Donne is at pains to avoid here, even in giving greater scope to human freedom, is the error of Pelagianism. In his third Prebend sermon, Donne writes that those persons who are disposed and qualified to God are "Not disposed by nature, without use of grace; that is flat and full Pelagianisme," and yet he cannot help but add, in opposition to strict Calvinism, that these persons are also "Not disposed by preventing grace, without use of subsequent grace, by Antecedent and anticipant, without concomitant and auxiliant grace; that is Semi-pelagianisme" (7:240).[25] Donne always struggles throughout the *Sermons* to secure, on the one hand, the self-sufficiency of God in initiating grace, and to remind in his auditors, on the other hand, "Thou art so necessary to God, as that God had no utterance, no exercise, no employment for his grace and mercy, but for thee" (9:374).[26] It is this interrelational understanding of reconciliation that also informs his view that justification comes through faith and works operating in concert.

THE ROOT AND FRUIT

Calvin's antinomianism is clearly expressed throughout the *Institutes*, but especially in III.xi.1–23. In particular, he contends that "faith righteousness so differs from works righteousness that when one is established the other has to be overthrown," and that, as a result, "so long as any particle of works righteousness remains some occasion for boasting remains with us," for as he reasons, "if faith excludes all boasting, works righteousness can in no way be

---

[24] For a similar statement of modification, see *Sermons* 7:353.

[25] For a similar explanation of full and semi-Pelagianism, see *Sermons* 9:67.

[26] See William Mueller's discussion of "Grace and Free Will" (*John Donne: Preacher*, pp. 178–94), in which he concludes:

> It is evident that Donne followed, and indeed helped to form, the Anglican position, the middle way between the Roman and the Reformed theologians. He shared with Luther and Calvin and their followers the fear that much of the apparatus of Roman belief and practice detracted from the glory of God. . . . But like many good things, the Reformed movement had, Donne felt, gone too far. In an effort to preserve the truth of God's omnipotence they had sacrificed God's best creation, man, depriving him of virtually all activity in the redemptive process. If Rome had seemed to overassess man's role, Geneva had seemed to reduce it by a ruthless logic to zero. (pp. 193–94)

associated with faith righteousness" (III.xi.13).[27] Later in this discussion, Calvin first reiterates, "it is clear that those who are justified by faith are justified apart from the merit of works – in fact, without the merit of works," and then asks, in the context of Romans 4:16 that grace is a free inheritance received by faith, "how is this so except that faith rests entirely upon God's mercy without the assistance of works?" (III.xi.18).[28]

In that section of the *Institutes* in which Calvin examines biblical passages that seem to relate justification with works (III.xvii.6–15), he entertains the notion that justification by works relies upon faith and concludes, "if works righteousness, whatever its character be finally reckoned, depends upon the justification of faith, the latter is by this not only not diminished but actually strengthened, while thereby its power shines forth even stronger" (III.x–vii.9).[29] The explanation Calvin offers for this reasoning is that "unless the justification of faith remains whole and unbroken, the uncleanness of works will be uncovered," for as he states earlier in this section, and as a consequence of his doctrine of total depravity, "no good work exists which is not so defiled both with attendant transgressions and with its own corruption that it cannot bear the honorable name of righteousness" (III.xvii.9).[30] In an earlier section of the *Institutes*, Calvin clarifies this point of all human works as defiled when he writes, "to man we assign only this: that he pollutes and contaminates by his impurity those very things which were good" and that "nothing proceeds from a man, however perfect he be, that is not defiled by some spot" (III.xv.3).[31] Although Calvin concedes, "good works, then, are pleasing to God and are not unfruitful for their doers," he goes on to affirm that those works "receive by way of reward the most ample benefits of God not because they so deserve but because God's kindness has of itself set this value on them" and that God "will indeed recognize in them his own righteousness but man's dishonor and shame!" (III.xv.3).[32]

In spite of Randolph Daniel's assertion that at the core of Donne's theology he unites a covenant theology with "the classical Protestant doctrine of salvation by faith alone,"[33] the *Sermons* forcefully argue against such an antinomian reading. In a late Paul's Cross sermon, preached on 22 November 1629, Donne first asks, "If a man pretend *Faith* to me, I must say to him, with Saint *James, Can his Faith save him?*" (James 2:14), and then responds that faith without works is "A *dead Faith*, as all Faith is that is inoperative, and workes not," for by analogy Donne explains that "if a man offer me the roote

---

[27] Calvin, *The Institutes of the Christian Religion*, I:743.

[28] Ibid., I:748.

[29] Ibid., I:812.

[30] Ibid., I:813, 812.

[31] Ibid., I:790–91.

[32] Ibid., I:791. For a similar discussion, see also II.iii.12.

[33] Daniel, "Reconciliation, Covenant and Election," pp. 29–30.

of a tree to taste, I cannot say this is such a Pear, or Apple, or Plum; but if I see *the fruit*, I can" (9:121). In another sermon, one of those on the Penitential Psalms, Donne cites Romans 4:4–5 ("to him that worketh, the reward is of debt, but to him that beleeveth, and worketh not, his faith is counted for righteousnesse") and then questions, "Doth the Apostle then, in this Text, exclude the Co-operation of Man?, . . . Doth S. *Paul* require nothing, nothing out of this Text, to be done by man?" (9:265). In short, Donne answers, "Surely he does." The long answer unfolds through metaphor and explanation as Donne seeks to establish that the propositions to believe alone and to do alone are all one:

> it is truly all one purpose, to say, If you live you may walke, and to say, If you stretch out your legges, you may walke. To say, Eat of this Tree, and you shall recover, and to say, Eat of this fruit, and you shall recover, is all one; To attribute an action to the next Cause, or to the Cause of that Cause, is, to this purpose, all one. And therefore, as God gave a Reformation to his Church, in prospering that Doctrine, That Justification was by faith onely: so God give an unity to his Church, in this Doctrine, That no man is justified, that works not; for, without works how much soever he magnifie his faith, there is *Dolus in spiritu, Guile in his spirit.* (9:265)[34]

Beyond the ways in which works are portrayed as integral to faith, this passage is also remarkable in Donne's assertion that the unity of the Church depends on this integrated understanding of justification.[35]

In the sermon Donne preached on the King's recently issued *Directions to Preachers*, the Dean of Paul's told those gathered at the Cross on 15 September 1622 that in this life "*God* requires something, some assistance, some concurrence, some cooperation, though," as he explains quoting his scripture text, "*he can fight from heaven, and the Starres, in their order, can fight against Sisera*" (4:186). This text forms the twentieth verse of Judges 5, the whole of which comprises the victory song of Deborah and Barak, which Donne holds up as a testimony to good works on equal footing with the catalogue of the faithful in Hebrews 11. Noting that God "gives them *their glorie*, that doe any thing for him, or for themselves," Donne goes on to elaborate that as God "hath laid up a record, for their glorie and Memoriall, who were remarkable for Faith (for the eleventh *Chapter* to the *Hebrewes*, is a *Catalogue* of them) So in this Song of *Deborah* and *Barake*, hee hath laide up a Record for their glorie, who expressed their faith in *Workes*, and assisted his service" (4:186). To the extent that James' *Directions* sought to put an end to the pulpit's being used to promote wrangling over matters of doctrinal indifference and revilings of a personal nature, Donne's insistence here that

---

[34] For complementary metaphors showing the relation of faith and works, see *Sermons* 3:286.

[35] See Stewart Dippel, *A Study of Religious Thought at Oxford and Cambridge, 1590–1640*, chapter II, in which he argues that throughout this period, "University theologians, then, did not emphasize faith at the expense of works" (p. 25).

justification is through both faith and works not only indicates that he views this doctrine as essential, but also implies, as revealed in the passage quoted above, that this understanding of faith and works actually serves to unify the Church.[36]

Donne further elaborates these views in his undated Candlemas Day sermon on Matthew 5:16, "Let your light so shine before men, that they may see your good works, and glorifie your Father which is in Heaven." At the end of the opening paragraph, Donne again employs the metaphor of a fruit tree, explaining, "Every good work hath faith for the roote; but every faith hath not good works for the fruit thereof" so that "good works presuppose faith" (10:85), and as he reasserts two paragraphs later, "though faith have a preheminence, because works grow out of it, and so faith (as the root) is first, yet works have the preheminence thus, both that they include faith in them, and that they dilate, and diffuse, and spread themselves more declaratorily, then faith doth" (10:87). Donne, however, proceeds further in this sermon contending that our works belong to us more than our faith: "Our faith is ours as we have received it, our worke is ours, as we have done it. Faith is ours, as we are possessors of it, the work ours, as we are doers, actors in it. Faith is ours, as our goods are ours, works, as our children are ours" (10:88). This last sentence is especially telling in aligning the acquisition of faith with inanimate objects (goods) and that of works with human relations (parents and children).

It is just this theological emphasis on communal participation that informs what Donne imagines as the chain of justification in a rather lengthy passage from his Whitsunday sermon on John 16:8–11:

> If it were possible to beleeve aright, and yet live ill, my faith should doe me no good. The best faith is not worth Heaven; The value of it grows *Ex pacto*, That God hath made that Covenant, that Contract, *Crede & vives*, onely beleeve and thou shalt be safe. Faith is but one of those things, which in severall senses are said to justifie us. It is truly said of God, *Deus solus justificat*, God only justifies us; *Efficienter*, nothing can effect it, nothing can worke towards it, but onely the meere goodnesse of God. And it is truly said of Christ, *Christus solus justificat*, Christ onely justifies us; *Materialiter*, nothing enters into the substance and body of the ransome for our sins, but the obedience of Christ. It is also truly said, *Sola fides justificat*, Onely faith justifies us; *Instrumentaliter*, nothing apprehends, nothing applies the merit of Christ to thee, but thy faith. And lastly it is as truly said, *Sola opera justificant*, Onely our works justifie us; *Declaratorie*, Only thy good life can assure thy conscience, and the World, that thou art justified. As the efficient justification, the gracious purpose of God had done us no good, without the materiall satisfaction, the death of Christ had

---

[36] For an extensive analysis of this sermon and its historical context, see Jeanne Shami, "'The Stars in their Order Fought Against Sisera,'" who emphasizes "the middle nature of Donne's divinity, the inclusiveness of his spirituality, and his respect for orderly processes and judicial means" (p. 21).

followed; And as that materiall satisfaction, the death of Christ would do me no good, without the instrumentall justification, the apprehension by faith; so neither would this profit without the declaratory justification, by which all is pleaded and established. God enters not into our materiall justification, that is onely Christs; Christ enters not into our instrumental justification, that is onely faiths; Faith enters not into our declaratory justification, (for faith is secret) and declaration belongs to workes. Neither of these can be said to justifie us alone, so, as that we may take the chaine in pieces, and thinke to be justified by any one link thereof; by God without Christ, by Christ without faith, or by faith without works; And yet every one of these justifies us alone, so, as that none of the rest enter into that way and that meanes, by which any of these are said to justifie us. (7:228)

It is typical of Donne to express doctrinal truth in such a paradoxical manner, for in doing so he seeks to hold these statements in tension in order to demonstrate more completely the inherent interrelation of justification by God alone, Christ alone, faith alone and works alone. Donne further establishes his point that, though distinct, these individual links are necessarily intertwined by means of the concatenating repetition he employs throughout this passage. The significance of Donne's insistence that faith and works are mutually related is most clearly revealed in his discussions of the Word and Sacraments, which for Donne together provide within the community of the visible Church the effectual means of grace.

THE DEW, AND BREATH IN THE AYRE

One of the central debates that persisted throughout the time of Donne's clerical career was that of the word-centered piety associated primarily with the Puritans versus the sacrament-centered piety attributed principally to the Laudians. In his recent studies of Donne's sermons, and the religious imagination they reveal, Daniel Doerksen asserts that Donne, whom he claims much more than such anticipators of Laudianism as Hooker and Andrewes, concentrates on "the Christian's relationship to God and its bearing on the experience of living – on 'conforming to the Word,'" and that Donne is "content to be associated with conforming puritanism, in part because he participates with it in the 'word-centered piety' that Hooker and the Laudians sought to replace."[37] Doerksen, however, overstates the case for Donne. There is no question that Donne views the dissemination and reception of the Word, most importantly through preaching (and common prayer), as essential for salvation; however, the *Sermons* testify that the sacraments are for Donne equally essential. It is for him neither the one over the other, nor the one more than the other, but

---

[37] Doerksen, *Conforming to the Word*, p. 112; and "'Saint Pauls Puritan': John Donne's 'Puritan' Imagination in the *Sermons*," p. 356.

both together through which the visible Church receives the invisible grace of God.

Throughout the *Sermons*, Donne espouses the efficacy of the Word by asserting that "There is no salvation but by faith, nor faith but by hearing, nor hearing but by preaching" (7:320)[38] and that "*Faith comes by hearing*, saith the Apostle; but it is by that hearing of the soul, *Hearkning, Considering*" (6:102). In addition, Donne writes in his sermon preached on the Sunday following the celebration of St. Paul's conversion, "Our Regeneration is by his Word; that is, by faith, which comes by hearing," and beyond the Word spoken at creation, God has provided "His written Word, his Scriptures" and, most importantly, "Our Principall, and Radicall, and Fundamentall security," that is "his Essentiall Word, his Son Christ Jesus" (6:216). Referring directly then to the biblical account of the conversion, he advises that the first step in Saul's cure and ours, he tells his auditors, is "That there was not onely a word, the Word, Christ himselfe, a Son of God in heaven, but a Voyce, the word uttered, and preached; Christ manifested in his Ordinance" (6:217). Nevertheless, Donne is equally firm in his assertions concerning the efficacy of the Sacraments, which are the "means to seal, and convey the graces, which accompany this Redemption of our souls, to our souls" (1:154). In another sermon, Donne cites Luther's comment on the Lord's Supper that it is *Venerabile & adorabile*, "for certainly," Donne explains, "whatsoever that is which we see, that which we receive, is to be adored; for, we receive Christ," who is "*Res Sacramenti*, The forme, the Essence, the substance, the soule of the Sacrament" (7:320).[39] Finally, in his Heidelberg sermon, Donne specifies that the Sacraments convey God's grace, "though not *ex opere operator*, not because that action is performed, not because that sacrament is administered, yet *ex pacto* and *quando opus operamur:* by Gods covenant, when soever that action is performed, whensoever that sacrament is administered, the grace of God is exhibited and offered" (2:258).[40] He further imagines for his Heidelberg auditors that grace "is such a light, such a torch, such a beacon, as where it is, it is easily seen" so that "whosoever receives this sacrament worthily, sees evidently an entrance, and a growth of grace in himself" (2:258).

Prior to examining Donne's views on God's Ordinances in the Church in

---

[38] In the remainder of this passage, Donne reinterprets the Keys of the Church and the doctrine of absolution in relation to preaching:

> and they that thinke meanliest of the Keyes of the Church, and speake faintliest of the Absolution of the Church, will yet allow, That those Keyes lock, and unlock in Preaching; That Absolution is conferred, or withheld in Preaching, That the proposing of the promises of the Gospel in preaching, is that binding and loosing on earth, which bindes and looses in heaven. (7:320)

[39] Donne continues this passage with a defense of kneeling during the service of Holy Communion.

[40] Hooker also, in his *Ecclesiastical Polity*, argues against *ex opere operator* (see especially, V.lvii.1–6).

more depth, it is first necessary to provide a broader perspective of the means for apprehending God's grace, beginning with human faculties. In his fourth Prebend sermon, preached at St. Paul's on 28 January 1628, Donne imagines God's grace and human faculties in relational terms, specifically as the Sun to the sphere "in which that Sun, that Grace moves" and as the soul to the body "which ministers Organs for that soule, that Grace to worke by" (7:305). Further, in the light of his understanding that the senses apprehend the grace of God, Donne writes in his sermon for the churching of Lady Doncaster:

> It is said often in Philosophy, *Nihil in intellectu, quod non prius in sensu;* till some *sense* apprehend a thing, the *Judgment* cannot debate it, nor discourse it; It may well be said in *Divinity* too, *Nihil in gratia, quod non prius in natura,* there is nothing in grace, that was not first in nature, so farre, as that grace always finds nature, and naturall faculties to work on. (5:176)[41]

While Donne insists that the grace of God can only be received by "a sweet, and souple, and tractable, and ductile disposition," he is quick to add that "This disposition is *no cause why* God gives his grace" (5:177). As a consequence of urging his auditors to prepare their natural faculties for receiving God's grace, a request that echoes his views on the interrelation of prevenient and subsequent grace, Donne then raises two concurrent and complementary questions: "How long shall we make this bad use, of this true doctrine, that, because we cannot doe *enough*, for our salvation, therefore we will doe *nothing?*" and "Shall I see any Man shut out of heaven, that did what he could upon earth?" (5:177). Donne's point here is that no one has any excuse for not apprehending God's grace, for all possess the requisite natural faculties.

Furthermore, Donne reminds his auditors in the second of his great two-part exegesis of Genesis 1:26 that "the meer naturall man, hath the Image of the King of Kings" (9:85) and then exhorts them, as a result, to apprehend the grace of God through their natural faculties, which he specifically aligns here with the workings of the tripartite soul: "Make thine understanding, and thy will, and thy memory (though but naturall faculties) serviceable to thy God; and auxiliary and subsidiary for thy salvation" (9:85). Although he explains that these powers of the soul "be not naturally instruments of grace," he nevertheless adds that "naturally they are susceptible of grace, and have so much in their nature, as that by grace they may be made instruments of grace" (9:85). Donne then concludes the paragraph, using a statement that

---

[41] Along these lines, see Peter Lake (*Anglicans and Puritans?*) who in his discussion of Hooker's theology states:

> throughout the *Polity* Hooker's emphasis had been on the compatibility between nature and grace. In dealing with man he had emphasized those elements in human nature which led naturally towards God, despite the fall. In dealing with God, too, he had tended to stress his role as the author of those hierarchies of law, desire and experience through which man could ascend to eternal life. (p. 182)

accords with his point in the questions from the churching sermon above, by insisting, "And doe not thinke that because a naturall man cannot doe all, therefore he hath nothing to doe for himselfe" (9:85). Donne's position that the natural faculties (including the three powers of the soul) can apprehend God's grace, along with his insistence on the need for human efforts in the workings of grace, points as a consequence to his distinctly inclusive understanding that salvation is offered by God to all.

In his sermon on Psalm 32:9, Donne expressly challenges, in its strictest sense, the Calvinist language of election and reprobation and the question of whether or not it is possible to fall from grace, stating, "Truly, Beloved, it is hard to conceive, how any height of sin in man should worke thus upon God, as to throw him away, without any purpose of re-assuming him againe, or any possibility of returning to him againe" (9:389). Further, Donne unequivocally articulates his theology of inclusion in a Whitsunday sermon preached at Lincoln's Inn:

> They are too good husbands, and too thrifty of Gods grace, too sparing of the Holy Ghost; that restraine Gods generall propositions, *Venite omnes*, Let all come, and *Vult omnes salvos*, God would have all men saved, so particularly, as to say, that when God sayes *All*, he meanes some of all sorts, some Men, some Women, some Jews, some Gentiles, some rich, some poore, but he does not meane, as he seemes to say, simply All. Yes; God does meane, simply All, so as that no man can say to another, God meanes not thee, no man can say to himselfe, God meanes not me. (5:53)

There is little doubt in the *Sermons* that Donne believes Christ's redeeming blood was shed "for all that will apply it" and that the Holy Ghost descends to disperse the salvific effects of the crucifixion "upon all that do not resist him" (5:54).

As commentary to the inclusive notions that each of the two passages above assert, Donne immediately follows up both with a straightforward attack on a supralapsarian understanding of election and reprobation. In the former, which serves as the conclusion for this sermon, he explains that "to impute that distemper to God" that would require God to hate and condemn those predestined as reprobate even before the Creation is "to impute to God, a sowrer and worse affected nature, then falls into any man" (9:389, 390). Donne then asks, in a series of rhetorical questions that requires his auditors to reflect on their own common-sense understanding of interpersonal relationships, "Doth any man desire that his enemy had a sonne, that he might kill him? Doth any man beget a sonne therefore, that he might dis-inherit him? Doth God hate any man therefore, because he will hate him?" (9:390). In the latter, from his Whitsunday sermon at Lincoln's Inn, Donne expresses to this primarily Calvinist auditory, "They are hard words, to say, That God predestinated some, not only *Ad damnationem*, but *Ad causas damnationis*, Not onely to damnation because they sinned, but to a necessity of sinning, that they might the more justly be damned" (5:53).

As these passages so clearly convey, John Carey is simply wrong in his assessment that "Donne, like most of his countrymen, believed that God, before he made the world or any souls to put in it, chose some souls for salvation and condemned others to eternal damnation."[42] More theologically informed critics such as David Nicholls, Paul Sellin, and Debora Shuger realize that throughout the *Sermons* Donne persistently argues against this supralapsarian position.[43] What Donne rejects in such an application of extreme Calvinism is the view that God's sovereignty must be maintained above all else, in contrast to his own understanding that the godhead, because of its communal and discursive nature, extends itself to humankind in ways that exhibit vulnerability. While Donne's theological vision portrays God struggling to woo humankind into a relationship with the divine community, he is no universalist. Natural faculties do in fact possess the capacity for apprehending God's grace; however, the effectual means for receiving the grace that God extends to all are made available only in the Church.

For example, at one point in his Heidelberg sermon, Donne quotes Calvin approvingly in order to affirm that God's grace can only be assured through tangible means:

> *quia nec oculis perspicitur, nec manibus palpatur spiritualis gratia,* because the grace of God it self cannot be discerned by the eye, nor distinguished by the touch, *non possumus nisi externis signis adjuti, statuere Deum nobis esse*

---

[42] Carey, *John Donne: Life, Mind and Art*, p. 241. As a further corrective to Carey's views, see Dewey Wallace's comments on the Synod of Dort (*Puritans and Predestination*, pp. 80–83), in which he explains, "in one of the major debates of the synod, that between supralapsarians and infralapsarians, the English delegates took the latter, more moderate, position" and, further, that "the synod as a whole did not canonize the more extreme views, most of the delegates apparently being content with the formulation that predestination had as its subject humankind after the fall" (pp. 81–82).

[43] Nicholls, "The Political Theology of John Donne," pp. 48–50; Sellin, *John Donne and "Calvinist" Views of Grace*, pp. 12–15; and Shuger, *Habits of Thought in the English Renaissance*, pp. 176–80, although I disagree with her view that Donne comes to this position in an attempt "to stabilize the terrifying freedom of God vis-à-vis mankind by denying reprobation" (p. 176). In addition, Sellin's position that Donne, in rejecting supralapsarianism, must by default be infralapsarian overstates the case, especially in the light of his definition of infralapsarianism:

> God – having decided to manifest his virtues in general – begins by creating man and for unknown reasons permits him to fall. Out of mankind lying thus in misery, God subsequently decrees the election of some men to salvation and the reprobation of the rest to eternal destruction, either because of the original sin they inherited from Adam or because of the sins they actively committed as fallen creatures. (p. 13)

In particular, Donne avoids making distinctions between the elect and, especially, the reprobate in strictly Calvinist terms, and, further, the language of reprobation stands in contrast to Donne's language of inclusion, that God offers his grace to all.

propitium, we could not assure our selves of the mercies of God, if we had not outward and sensible signs and seals of those mercies. (2:254)

As a result, God provided for humankind "such external and visible means and seals of grace" (2:254), but these are made available only in the Church in order to bring individuals into a conforming unity with the godhead. While Donne then expresses the difficulty of knowing how visible signs confer God's grace, he is nevertheless clear that "God hath covenanted with his people, to be present with them in certain places, in the Church at certain times, when they make their congregation, in certain actions, when they meet to pray" (2:255). Donne explains further that although God is not bound to extend his grace simply because certain actions have been performed, "yet he is bound in his covenant to exhibit grace, and to strengthen grace, in certain sacrifices, and certain sacraments; and so other sacramental, and ritual and ceremonial things ordained by God in the voice of his Church, because they further salvation" (2:255). In the shadow of the Synod of Dort, Donne uses the language of covenant theology for his auditors at Heidelberg to emphasize his own theological concerns both for the relationship God desires with humankind and for the contractual promises that define that relationship.

As a result of the initial, prevenient grace God offers to all and the Covenant that secures the administration and reception of God's grace in the Church, Donne insists that humankind has an obligation to foster the growth of the relationship God began. In a sermon preached on Christmas Day (1629?), Donne argues that because God "hath given us meanes to be better to day then yesterday, and to morrow then to day" and because the grace God offers us in the Church "does not onely fill that capacity, which we have, but give[s] us a greater capacity then we had," it is, therefore, "an abuse of Gods grace, not to emprove it, or not to procure such farther grace, as that present grace makes us capable of" (9:150). Donne then warns his auditors that it is dangerous "to rely upon that portion of grace, which I thinke I had in my election, or that measure of Sanctification, which I came to in my last sicknesse" (9:150). Because Donne believes that the essential nature of the godhead is communal and that the Church is the reflection and extension of that divine unity, the Word and Sacraments are for him the tangible expressions of the loving relationship between God and the Church.

The extended discussions above on human faculties and on his theology of inclusion, as well as his rejection of supralapsarianism, all inform a proper reading of Donne's understanding of the Word and Sacraments as the effectual means of God's grace. In the Valediction Sermon for his last going into Germany, Donne reads the six days of creation as the typological pattern for the manner in which God reveals himself in the Church. In particular, Donne interprets God's establishment of the firmament on day two, "to divide between the waters above, and the waters below," as "*terminus cognoscibilium*, the limit of those things which God hath given man meanes and faculties to conceive and understand of him" (2:381).[44] He then explains that the firmament consists of "those stars whom he hath kindled in his Church, the Fathers and Doctors [who] have ever from the beginning proposed as things necessary to be explicitely beleived [sic] for the salvation of our soules" (2:381), and that such persons have been raised up by God "to convay to us the dew of his grace, by waters under the firmament, by visible meanes, by Sacraments and by the word soe preached, and so explicated, as it hath beene unanimly [sic] and constantly from the beginning of the Church" (2:382).[45] In a similar act of typological interpretation, Donne recounts that on the third day God not only gathered the waters of life into one place, which he reads as "all the doctrines necessary for the life to come into the Catholique Church" so that "noe doctrine should be taught that had not been received in the Church," but also God produced all the herbs and fruits necessary to sustain humankind, by which he understands that "in the visible Church should be all things necessary for the spirituall food of our Soules" and that "All doctrines that were to be seminal, to be proseminated and propagated and continued to the end, should be taught in the Church" (2:382).

In proposing as he does that the Word and Sacraments together provide the effectual means of God's grace that can be enjoyed only in the community of the Church, Donne has a great deal in common with both Hooker and Calvin. Relying on a metaphor of regeneration and sustenance, Hooker writes in his *Ecclesiastical Polity*:

> The Church is to us that verie mother of our new birth in whose bowels wee are all bredd, at whose brestes wee receyve nourishment. As many therefore as are apparentlie to our judgment born of God, they have the seede of theire regeneration by the ministerie of the Church, which useth to that ende and purpose not only the word but the sacramentes, both havinge generative force and vertue. (V.l.1)[46]

The language in this passage complements Donne's own understanding of grace as a relationship between the divine and human that requires nurturing. In the *Institutes*, Calvin by and large employs metaphors that emphasize the Word and Sacraments as tangible expressions of God's grace. For example, he begins one section by straightforwardly asserting, "let it be regarded as a settled principle that the sacraments have the same office as the Word of God: to offer and set forth Christ to us, and in him the treasures of heavenly grace"

---

[44] As with the extended discussion of the Valediction Sermon in chapter 4, I am quoting from the earlier version that appears as Appendix B in Volume 2 of the Simpson and Potter edition.

[45] Simpson and Potter do not provide any textual notes for this earlier text of the sermon, which is printed as Appendix B in volume 2 and about which they explain that they "decided to print in full the earlier form of the sermon, basing [the] text on the two best manuscripts, *M* and *E*" (2:373).

[46] *The Folger Library Edition of the Works of Richard Hooker*, II:207.

(IV.xiv.17).[47] Adding that the Word and Sacraments "avail and profit nothing unless received by faith," Calvin then writes, "as with wine or oil or some other liquid, no matter how much you pour out, it will flow away and disappear unless the mouth of the vessel to receive it is open" (IV.xiv.17).[48] Calvin further imagines the Word and Sacraments as a government document secured by a wax seal (IV.xiv.5), as the foundation and supporting columns for faith (IV.xiv.6), and as the rays of the sun metaphorically illuminating our minds (IV.xiv.10).[49]

Similar to Hooker and Calvin, Donne writes that in the exercises of holy convocations, the "Sonne shines out as at noone, the Grace of God is in the Exaltation, exhibited in the powerfullest and effectuallest way of his Ordinance" (5:282), that as one who informs us that our debts are paid, God "returns to us in the dispensation and distribution of his graces, in his Word and Sacraments" (5:372), and that by his grace, God "feeds us with his Word, and cloaths us with his Sacraments, and warms us with his Absolutions" (1:154). Further, Donne establishes in his 1628 Easter sermon preached at St. Paul's that the knowledge of God in this world is "*Gratiæ communis*, it is an effect and fruit of that Grace which God shed upon the whole communion of Saints, that is, upon all those who in this Academy, the Church, do embrace the *Medium*, that is, the Ordinances of the Church" (8:229). Finally, in his sermon on Psalm 51:7 ("Purge me with Hyssope, and I shall be cleane"), Donne writes of his scripture text, "This *Cleansing* then implies that, which wee commonly call the enwrapping in the Covenant," which places us, Donne tells his auditors, "within the reach of our spirituall food, the Word and Sacraments" (5:310). He elaborates in the paragraph following that in order to prevent falling from this grace, this cleansing is "To be continued in the disposition, and working of the meanes of cleansing, that he may alwayes grow under the dew, and breath in the ayre of Gods grace exhibited in his Ordinance" (5:311).

Though at times Donne discusses either the Word or the Sacraments without the other, yet persistently throughout the *Sermons* he urges his auditors to the efficacy of both equally, even as his preaching occurred within the liturgical context of the Prayer Book and his own administration of the Sacraments. It is tempting for critics to overstate the importance of preaching for Donne because we have his sermons. However, it is incumbent on those who read these texts also to imagine Donne performing the liturgy, to balance as he does his comments on the Word he preached with those on the Sacraments he administered. For Donne, the Word and the Sacraments are together the visible means for conforming the visible Church to God through Christ, for in both, the Church receives a manifestation and infusion of God's

---

[47] *Institutes of the Christian Religion*, II:1292.
[48] Ibid., II:1292.
[49] Ibid., II:1280, 1281, and 1286.

grace that, in Augustinian fashion, leads to a relationship of knowing and loving.[50]

GUSTATE & VIDETE

With regularity, Donne imagines the human response to God's grace in terms of appetite and consumption, such as in his sermon to Charles at Whitehall on 15 April 1628, when he writes that "Grace is not grace to me, till it make me know that I have it" and that, as a result, God has "given that soule an appetite, and a holy hunger and thirst to take in more of him; for I have no Grace, till I would have more" (8:250). To acknowledge, and then act on, the human need to feed on God's grace is for Donne the very idea of wisdom. In contrast to his assertion that "Ignorance may be said to worke, as an in-appetency in the stomach, and as an insipidnesse, a tastelessnesse in the palate" (8:257), that person is wise who can, Donne writes, follow the good rule of St. Bernard: "*Cui quæque res sapiunt prout sunt, is sapiens est*: He that tasts, and apprehends all things in their proper and naturall tast, he that takes all things aright as they are, *Is sapiens est*, nothing distasts him, nothing alters him" (7:338–39). Donne explains that natural reason allows one to "digest" this rule into an understanding that both those who are good and those who are evil feel the want of riches, health and reputation; however, the greater wisdom arises from the higher contemplation that the need to satisfy these pangs of hunger draws one more readily to God.

The passage above highlights Terry Sherwood's contention that, in general, "Donne found in Bernard a conception of man congenial to his own belief in a dualism of body and soul made intimate by definable correpondences" and that, in particular, Donne's depiction of saving knowledge "embraces the processes of spiritual digestion, filling, assimilation: the soul gradually digests knowledge that fills the soul, increasingly assimilating, likening him to God."[51] Sherwood's further assertion that "for both Donne and Bernard, digestion into fullness describes participation in God through erected human faculties" accurately addresses the means through which Donne seeks to portray the salvific unity of body and soul.[52] While the center of Donne's theology is the essential community of God revealed in the doctrine of the Trinity, the theological goal divulged in his preaching, as well as in his administration of the sacraments, is to bring the individual, through the visible Church, into loving conformity with God. To that end, the tasting and seeing by which one receives the grace offered to all in Christ's passion serves as the antitype to the eating of the forbidden fruit and the resultant knowing of good and evil that ensnared all humanity in original sin.

---

[50] Cf. p. 36 ns 72, 73 above.

[51] Sherwood, *Fulfilling the Circle*, pp. 96, 97.

[52] Ibid., p. 97.

Donne's articulation of saving grace in terms of appetite and consumption leads naturally to a discussion of his views on the Lord's Supper, in which, through an act of eating, the body and soul are united by sharing in the sufferings of Christ, in whom the divine and human are conjoined. In his Easter sermon preached to the Lords at Communion, Donne confronts his auditors with the truth that all hunger signifies human mortality: "As Christ sayes, that as often as wee eate the Sacramentall Bread, we should remember his Death, so as often, as we eate ordinary bread, we may remember our death; for even hunger and thirst, are diseases; they are *Mors quotidiana*, a daily death, and if they lasted long, would kill us" (2:203). Therefore, as reparation for the eating by Adam and Eve that brought death, Christ comes to fallen humanity and, as Donne writes, "he knocks and he enters, and he sups with them, and he is supper to them" (2:224).[53]

With regard to the Lord's Supper, the most profound theological issue during this period was, of course, the controversy over the mode of Christ's presence in the sacrament. Donne does not trouble himself in the *Sermons* to locate the presence of Christ with any more precision than necessary for the purpose of demonstrating his moderate conformity. Furthermore, Eleanor McNees clarifies that with Donne "the debate about the nature of Real Presence has shifted from the presence of Christ in the elements to the presence of Christ in one who has partaken of these elements" so that "conformity with Christ is Donne's definition of Real Presence."[54] The closest Donne comes to a detailed elaboration of this controversy occurs in his 1626 Christmas sermon delivered at St. Paul's. The sermon text consists of the words spoken by Simeon on witnessing the presentation of the infant Christ at the Temple: "Lord now lettest thou thy servant depart in peace, according to thy word: for mine eyes have seen thy salvation" (Lk. 2:29, 30). Repeatedly throughout the early pages of this sermon, Donne compares Simeon's epiphany to the manifestation of Christ's body and blood in the sacraments (cf. 7:279–84) and, as a result, urges his auditors, "Make good your Christmas day, that Christ by a worthy receiving of the Sacrament, be born in you" (7:280).

Later in the sermon, Donne articulates his views on Christ's presence by specifying that the sacramental bread does not alter in substance, but in use:

> Beloved, in the blessed, and glorious, and mysterious Sacrament of the Body and Blood of Christ Jesus, thou seest *Christum Domini*, the Lords Salvation, and thy Salvation, and that, thus far with bodily eyes; That Bread which thou seest after the Consecration, is not the same bread, which was presented before; not that it is Transubstantiated to another substance, for it is bread still, (which is

---

[53] For comparable statements, see also *Sermons* 7:147–48, 152–53.
[54] McNees, "John Donne and the Anglican Doctrine of the Eucharist," p. 101.

the hereticall Riddle of the Roman Church, and Satans sophistry, to dishonour miracles, by the assiduity and frequency, and multiplicity of them) but that it is severed, and appropriated by God, in that Ordinance to another use; It is other Bread, so, as a Judge is another man, upon the bench, then he is at home, in his owne house. (7:294)

In this passage, Donne aligns himself with the Church of England's rejection of the Roman Catholic doctrine of transubstantiation (for the bread does not change substance to become the actual flesh of Christ), of the Lutheran position of consubstantiation (for the Lord's salvation is not hidden, but can be seen with bodily eyes), and of the memorialism attributed to Zwingli (for there is a distinctive presence of Christ in the sacrament).[55] Donne also rejects in this section of the sermon the doctrine of ubiquity, "that Christ is present in the eucharist in body as well as in spirit, and that his body is not therefore confined to one place, but can be everywhere (*ubique*),"[56] and he then reaffirms, "We say the Sacramentall bread is the body of Christ, because God hath shed his Ordinance upon it, and made it of another nature in the use, though not in the substance" (7:296). Finally, Donne asserts that those who deny the presence of Christ in the sacrament and those who find it necessary to prescibe the precise manner of Christ's presence are both without a scriptural foundation for their positions, and he then concludes in a statement that seeks for unity in the Church by focusing Christ's presence in the communicant:

> so the Roman Church hath catched a *Trans*, and others a *Con*, and a *Sub*, and an *In*, and varied their poetry into a Transubstantiation, and a Consubstantiation, and the rest, and rymed themselves beyond reason, into absurdities, and heresies, and by a young figure of *similiter cadens*, they are fallen alike into error, though the errors that they are fallen into, be not of a like nature, nor danger. We offer to goe no farther, then according to his Word; In the Sacrament our eyes see his salvation, according to that, so far, as that hath manifested unto us, and in that light wee depart in peace, without scruple in our owne, without offence to other mens consciences. (7:296)

What Donne affirms in this controversy is that the bread and wine are actual and that to avoid an absurd contradiction of the senses and of reason, these elements must be understood to retain their physical substance. Nevertheless, Donne is equally insistent that Christ is "*Res Sacramenti*, The

[55] For an overview of these distinctions, see Horton Davies, *Worship and Theology in England*, I:80–85.

[56] Anthony Milton, *Catholic and Reformed*, p. 385. In this context, he contends that

> for Romanists and Lutherans, and indeed for some irenical writers, the Church of England was understood to be Calvinist principally because of her doctrine of the eucharist, which disowned Lutheran consubstantiation [and the related doctrine of ubiquitarianism] – one of the fundamental divisions between the Lutheran and Calvinist worlds. (p. 385)

forme, the Essence, the substance, the soule of the Sacrament" so that for him "*Sacramentum sine re Sacramenti, mors est,* To take the body, and not the soule, the bread, and not Christ, is death" (7:320). There is actual bread and wine that feeds the body, there is the flesh and blood of Christ that nourishes the soul, and therefore, he writes, "There is the true Transubstantiation, that when I have received it worthily, it becomes my very soule; that is, My soule growes up into a better state, and habitude by it, and I have the more soule for it, the more sanctified, the more deified by that Sacrament" (7:321). In his article discussing self-love and the Passion, Paul Harland states that for Donne "the ultimate goal of the Christian is to conform the self to Christ so perfectly that the restored divine image mirrors Christ completely, or *is* Christ" and that such conformity occurs "by mirroring the active, suffering Christ of history, not the glorious Christ of heaven."[57] It is the crucified Christ that is reborn in those who receive the bread and wine.

Donne's view that the body and soul, even as the divine and human, are united by Christ's presence in the worthy communicant has a great deal in common with the views expressed by Calvin and Hooker. In the midst of his lengthy discussion in the *Institutes* of the Lord's Supper (IV.xvii.1–50), Calvin directly asserts, "our souls are fed by the flesh and blood of Christ in the same way that bread and wine keep and sustain physical life" so that "Christ truly grows into one with us, and refreshes us by the eating of his flesh and the drinking of his blood" (IV.xvii.10).[58] While he acknowledges that "it seems unbelievable that Christ's flesh, separated from us by such great distance, penetrates to us, so that it becomes our food," Calvin goes no further to particularize Christ's presence than to assent what faith alone can conceive, "that the Spirit truly unites things separated in space" (IV.xvii.10).[59] In a similar fashion, Hooker explains in his *Ecclesiastical Polity,*

> wee understande that the strengthe of oure life begun in Christe is Christe, that his fleshe is meate, and his blood drinke, not by surmised imagination but trulye, even so trulie that throughe faithe wee perceive in the bodie and bloode sacramentallye presented the verye taste of eternall life, the grace of the sacramente is heere as the foode which wee eate and drinke. (V.lxvii.1)[60]

Furthermore, Hooker concludes that in this controversy over Christ's presence, "the reall presence of Christes most blessed bodie and bloode is not therefore to be sought for in the sacrament, but in the worthie receiver of the sacrament" (V.lxvii.6).[61] Along with Calvin and Hooker, Donne espouses that when the ordinary, domestic act of eating bread and drinking wine

---

[57] Harland, "'A true transubstantiation': Donne, Self-love, and the Passion," p. 165.
[58] *Institutes of the Christian Religion*, II:1370.
[59] Ibid., p. 1370.
[60] *The Folger Library Edition of the Works of Richard Hooker*, II:331.
[61] Ibid., II:334.

occurs in the liturgy of the visible Church, the worthy communicant comes to the epiphany that in these elements Christ nourishes the soul.

As part of the communicants' recognition of Christ in the elements, Donne believes that Holy Communion is properly received in a kneeling position, for as he writes in his fourth Prebend Sermon, "he that feels Christ, in the receiving of the Sacrament, and will not bend his knee, would scarce bend his knee, if he saw him" (7:320).[62] Donne elaborates his views on this controversy over kneeling in one of his Candlemas sermons, in which he observes that the objection to kneeling by Puritan dissenters cannot be based on scripture since during the Last Supper, "it is cleare, that Christ did not continue one position all this while, but he arose and did some actions between" (7:332). In addition, Donne argues that the position of the body that one assumed in Christ's day for the purpose of dining could not be described, strictly speaking, as sitting, for, Donne informs his auditors, "it was rather a lying, a reclining, a leaning upon a bed" (7:332). As one last point in this controversy, Donne adds that although kneeling is not absolutely necessary for salvation, he asserts that it is "yet necessary *Ratione præcepti*, as it is enjoyned by lawfull authority, and to resist lawfull authority, is a disobedience, that may endanger any mans salvation" (7:333). The larger theological point for Donne is that kneeling places the body of the communicant in a position that more readily informs the soul of the need to be conformed to the image of God in Christ.

In keeping with his theological position that the Sacraments and the Word both offer the effectual means of grace, Donne often expresses in the *Sermons* that the Church may also "Taste and see that the Lord is good" (Ps. 34:8) by digesting the words of the scriptures and of sermons. For example, in a Whitsunday sermon he preached at Lincoln's Inn, Donne asserts, "For, *Si adsit palatum fidei, cui sapiat mel Dei*, saies S. *Augustine*, To him who hath a spirituall taste, no hony is so sweet, as the word of God preached according to his Ordinance" (5:38–9). In another sermon, Donne alludes to the book "of lamentation and mourning and woe" Ezekiel was given by God to eat that tasted as sweet as honey (Ez. 2:8–3:3), which Donne explains to his auditors in terms of their own reading of the scriptures: "if we can bring it to the first concoction, the first digestion, to that mastication, that rumination, which is the consideration of Gods purpose upon us in that Judgement, we shall change our taste, for we shall *Taste and See, Quam suavis Dominus, How good, and how sweet the Lord is*; for even this Judgement is Mercy" (9:408).

In addition, Donne also cautions those gathered for his sermon on the anniversary of the Gunpowder Plot (5 November 1622) that "a vehement zeale on Sunday, doth not rectifie the six dayes sinner," that "to fast all weeke long, so as never to taste how sweet the Lord is," to be starved for a

---

[62] For a summary of the Puritan objections to kneeling for the service of Holy Communion, see Horton Davies, *Worship and Theology in England*, II:207–09.

sermon, is "no good diet" (4:261).[63] In the light of exhorting his auditors to feed on God's Word, Donne recognizes for himself that his work of exegesis is to "crack a shell, to tast the kernell, cleare the words, to gaine the Doctrine" (9:226). Along similar lines, in his sermon on calling delivered at The Hague, Donne alludes at one point to the manna God provided the Israelites as that which was "agreeable to every mans taste, and tasted to every man like that, that that man liked best" in order to establish that preachers are "to deliver the bread of life agreeable to every taste, to fit our Doctrine to the apprehension, and capacity, and digestion of the hearers" (2:276). It is, Donne continues, the responsibility of the preacher to "Let the Congregation see that thou studiest the good of their soules, and they will digest any wholesome increpation, any medicinall reprehension at thy hands" (2:277). Finally, as preparation for enumerating in one Christmas sermon the places in scripture that name the Lord as shepherd, Donne invites his auditors, "Be pleased to taste a few of them" (9:132). He then culminates his delineation of Christ's pastoral care by stating, "he feeds not one Parish, nor one Diocesse, but *humanum genus*, all Mankinde, the whole world, and then feeds us so, as that he is both our *Pastor*, and our *Pasture*, he feeds us, and feeds us with himself, for, *His flesh is meat indeed, and his bloud is drink indeed*" (9:133). As present in both effectual means of grace, Christ is to be consumed in the Word that he is and in the Sacraments that enact his Passion.

The end of all this eating, "The end of all digestions, and concoctions," Donne writes, "is assimilation, that that meate may become our body," so that, as he confides with his auditors in this 1626 Christmas sermon, if they have offered themselves to God truly, then "God hath given thee thy selfe back, so much mended, as that thou hast received thy self and him too" (7:280, 283). In addition, to the royal auditors at Whitehall on 4 March 1624, Donne specifies that the feast to which God has directed them to participate in the immediacy of the present liturgy is a continuation of a great feast, in which, Donne explains, "the first course (that which we begin to serve in now) is Manna, food of Angels, plentifull, frequent preaching; but the second course, is the very body and blood of Christ Jesus, shed for us, and given to us, in that blessed Sacrament, of which himselfe makes us worthy receivers at that time" (6:223). Donne then concludes this opening paragraph of the sermon by providing the theological interpretation for his metaphor:

> Now, as the end of all bodily eating, is Assimilation, that after all other concoctions, that meat may be made *Idem corpus*, the same body that I am; so the end of all spirituall eating, is Assimilation too, That after all Hearing, and all Receiving, I may be made *Idem spiritus cum Domino*, the same spirit, that my God is: for, though it be good to Heare, good to Receive, good to Meditate, yet,

---

[63] There are no substantive differences in this passage between the Simpson and Potter edition (quoted here) and Shami's edition of this sermon (cf. p. 175, ll. 1420–27)

(if we speake effectually, and consummatively) why call we these good? there is nothing good but One, that is, Assimilation to God. (6:223–24)

The assimilation that Donne articulates throughout the *Sermons* is not accomplished in a single moment or in an isolated act, but in a gradual, life-long turning of the self to God. It is for Donne a process of growth requiring nurturing, as he insists to those gathered at the Spittle on Easter Monday 1622:

Measure not thou therefore the growth and forwardness of thy Child, by how soon he could speak, or go; how soone he could contract with a man, or discourse with a woman: but how soon he became sensible of that great contract which he had made with Almighty God, in his Baptism: how soon he was able to discharge those sureties, which undertook for him, then, by receiving his confirmation, in the Church: how soon he became to discern the Lords Spirit, in the preaching of his Word, and to discern the Lords body, in the Administration of the Sacrament. (4:121)

As this passage makes clear, the assimilation that defines for Donne the purpose of life must occur within the visible Church, for it is there that the communal unity of the godhead manifests itself in the Word and Sacraments that effectually communicate God's grace.

*

Assimilation is for Donne another way of talking about relationship and of imagining, specifically, the response of humankind for that love extended first by God. The goal of loving conformity, then, illustrates all the more clearly that Donne's understanding of the nature of God in the doctrine of the Trinity informs every aspect of his theology. As his theological first principle, Donne believes that the essential nature of God is communal, which the godhead itself reveals in the discursive concurrence of creating humankind (*faciamus hominem*), and God's desire to create displays for Donne the intention of the Trinity to dilate its own community. The godhead, therefore, exposes its vulnerability (a necessary condition in any relationship) by calling for human efforts to complete the motion initiated by God, who even provides for the salvation of all the image of its triune self imprinted in the soul. The doctrine of the Trinity is for Donne the seminal Christian belief, and it is in the context of this belief that he practices "the art of memory," which, informed by the Holy Spirit, is "the art of salvation" (2:73). The knowledge of the Trinity, however, cannot be reached through reason and natural philo-sophy, but is revealed in the scriptures and realized through participation in the visible Church.

The communal nature of God necessitates that the human reflection of the Creator manifests itself in the world as community. It is, therefore, the earthly trinity of prayer, preaching, and the Sacraments that, Donne specifies, "must bring thee to the Trinity in heaven" (9:315). From within the liturgical pattern of common prayer, the invisible grace of God is made visible in the Word and Sacraments, and thus, the divine/human relationship, severed because of original and habitual sin, is restored. The Church is for Donne the nexus for that reconciliation, which achieves its spiritual significance by means of a physical participation. Because the eternal God entered time and space and became human, those individuals who, in the means afforded by the Church, align their bodies with the divine image in their souls conform themselves to God, even as they realize the presence of Christ anew. It is not surprising then that Donne insists on the preeminence of sight, not simply because it is the highest of the human senses, but primarily because the eye instructs the soul, or as he learned from Augustine, seeing leads to knowing, which in turn is the condition for loving.

Donne is fond of reminding his auditors that God did not proceed in the Creation without a pattern, and neither should the Church. Common prayer is the pattern that defines the Church and, thereby, the pattern to which everyone is called to participate. In the Church, Donne contends, human efforts find meaning and purpose, and it is here that individuals are to engage in the "religious impudency" and "holy importunity" encouraged by God. Furthermore, Donne relates his own personal sense of calling to his responsibility as a priest in the Church of England for preaching the gospel of repentance. Through his exegesis of the scriptures, Donne sounds the need for all to humble themselves in the mystery of confession. He urges his auditors to a tearful acknowledgment of their sins that, through this purifying second baptism, reunites them with God. Finally, in the administration and reception of the Sacraments, Donne finds the union of body and soul, as well as of divine and human, perfected. Baptism, including the signing of the cross, initiates the individual into the community of those united by participating in Christ's sufferings, and the Lord's Supper, by which Christ's presence is manifested in the communicant, continues this process of conformity through assimilation.

Donne's theology is marked by an eclecticism that defies assigning him too precise a sectarian designation, as revealed by the various discussions of his religious prose and verse that have reached markedly different conclusions. His theology develops from an idiosyncratic blend of ideas and authors that attests to his own desire to locate and nurture what unifies the Church, and to condemn only what he believes leads to "schismaticall singularity." The difficulty in describing Donne's theology is that his *Sermons*, the most extensive record of his mature thought, are not polemic tracts, and as such, they represent, to a great extent, the fruit of his theological vision rather than a defense of it. The result is that Donne's theology develops from and exists in the complexities of his own personal history, the particular circumstances of Church and State during this period, and the theological controversies at this time that shaped faith and practice. Donne weaves together such disparate elements as his own Catholic background, the Synod of Dort, the need to provide orthodox correctives to his King and patrons, the churching of women, the iconoclastic controversy, and his assuming the vicarage of St. Dunstan's into a theology anchored in the unifying concurrence of the Trinity. From "so steepy a place" as this, Donne attains a theological perspective from which to reconcile himself both to the Church of England and, along with those to whom he preached and administered the Sacraments, to God.

BIBLIOGRAPHY

Aers, David and Gunther Kress. "Vexatious Contraries: A Reading of Donne's Poetry." *Literature, Language and Society in England, 1580–1680.* Totowa, NJ: Barnes & Noble, 1981. 49–74.

Akrigg, G. P. V. *Jacobean Pageant, or the Court of King James I.* Cambridge: Harvard U P, 1962.

Aquinas, Saint Thomas. *Summa Theologiae.* Trans. Kevin D. O'Rourke, O.P. 61 Vols. London: Eyre & Spottiswoode, 1964–80.

Asals, Heather. "John Donne and the Grammar of Redemption." *English Studies in Canada* 5 (1979): 125–39.

Augustine, Saint. *The Trinity.* Trans. Stephen McKenna, C.SS.R. Washington, DC: Catholic U of America P, 1963.

Baker-Smith, Dominic. "John Donne's *Critique of True Religion."* *John Donne: Essays in Celebration.* Ed. A. J. Smith. London: Methuen, 1972. 404–32.

Bald, R. C. *John Donne: A Life.* Oxford: Clarendon P, 1970.

Bernard of Clairveaux, Saint. *Selected Works.* New York: Paulist P, 1987.

Booty, John, ed. *The Book of Common Prayer, 1559.* Charlottesville: U of Virginia P, 1976.

Boulton, Jeremy. *Neighborhood and Society: A London Suburb in the Seventeenth Century.* Cambridge: Cambridge U P, 1987.

Bromiley, G. W. *Baptism and the Anglican Reformers.* London: Lutterworth P, 1953.

Brooks, Helen B. "Donne's 'Goodfriday, 1613. Riding Westward' and Augustine's Psychology of Time." *John Donne's Religious Imagination: Essays in Honor of John T. Shawcross.* Eds. Raymond-Jean Frontain and Frances M. Malpezzi. Conway: U of Central Arkansas P, 1995. 284–305.

Calvin, John. *Institutes of the Christian Religion.* Ed. John T. McNeill. 2 Vols. Philadelphia: The Westminster P, 1960.

Carey, John. *John Donne: Life, Mind and Art.* London: Faber and Faber, 1981.

Carrithers, Gale H., Jr. *Donne at Sermons: A Christian Existential World.* Albany: SUNY P, 1972.

Carrithers, Gale H., Jr. and James D. Hardy, Jr. "Love, Power, Dust Royall, Gavelkinde: Donne's Politics." *John Donne Journal* 11 (1992): 39–58.

Chamberlain, John. *The Chamberlain Letters: A Selection of the Letters of John Chamberlain Concerning Life in England from 1597 to 1626.* Ed. Elizabeth McClure Thomson. New York: Putnam, 1965.

Chambers, A. B. "'Goodfriday, 1613. Riding Westward' Looking Back." *John Donne Journal* 6 (1987): 185–201.

———. "'Goodfriday, 1613. Riding Westward': The Poem and the Tradition." *ELH* 28 (1961): 31–53.

Chanoff, David. "Donne's Anglicanism." *Recusant History* 15 (1980): 154–67.

Charles, R. H., ed. *Apocrypha and Pseudepigrapha of the Old Testament.* 2 Vols. Oxford: Clarendon P, 1973.

Clucas, Stephen. "'Noble virtue in extremes': Henry Percy, Ninth Earl of Northumberland, Patronage and the Politics of Stoic Consolation." *Renaissance Studies* 9 (1995): 267–91.

Coster, William. "Purity, Profanity, and Puritanism: The Churching of Women, 1500–1700." *Women in the Church.* Eds. W. J. Sheils and Diana Wood. Studies in Church History, vol. 27. Oxford: Basil Blackwell, 1990. 377–87.

Coudert, Allison. *Alchemy: The Philosopher's Stone.* Boulder, CO: Shambala Publications, 1980.

Crawford, Patricia. *Women and Religion in England, 1500–1720.* London and New York: Routledge, 1993.

Daniel, E. Randolph. "Reconciliation, Covenant and Election: A Study in the Theology of John Donne." *Anglican Theological Review* 48 (1966): 14–30.

Davies, Godfrey. *The Early Stuarts, 1603–1660.* Oxford: Clarendon P, 1959.

Davies, Horton. *Worship and Theology in England.* Vols. I (from Cranmer to Hooker, 1534–1603) and II (from Andrewes to Baxter to Fox, 1603–1690). Princeton: Princeton U P, 1970 and 1975.

Dippel, Stewart A. *A Study of Religious Thought at Oxford and Cambridge, 1590–1640.* New York and London: U P of America, 1987.

Doerksen, Daniel W. *Conforming to the Word: Herbert, Donne, and the English Church before Laud.* Lewisburg, PA: Bucknell U P, 1997.

——. "'Saint Pauls Puritan': John Donne's 'Puritan' Imagination in the *Sermons.*" *John Donne's Religious Imagination: Essays in Honor of John T. Shawcross.* Eds. Raymond-Jean Frontain and Frances M. Malpezzi. Conway: U of Central Arkansas P, 1995. 350–65.

Donne, John. *The Complete Poetry of John Donne.* Ed. John T. Shawcross. Garden City, NY: Anchor Books, 1967.

——. *Devotions upon Emergent Occasions.* Ed. Anthony Raspa. Oxford: Oxford U P, 1987.

——. *The Divine Poems of John Donne.* Ed. Helen Gardner. Oxford: Clarendon P, 1952.

——. *Essays in Divinity.* Ed. Evelyn M. Simpson. Oxford: Clarendon P, 1952.

——. *Letters to Severall Persons of Honour (1651).* Ed. M. Thomas Hester. Delmar, NY: Scholars' Facsimiles, 1977.

——. *Pseudo-Martyr.* Ed. Anthony Raspa. Montreal: McGill-Queen's U P, 1993.

——. *The Sermons of John Donne.* Eds. Evelyn M. Simpson and George R. Potter. 10 Vols. Berkeley: U of California P, 1953–62.

——. *The Variorum Edition of the Poetry of John Donne.* Gen. ed. Gary A. Stringer. Vols. 6 (The Anniversaries and the Epicedes and Obsequies) and 8 (The Epigrams, Epithalamions, Epitaphs, Inscriptions, and Miscellaneous Poems). Bloomington: Indiana U P, 1995.

Donnelly, M. L. "Saving the King's Friend and Redeeming Appearances: Dr. Donne Constructs a Scriptural Model for Patronage." *Yearbook of English Studies* 21 (1991): 107–20.

——. "'To furder or represse': Donne's Calling." *John Donne Journal* 8 (1989): 115–24.

Dubinski, Roman R. "Donne's Holy Sonnets and the Seven Penitential Psalms." *Renaissance and Reformation* 10 (1986): 201–16.

——. "Donne's 'A Litanie' and the Saints." *Christianity & Literature* 41 (1991): 5–26.

Eliot, T. S. *Selected Essays*. London: Faber and Faber, 1972.

Emisson, F. G. *Elizabethan Life: Morals & the Church Courts*. 2 Vols. Colchester, England: Benham & Co., 1973.

Fincham, Kenneth, ed. *The Early Stuart Church, 1603–1642*. Stanford: Stanford U P, 1993.

——. "Ramifications of the Hampton Court Conference in the Dioceses, 1603–1609." *Journal of Ecclesiastical History* 36 (1985): 208–27.

Fincham, Kenneth and Peter Lake. "The Ecclesiastical Policies of James I and Charles I." *The Early Stuart Church, 1603–1642*. Ed. Kenneth Fincham. Stanford: Stanford U P, 1993. 23–49.

Flynn, Dennis. "Donne's Catholicism: I and II." *Recusant History* 13 (1975): 1–17, 178–95.

——. "Donne's *Ignatius His Conclave* and Other Libels on Robert Cecil." *John Donne Journal* 6 (1987): 163–83.

——. *John Donne and the Ancient Catholic Nobility*. Bloomington: Indiana U P, 1995.

Foxell, Nigel. *A Sermon in Stone*. London: Menard P, 1978.

Frere, W. H. and C. E. Douglas, eds. *Puritan Manifestoes: A Study of the Origin of the Puritan Revolt*. London: S.P.C.K., 1954.

Friedman, Donald M. "Memory and the Art of Salvation in Donne's Good Friday Poem." *English Literary Renaissance* 3 (1973): 418–42.

Frontain, Raymond-Jean. "'With Holy Importunitie, with a Pious Impudencie': John Donne's Attempts to Provoke Election." *Journal of the Rocky Mountain Medieval and Renaissance Association* 13 (1992): 85–102.

Frontain, Raymond-Jean and Frances M. Malpezzi, eds. *John Donne's Religious Imagination: Essays in Honor of John T. Shawcross*. Conway: U of Central Arkansas P, 1995.

Gilman, Ernest B. *Iconoclasm and Poetry in the English Reformation: Down Went Dagon*. Chicago and London: U of Chicago P, 1986.

——. "'To adore, or scorne an image': Donne and the Iconoclastic Controversy." *John Donne Journal* 5 (1986): 63–100.

Guibbory, Achsah. "John Donne and Memory as 'the Art of *Salvation*.'" *Huntington Library Quarterly* 43 (1980): 261–74.

Guite, A. M. "The Art of Memory and the Art of Salvation: The Centrality of Memory in the Sermons of John Donne and Lancelot Andrewes." *Seventeenth Century* 4 (1989): 1–17.

Hall, Michael. "Circles and Circumvention in Donne's Sermons." *JEGP* 82 (1983): 201–14.

Harland, Paul W. "Donne's Political Intervention in the Parliament of 1629." *John Donne Journal* 11 (1992): 21–37.

——. "'A true transubstantiation': Donne, Self-love, and the Passion." *John Donne's Religious Imagination: Essays in Honor of John T. Shawcross*. Eds. Raymond-Jean Frontain and Frances M. Malpezzi. Conway: U of Central Arkansas P, 1995. 162–80.

Herbert, George. *The Works of George Herbert*. Ed. F. E. Hutchinson. Oxford: Clarendon P, 1972.

Hill, Christopher. *Economic Problems of the Church: from Archbishop Whitgift to the Long Parliament*. Oxford: Clarendon P, 1956.

Hooker, Richard. *The Folger Library Edition of the Works of Richard Hooker.* Gen. ed. W. Speed Hill. 5 Vols. Cambridge: Belknap P, 1977–90.

Hylson-Smith, Kenneth. *The Churches in England from Elizabeth I to Elizabeth II.* Vol. I, 1558–1688. London: SCM P, 1996.

Jackson, Robert S. *John Donne's Christian Vocation.* Evanston, IL: Northwestern U P, 1970.

Johnson, Jeffrey. "Gold in the Washes: Donne's Last Going into Germany." *Renascence* 46 (1994): 199–207.

——. "Spectacle, Patronage, and Donne's Sermon at Hanworth, 1622." *Studies in Philology* 96 (1999): 96–108.

——. "Wrestling with God: John Donne at Prayer." *John Donne's Religious Imagination: Essays in Honor of John T. Shawcross.* Eds. Raymond-Jean Frontain and Francis M. Malpezzi. Conway: U of Central Arkansas P, 1995. 306–23.

Kaufman, Peter Iver. *Prayer, Despair, and Drama: Elizabethan Introspection.* Urbana and Chicago: U of Illinois P, 1996.

Klinck, Dennis. "John Donne's 'knottie Trinitie.'" *Renascence* 33 (1981): 240–55.

——. "*Vestigia Trinitatis* in Man and His Works in the English Renaissance." *Journal of the History of Ideas* 42 (1981): 13–27.

Lake, Peter. *Anglicans and Puritans?: Presbyterianism and English Conforming Thought from Whitgift to Hooker.* London: Unwin Hyman, 1988.

——. "Calvinism and the English Church, 1570–1635." *Past and Present* 114 (1987): 32–76.

MacLure, Millar. *The Paul's Cross Sermons, 1534–1642.* Toronto: U of Toronto P, 1958.

Malpezzi, Frances. "'As I Ride': The Beast and His Burden in Donne's 'Goodfriday.'" *Religion & Literature* 24 (1992): 23–31.

——. "Christian Poetics in Donne's 'Upon the Translation of the Psalmes.'" *Renascence* 32 (1980): 221–28.

Maltby, Judith. "'By this Book': Parishioners, the Prayer Book and the Established Church." *The Early Stuart Church, 1603–1642.* Ed. Kenneth Fincham. Stanford: Stanford U P, 1993. 115–37.

Marotti, Arthur F. *John Donne, Coterie Poet.* Madison: U of Wisconsin P, 1986.

Martz, Louis. *The Poetry of Meditation.* New Haven: Yale U P, 1954.

McNees, Eleanor. "John Donne and the Anglican Doctrine of the Eucharist." *Texas Studies in Literature & Language* 29 (1987): 94–114.

Milgate, Wesley. "Dr. Donne's Art Gallery." *Notes & Queries* 194 (1949): 318–19.

Miller, V. C. *The Lambeth Articles: Doctrinal Development and Conflict in 16th Century England.* Oxford: Latimer House, 1994.

Milton, Anthony. *Catholic and Reformed: The Roman and Protestant Churches in English Protestant Thought, 1600–1640.* Cambridge: Cambridge U P, 1995.

Mueller, Janel. *Donne's Prebend Sermons.* Cambridge: Harvard U P, 1971.

Mueller, William R. *John Donne: Preacher.* Princeton: Princeton U P, 1962.

New, John F. H. *Anglican and Puritan: The Basis of Their Opposition, 1558–1640.* London: Adam & Charles Black, 1964.

Nicholls, David. "Divine Analogy: The Theological Politics of John Donne." *Political Studies* 32 (1984): 570–80.

——. "The Political Theology of John Donne." *Theological Studies* 49 (1988): 45–66.

Novarr, David. *The Disinterred Muse.* Ithaca, NY: Cornell U P, 1980.

Bibliography

O'Connell, Patrick F. "'Restore Thine Image': Structure and Theme in Donne's 'Goodfriday.'" *John Donne Journal* 4 (1985): 13–28.

Oliver, P. M. *Donne's Religious Writing: A Discourse of Feigned Devotion.* London and New York: Longman, 1997.

Patterson, Annabel. "Afterword." *John Donne Journal* 14 (1995): 219–30.

——. "John Donne, Kingsman?" *The Mental World of the Jacobean Court.* Ed. Linda Levy Peck. Cambridge: Cambridge U P, 1991. 251–72.

Phillips, John. *The Reformation of Images: Destruction of Art in England, 1535–1660.* Berkeley: U of California P, 1973.

Pollock, John J. "A Hymne to Christ, at the Authors last going into Germany." *Explicator* 38 (1980): 20–22.

Reeve, L. J. *Charles I and the Road to Personal Rule.* Cambridge: Cambridge U P, 1989.

Russell, Conrad. *Parliaments and English Politics, 1621–1629.* Oxford: Clarendon P, 1979.

Sanders, Wilbur. *John Donne's Poetry.* Cambridge: Cambridge U P, 1971.

Schleiner, Winfried. *The Imagery of John Donne's Sermons.* Providence, RI: Brown U P, 1970.

Seelig, Sharon Cadman. "In Sickness and in Health: Donne's *Devotions upon Emergent Occasions.*" *John Donne Journal* 8 (1989): 103–13.

Sellin, Paul. *John Donne and "Calvinist" Views of Grace.* Amsterdam: VU Boekhandel/ Uitgeverij, 1983.

——. *So Doth, So is Religion: John Donne and Diplomatic Contexts in the Reformed Netherlands, 1619–1620.* Columbia: U of Missouri P, 1988.

Shami, Jeanne M. "Anatomy and Progress: The Drama of Conversion in Donne's Men of a 'Middle Nature.'" *University of Toronto Quarterly* 53 (1984): 221–35.

——. "Donne on Discretion." *ELH* 47 (1980): 48–66.

——. "Donne's Protestant Casuistry: Cases of Conscience in the Sermons." *Studies in Philology* 80 (1983): 53–66.

——. "Donne's *Sermons* and the Absolutist Politics of Quotation." *John Donne's Religious Imagination: Essays in Honor of John T. Shawcross.* Eds. Raymond-Jean Frontain and Frances M. Malpezzi. Conway: U of Central Arkansas P, 1995. 380–412.

——, ed. *John Donne's 1622 Gunpowder Plot Sermon: A Parallel-Text Edition.* Pittsburgh, PA: Duquesne U P, 1996.

——. "'Kings and Desperate Men': John Donne Preaches at Court." *John Donne Journal* 6 (1987): 9–23.

——. "'The Stars in their Order Fought against Sisera': John Donne and the Pulpit Crisis of 1622." *John Donne Journal* 14 (1995): 1–58.

Sharpe, Kevin. *The Personal Rule of Charles I.* New Haven: Yale U P, 1992.

Shawcross, John T. "The Concept of *Sermo* in Donne and Herbert." *John Donne Journal* 6 (1987): 203–12.

——. *Intentionality and the New Traditionalism: Some Liminal Means to Literary Revisionism.* University Park: Penn St. U P, 1991.

Sherwood, Terry. *Fulfilling the Circle: A Study of John Donne's Thought.* Toronto: U of Toronto P, 1984.

Shuger, Debora. *Habits of Thought in the English Renaissance.* Berkeley: U of California P, 1990.

Simpson, Evelyn M. *A Study of the Prose Works of John Donne*. Oxford: Clarendon P, 1948.

Stachniewski, John. "John Donne: The Despair of the 'Holy Sonnets.'" *ELH* 48 (1981): 677–705.

Stanwood, P. G. "Donne's Earliest Sermons and the Penitential Tradition." *John Donne's Religious Imagination: Essays in Honor of John T. Shawcross*. Eds. Raymond-Jean Frontain and Frances M. Malpezzi. Conway: U of Central Arkansas P, 1995. 366–79.

Stanwood, P. G. and Heather Ross Asals, eds. *John Donne and the Theology of Language*. Columbia: U of Missouri P, 1986.

Stone, Lawrence. *The Crisis of the Aristocracy, 1558–1641*. Oxford: Clarendon P, 1965.

Strier, Richard. "John Donne Awry and Squint: The 'Holy Sonnets,' 1608–1610." *Modern Philology* 86 (1989): 357–84.

Tebeaux, Elizabeth. "Memory, Reason, and the Quest for Certainty in the *Sermons* of John Donne." *Renascence* 43 (1991): 195–213.

Thomas, Keith. *Religion and the Decline of Magic: Studies in Popular Beliefs in 16th and 17th Century England*. London: Weidenfeld and Nicolson, 1971.

Thompson, Christopher. "The Divided Leadership of the House of Commons in 1629." *Faction and Parliament: Essays on Early Stuart History*. Ed. Kevin Sharpe. Oxford: Clarendon P, 1978. 245–84.

Tyacke, Nicholas. *Anti-Calvinists: The Rise of English Arminianism, c. 1590–1640*. Oxford: Clarendon P, 1987.

Vaughan, Henry. *The Works of Henry Vaughan*. Ed. L. C. Martin. Oxford: Clarendon P, 1957.

Verkamp, Bernard J. *The Indifferent Mean: Adiaphorism in the English Reformation to 1554*. Athens and Detroit: Ohio U P and Wayne State U P, 1977.

Wallace, Dewey D., Jr. *Puritans and Predestination: Grace in English Protestant Theology, 1525–1695*. Chapel Hill: U of North Carolina P, 1982.

Walton, Izaak. *The Lives of John Donne, Sir Henry Wotton, Richard Hooker, George Herbert, and Robert Sanderson*. London: Oxford U P, 1927.

Webber, Joan. *Contrary Music*. Madison: U of Wisconsin P, 1963.

White, Peter. *Predestination, Policy and Polemic: Conflict and Consensus in the English Church from the Reformation to the Civil War*. Cambridge: Cambridge U P, 1992.

——. "The *via media* in the Early Stuart Church." *The Early Stuart Church, 1603–1642*. Ed. Kenneth Fincham. Stanford: Stanford U P, 1993. 211–30.

Williams, Arnold. *The Common Expositor: An Accord of the Commentaries of Genesis, 1527–1633*. Chapel Hill: U of North Carolina P, 1948.

Wright, Nancy E. "The *Figura* of the Martyr in John Donne's Sermons." *ELH* 56 (1989): 293–309.

Yates, Francis A. *The Art of Memory*. Chicago: U of Chicago P, 1966.

INDEX TO DONNE'S *SERMONS*

The references listed below identify the sermon numbers for each volume from the Simpson and Potter edition and indicate where these sermons have been cited in this study.

GENERAL INDEX

Ingram Content Group UK Ltd.
Milton Keynes UK
UKHW021820220323
419000UK00005B/334